LASTING
VALUE

LASTING VALUE

LESSONS FROM A CENTURY OF AGILITY AT LINCOLN ELECTRIC

JOSEPH A. MACIARIELLO

JOHN WILEY & SONS, INC.

New York • Chichester • Weinheim • Brisbane • Singapore • Toronto

This publication is designed to provide accurate and authoritative information in
regard to the subject matter covered. It is sold with the understanding that the
publisher is not engaged in rendering legal, accounting, or other professional services.
If legal advice or other expert assistance is required, the services of a competent
professional person should be sought.

ISBN: 0-471-33025-6

Printed in the United States of America.

10 9 8 7 6 5 4 3 2 1

To the Legacy James F. Lincoln

Contents

Preface

Despite intense domestic and foreign competition from some of the world's most aggressive companies, the Lincoln Electric Company has managed to sustain its status as the world's leader in welding technology. This prompted George Willis, who retired as chairman and CEO of Lincoln in 1992, to say: "We're not a marketing company, we're not an R&D company, and we're not a service company. We're a manufacturing company, and I believe we are the best manufacturing company in the world."[1]

What has helped Lincoln to establish and sustain its competitive advantage during its 104-year history? Why have many other companies been unsuccessful in duplicating Lincoln's approach? In a recent article, Milgrom and Roberts proposed that other companies fail to comprehend Lincoln's *mutually reinforcing set of management systems.*[2] *One aspect of this management system reinforces the others to create a synergy that boosts overall performance.*

Milgrom and Roberts, by using the highly advanced mathematical technique of "supermodular optimization," demonstrated that the multiple aspects of the rewards and recognition systems at Lincoln create synergy, and this synergy makes it difficult for other companies to duplicate Lincoln's management system.

This book supports Milgrom and Roberts's findings. Attempts to mimic one aspect of Lincoln's management system apart from the context of mutually enhancing elements are bound to fail. Milgrom and Roberts limit their concern to the complementarity of the various aspects of the rewards and recognition subsystem. They state:

> The complementarity perspective suggests a quite different answer. Other explanations focus on piece rates almost exclusively. Our discussion

suggests that Lincoln's piece rates are a part of a system of mutually enhancing elements, and that one cannot simply pick out a single element, graft it onto a different system without the complementary features, and expect positive results. Analyses of Lincoln that focus on the piece rates and fail to appreciate that their value is dependent on their being supported by the bonus scheme, the ownership structure, the inventory policy, and so on, cannot explain the failures of other companies to mimic Lincoln's system successfully.[3] (p. 204)

When Lincoln's *mutually reinforcing* management systems are described and developed in their entirety, it becomes clear that the company's sustained success is due to its *natural development of agility.*

By "agility" I mean that the management systems of Lincoln have been designed and developed to allow the company, in most cases, to change rapidly and to do things differently than in the past. Agility has been defined formally by Bahrami as the ability to move rapidly, to "change course to take advantage of an opportunity or to sidestep a threat" (p. 35).[4] Management systems that are agile can make rapid changes to respond to either opportunities or threats.

Lincoln's agility, in turn, can be attributed to its executive leadership and management systems, including its highly publicized incentive systems and cultural environment. The cultural environment of the company includes its strong ethical underpinnings.

The purpose of this book is to describe, in detail, the management systems at the Lincoln Electric Company, as they exist after a century of successful practice; our fundamental premise is that, when properly understood, the Lincoln system is transferable to many other companies.

I describe Lincoln's approach to management in a systematic manner and demonstrate why the company has been so effective, both economically and ethically, over a period of 104 years. In the process, I identify the specific aspects of Lincoln's management systems that have helped to establish and maintain the company's leadership position in welding technology in a highly competitive global environment.

A few other companies have evolved management systems that are similar in design to those at Lincoln Electric. I describe the management systems of two of these companies. When other successful companies use similar systems, it becomes obvious that the experiences at Lincoln are not unique, nor do they represent a historical accident. They may be duplicated by many other companies. The century-long experience at Lincoln is not a "historical accident." It should be taken seriously by American management.

The primary purpose of the book is to provide a systematic analysis of Lincoln's management system, to clarify *the genius of its design*. This in turn *allows additional companies to apply* pertinent aspects of these management systems to their operations.

In describing the management systems at Lincoln, I use the general approach to the design of adaptive management systems presented in J. Maciariello and C. Kirby, *Management Control Systems: Using Adaptive Systems to Attain Control*.[5] Within this general approach, I identify the attributes of the management systems at Lincoln that are compatible with the management practices necessary to create and sustain an agile and competitive organization.[6]

JOSEPH A. MACIARIELLO

NOTES

1. Christopher A. Bartlett and Jamie O'Connell, *Lincoln Electric: Venturing Abroad* (Boston: Harvard Business School, Case 9-398-095) (April 22, 1998): 4.

2. Paul Milgrom and John Roberts, "Complementarities and Fit: Strategy, Structure and Organizational Change in Manufacturing," *Journal of Accounting and Economics* (March–May 1995): 179–208.

3. Reprinted from Paul Milgrom and John Roberts, "Complementarities and Fit: Strategy, Structure and Organizational Change in Manufacturing," *Journal of Accounting and Economics,* 1995:179–208 with permission from Elsevier Science.

4. Homa Bahrami, "The Emerging Flexible Organization: Prospectives from Silicon Valley," *California Management Review* (summer 1992): 33–52.

5. Joseph Maciariello and Calvin Kirby, *Management Control Systems: Using Adaptive Systems to Attain Control* (Englewood Cliffs, NJ: Prentice Hall, 1994).

6. See Steven Goldman, Roger Nagel, and Kenneth Preiss, *Agile Competitors and Virtual Organizations* (New York: Van Nostrand-Reinhold, 1995). These authors include additional examples of these attributes of agility described in the CEO Brief *published by the Agility Forum and reproduced in Appendix A to this book.*

Acknowledgments

My greatest debt on this book is owed to Richard S. Sabo, long time assistant to the CEO at The Lincoln Electric Company, who retired from the company on May 7, 1999, after over 40 years of service in numerous capacities. Dick has provided access to the operations of the company and its management systems. He has taken time to read and correct drafts of my work. He has secured permission from the company for me to complete this book. He has made suggestions as to other companies that use management systems similar to those used by Lincoln Electric. I treasure his wisdom, his knowledge of management, his knowledge of Lincoln Electric, and his friendship. I would not have been able to complete this book without his help. I am truly grateful to him.

Mr. Roy Morrow, Director of Corporate Relations at Lincoln Electric, reviewed the manuscript and suggested corrections to remove tactual errors in a previous draft. I am grateful to him for his effort and kindness.

I began work on this book and visits to Lincoln Electric while on sabbatical at the University of Notre Dame during the Fall Semester, 1996. I want to express my gratitude to the Reverend Oliver Williams and to John Houck (deceased) of the Institute for Ethics and Religious Values in Business for their advice and kindness to me during my sabbatical and during the period over which much of the data for this book were collected. I also want to thank the students of the Society for Responsible Business at Notre Dame for sponsoring a talk I gave on the management systems at Lincoln Electric at the University during the Fall of 1998. Preparation for the talk became foundational to preparation of the book.

My editor at John Wiley, Jeanne Glasser, provided motivation, help, and encouragement during the entire time this book was prepared. I am grateful to her for her confidence in the project and for her sustaining spirit. I also want to thank Debra Alpern of John Wiley for her frequent assistance. And I would like to express my gratitude to Nancy Marcus Land and her staff at Publications Development Company for the wonderful support they provided during the production process.

Frederick Mackenbach, former president, chief operating officer, and member of the Board of Directors of Lincoln Electric, provided me with insights into the foreign operations of the firm. He was very generous with his time in our meeting on June 15, 1999, in Pasadena, California. I am grateful to him for his help and to Dr. William Opel, executive director of the Huntington Memorial Research Institute, for arranging the meeting and for providing a convenient meeting place.

Mr. Donald F. Hastings, chairman emeritus of the Lincoln Electric Company, provided me with valuable insights into the impact of ethical and moral values on the operations of Lincoln Electric both during and after the tenure of James F. Lincoln. Mr. Hastings was CEO of Lincoln Electric from 1992 to 1996 and retired as chairman of the Board of Lincoln Electric in 1997. I was delighted to receive a letter from Mr. Hastings and minutes of the 1997 Meeting of the Board of Directors of Lincoln Electric. The transcript of this meeting provided examples of the lasting impact of the values and practices of James Lincoln on the company.

I am grateful to John Correnti, then CEO, president, and vice chairman of Nucor Corporation for providing me with help on the material in this book pertaining to Nucor Corporation. I also want to thank David Aycock, chairman, and Samuel Siegel, chief financial officer of Nucor, for their insights into the history and operations of the company. I am grateful for the gracious treatment I received at Nucor and I want to thank Cornelia Wells of Nucor for arranging my visit to corporate headquarters on February 18, 1999. I did not get to meet with Ken Iverson, chairman emeritus of Nucor Corporation, because of his illness, but I have gained much from him by studying his managerial and technological innovations. He and James Lincoln had much in common.

Three people were instrumental in my work at Worthington Industries. I would like to thank Mark H. Stier, vice president, Corporate Human Resources for his generous help in explaining the values and management systems in place at Worthington. I also would like to thank Cathy Mayne Lyttle, vice president, Corporate Communications, for her suggestions on the material in Chapter 11 pertaining to Worthington Industries and for her corrections to an earlier draft of the chapter. Finally, I want to acknowledge the help I received from Sonya L. Lowmiller, Community Relations Coordinator, in arranging my interviews at Worthington on Tuesday, March 16, 1999. I did not have an opportunity to meet with John H. McConnell, founder of Worthington Industries, but through a study of materials made available to me, I find a striking similarity between the values and management practices he established at Worthington and those instituted by James Lincoln at Lincoln Electric.

The Drucker School of Management of Claremont Graduate University provided much of the financial support that was necessary to get this project under way and to sustain it. I am grateful to the school for help on the overall research project from which this book and related articles have been derived. Elizabeth Rowe, my secretary for many years, performed miracle after miracle in paving the way for the timely completion of this book. I have been very fortunate to have her assistance and I thank her for it. Cindy Chen served as my research assistant at the Drucker School during the 1998–1999 academic year. She provided assistance in gathering information on these three companies and on making the necessary financial calculations. I thank her for the dedicated assistance she provided me in preparing this book.

My wife Judy has been a constant source of encouragement on this project. She has listened carefully and has provided suggestions along the way. She has made the project worthwhile and has always understood its significance to me.

Last, I dedicate this book to the legacy of James Finney Lincoln, the architect of the values and management systems at The Lincoln Electric Company. His life, work, and company have ignited a flame in me that has sustained me throughout this project. I hope the book will encourage corporate executives and other students of management "to go and do likewise."

J.A.M.

Chapter
1

Lincoln Electric: The Company, Its Operations, and Its Values

Lincoln Electric was founded by John C. Lincoln in 1895 and was initially involved in the repair and manufacture of electric motors. The company was incorporated in Cleveland, Ohio, in 1906. When James Finney Lincoln, John's brother, joined the company in 1907, John, the president and innovator, began to devote his efforts to the development and use of welding machines and welding products. James, the vice president of the company, became the general manager and operating head in 1911. In 1914, at the beginning of World War I, James began to demonstrate the advantages of arc welding over riveting for attaching two metals in construction and in manufacturing. Previously, John had used welding as a repair tool, but the war provided an opportunity to demonstrate the superiority of arc welding for the joining of two metals.

Arc welding is a technique in which an electric cable is attached to an electrical motor. At the end of the cable, an electrode is placed; usually it is a wire that is similar to the two metals being joined. The electrode is placed in an appropriate holder. When electricity is passed through the cable to within a fraction of an inch of the metals to be joined, the electricity jumps over the electrode and creates a spark or an "arc." In the process, the electrode melts and flows into the space where the metals are to be joined.

Since those early days, Lincoln Electric has become a world leader in the manufacture of welding products and equipment. It has also produced a whole range of electric motors varying in size from one third to 1,250 horsepower for various niche markets. Welding products include arc-welding machines, robotic welding systems, welding electrodes, welding power sources, welding wire and feeding systems, and environmental systems for handling the fumes from industrial welding processes. Lincoln's products are used for cutting, manufacturing, and repairing metal products.

In 1995, Lincoln's hundredth year of operation, sales exceeded $1 billion for the first time in the company's history. Net income in 1995 was $61.5 million. Sales in 1996 were $1.1 billion, and net income in 1996 increased to $74.3 million, or 20.8 percent over 1995. In 1997, sales were $1.2 billion; net income in 1997 increased 15.0 percent to $85.4 million. For the year ended December 31, 1998, net sales were $1.2 billion, an increase of 2.4 percent. Net income in 1998, however, increased 9.7 percent to $93.7 million.

Lincoln operates three manufacturing facilities in the United States—in Cleveland, Ohio (the Ohio Company); Gainesville, Georgia; and Monterey Park, California—and as of December 31, 1998 seventeen manufacturing facilities in fourteen foreign countries. Foreign manufacturing operations currently exist in Sydney, Australia; Toronto, and Mississauga, Canada; Sheffield, England; Grand-Quevilly, France; Rathnew, Ireland; Pianoro, Milano, and Celle Ligure, Italy; Essen, Germany; Mexico City, Mexico; Nijmegen, Netherlands; Andebu, Norway; Shanghai People's Republic of China; Istanbul, Turkey; and Barcelona, Spain. Lincoln has recently added manufacturing capacity in Cikarang, Indonesia. Lincoln had a direct worldwide employment level of approximately 6,400 at the end of 1998.

Lincoln's welding products and welding consumables are marketed throughout the world. In total, the company maintains a worldwide network of distributors and sales offices in 160 countries.[1]

In the United States, the company's products are sold by its own sales force and by independent distributors. In international markets, the company's products are sold primarily by its foreign subsidiary companies. The company also operates an international export sales organization, using company employees who sell products from various manufacturing facilities to mass retailers, agents, distributors, and dealers.

Although Lincoln Electric became a public company in 1995 and is traded on the NASDAQ, more than 60 percent of its shares are owned by members of the Lincoln "family"—descendants of the founders, members of Lincoln's board of directors, and present and past employees.

How the Founding Values Influence Lincoln's Management Systems

The company values, which were developed by James F. Lincoln and described in three books that he authored, have had a powerful influence on the design of the management systems at Lincoln Electric. They have also contributed significantly to the company's agility and long-term success. In James Lincoln's *A New Approach to Industrial Economics,* the values are stated very explicitly and in considerable detail.[2] These values have had a significant effect on the design of the management systems at Lincoln and have contributed materially to the company's long-term agility, competitiveness, and success.

At the heart of the company's values is Christ's Sermon on the Mount, particularly the golden rule (Matt. 7:12): "So in everything, do to others what you would have them do to you, for this sums up the Law and the Prophets."[3] James Lincoln attempted to guide the development of the business operations of Lincoln Electric by this rule. He saw no reason why the behavior of other companies could not be guided similarly. He believed the golden rule to be *as natural to the functioning of human nature as gravity is to the functioning of material nature.*

James Lincoln sought to apply the golden rule first to Lincoln Electric's customers and then to its employees. Stockholders were prioritized third, but he believed that if the golden rule were applied to customers and employees, shareholders would end up in better shape than if the firm attempted primarily to serve stockholders' interests. In addition, he sought to make employees owners through employee stock ownership programs.

James did not see any final conflict among the three interests, but saw to it that they were congruent with one another, *at least in the long run.* The financial returns to stockholders, reviewed in Chapter 5, demonstrate that Lincoln's shareholders have indeed enjoyed above-average returns.

From his lifelong study of the Sermon on the Mount, James believed that life consists of relationships. The important relationships were between God and human beings, and between human beings—in other words, life was not to be lived as a "solo performance" but as one in which *right relationships* with God and with others were central to happiness and success.[4]

James also believed that workers should be treated with *dignity* and *respect* and that they should be rewarded fairly and in direct proportion to the value of their work. This was a simple matter of social justice, which led him to devise an *incentive management system* that sought to give labor a share in the output and profits of the company. This share was to be in direct proportion to the diligence, ingenuity, productivity, and cooperation of each worker.

In Lincoln's overall view of the appropriate relations between labor and management, he saw collective bargaining and governmental support of it as legalized "civil war." Both labor and management had the same interests: *to serve the customer* and, in the process, to benefit from their work in a fair and just manner. By establishing rules for conducting union–labor conflict, the government was, in a sense, writing rules for "war" between labor and management. Lincoln saw this as counterproductive to an attempt to serve the company's customers. Although they were never represented in these labor–management negotiations, the customers paid for both management and labor.

Lincoln believed that the Sermon on the Mount had six applications to labor relations:

1. Recognize that workers' greatest economic need is for income and security in that income, and that both labor and management have the same interests. But the workers' need for security in income can only be met by satisfying the needs of customers on a continuous basis. *Therefore, the customer is the key stakeholder whose needs are to be satisfied, and this should be done by applying the golden rule in the relations of the company to its customers.* He believed this should be the *goal of industry.*

This goal—as well as the deliberately cooperative relationships among customers, labor, and management—contrasts with the widely accepted view on the economic nature of the firm, as stated by Milton Friedman:[5]

In such an economy [one that is free], there is one and only one so-cial responsibility of business—to use its resources and engage in ac-tivities designed to increase its profits so long as it stays within the rules of the game, which is to say engages in open and free competi-tion, without deception or fraud. Similarly, the "social responsi-bility" of labor leaders is to serve the interests of the members of their unions. . . . Few trends could so seriously undermine the very foundations of our free society as the acceptance by corporate offi-cials of a social responsibility other than to make as much money for stockholders as possible. This is fundamentally a subversive doctrine.

2. Achieve the needs of the customer on a continuous basis by staying in touch with and in front of the needs of the customer. This happens when both management and the workforce apply continuous efforts to increasing *quality, customer service,* and *productivity,* which in turn provide the customer with new and improved products, higher quality products, and reduced prices. Thus, Lincoln advocated a "cost-based approach" to pricing.

This cost-based approach was (and still is) carried out alongside an effort to continuously improve the quality of the company's prod-ucts. Unlike many other U.S. companies, Lincoln Electric did not have to reengineer its production and quality control processes, or establish quality circles, to adopt a *total quality management* (TQM) process. The company has always focused on producing high-quality products at a low cost.

To James Lincoln, the goal was to produce more and more prod-uct, at better and better quality, at lower and lower prices, for more and more people. Following his example, the company has always re-garded this approach to the needs of the customer as the right and completely natural thing to do.

3. Provide the workers with the most modern tools of production (materials, methods, and machines) and with continuous train-ing and skill development, and encourage them to participate in solutions to all kinds of work-related problems. Besides raising the productivity of the workers and the quality of their work, these efforts also develop their talents and raise their *dignity, creativity, and self-respect.*

James Lincoln had a very high view of human beings and believed that, with proper management, training, and equipment, there was virtually no limit to the extent to which people could develop. His view on the "unlimited" potential of production workers was a radical change from the thinking of Henry Ford, who built his first plant for the mass production of automobiles in 1908.

4. Achieve continuous cost reduction and pass its benefits on to the customers in the form of lower prices. When combined with continuous increases in quality and the development of new and improved products, the golden rule is fulfilled as far as the customer is concerned.

5. Reward increased productivity, quality, and innovation via a merit system that puts *no upper limit* on what a worker can earn. On the other hand, workers should bear the penalty for lack of productivity, poor quality, absenteeism, and the absence of teamwork in fulfilling company goals. The incentive system should provide strong formal rewards according to variables that matter a great deal to the customer and increase the *economic and social status* of the worker. In the process, the worker becomes an entrepreneur.

When the workers contribute to progress and when a cooperative and trusting relationship is maintained between management and the workers, customers' needs are fulfilled and continuous employment can be achieved.

6. Recognize that the shareholders deserve a fair return on their investment. James Lincoln differentiated between a shareholder who helps to finance a new operation and one who simply trades shares for gain. Lincoln believed that to the extent a company is already launched and profitable, *a passive shareholder really does not contribute much to its success and is not deeply committed to its customers or its workers.* A shareholder who finances a new venture, however, adds great value and deserves a return commensurate with the risk of the new venture.

Potential conflict with shareholders has been largely avoided at Lincoln because most of the company's stock has traditionally been held by the Lincoln family and by the employees. That is true to this day, even though Lincoln Electric is now a public company. Conflict has also been avoided because the Lincoln philosophy has produced strong financial returns for the shareholders. (The financial returns earned by the shareholders of the company are discussed in Chapter 5.)

James Lincoln had a strong conviction that the concepts in the Sermon on the Mount could be successfully applied in business practice and *had in fact been applied successfully at the Lincoln Electric Company.* The operating values of the company are summarized in Table 1.1.

Table 1.1   Principal Operational Values of Lincoln Electric

Toward the Lincoln Customer
- Focus on customer service and customer satisfaction
- Focus on high-quality products (including ISO 9000 certifications)
- Focus on cost and price reductions—Guaranteed Cost Reduction Program
- Focus on continuous improvement and innovation

Toward the Lincoln Worker
- Strong employee focus
- Dignity of work and of the worker
- Openness and trust between management and workers
- Open-door policy between workers and top management and between middle and top management
- Continuous employment after probation period in domestic operations
- Focus on merit and accountability in performance measurement
- Egalitarian wage and salary structure
- Modest executive perquisites
- Strong focus on challenge, training, and development

Toward the Lincoln Stockholder
- Fair return to owners, most of whom are executives, board members, relatives of the Lincoln family, and workers

Some Problems
- Difficulty in transferring values to some acquisitions in foreign countries to implement global strategy
- Some need to phase in and adjust company culture to cultures of acquired foreign companies

The credo of the company—"The actual is limited, the possible is immense"—is engraved on the wall at the main entrance to the corporate headquarters in Cleveland, Ohio. This short form of the well-developed philosophy of James F. Lincoln supports his view of human nature. My analysis of his writings, especially his book *A New Approach to Industrial Economics,* reveals four assumptions that underlie his philosophy of human nature:

1. Humans have *endless abilities* if we will only recognize this fact and encourage individual development. Humans will then develop a continually greater economy.

2. There is no limit to the development of the human person and human cooperation, because humans are made in the image of their Creator.

3. There are many persons who, because of a greater effort, sparked by a handicap of lack of education, will develop themselves more than educated persons who feel that they have at least partially arrived. Genius is not merely the result of education.

4. The possibilities for humans, through development, are almost limitless. There may be limitations to an individual's possible development, but no one person yet has fully developed all of his or her latent abilities.

The attitude of management toward its workforce is central to workers' development and to the accomplishment of continuous improvement within the company. First and foremost, management must secure cooperative relationships with workers. Lincoln himself instituted numerous devices to accomplish this harmony.

Next, incentives that are meaningful to the workers must be developed. They include the potential for unlimited monetary rewards and promotion, depending on the worker's accomplishments. Financial rewards should represent distributive justice. Workers should receive rewards earned by their own physical strength, motivation, talents, and ability.

Lincoln did not believe that financial incentives were sufficient. Nonfinancial rewards, such as a sense of accomplishment, self-respect, status, recognition, and publicity, were also important—and sometimes more important—than monetary rewards to motivate workers.

Production workers are no different than managers, in this respect, and managers are most effective in bringing forth cooperation when they understand that their staff members have motivations similar to their own.

Nevertheless, formal and informal rewards, are not enough in themselves to bring forth cooperation. Communications must be open, free, and candid between management and labor. All parties must be seen as possessing similar interests. The workers' interests include a constant flow of income, and the managers' interests include a constant flow of profits. The interests of these two groups can only be met when they cooperate in meeting the genuine needs of the customer. Serving the customer is the primary goal of the enterprise, and effective service hinges on providing high-quality products at ever lower prices. Serving the customer also involves being knowledgeable about and solving problems. Sometimes this involves customer education, which, along with service, is the responsibility of the advertising and distribution functions of the company. The function of advertising is to inform potential customers about how the company's products might help solve their problems.

Serving the shareholders was Lincoln's last priority because, beyond providing venture capital to start or expand a business, they contributed little to satisfying the needs of the customer. Shareholders who purchase shares merely to collect dividends and capital gains contributed little to meeting customers' needs. Nevertheless, James Lincoln felt that even the shareholder would be better served if the needs of the customer and the worker were given primacy.

Continuous employment was the first step to *continuous improvement of operations.* If employees were laid off as a result of efficiency measures, there would be little incentive to create these efficiencies. And because the production workers are often in the best position to recommend improvements, workers must feel secure in their jobs if they are being asked to provide continuous improvements in operations.

Continuous improvement also requires management to add new tools and machinery to increase the workers' productivity. Every engineering design can be enhanced, every production and distribution method can be bettered, and every material used in production can be improved. Recessions may be used to rationalize and improve operations. Workers should not be discharged during difficult economic times. Their efforts along with those of management during these inevitable periods should be focused on improving operations and creating new markets.

Additional opportunities for production and sales may exist in new and foreign markets. James Lincoln himself started manufacturing and sales operations in Canada, Australia, and France during his life and tenure as Lincoln's chief executive.

Hours may be cut back so that no one is paid for being idle, but lean times should be used to improve operations and the company's products. Times of prosperity often create slack and inefficiencies that should be removed during leaner times. Thus, Lincoln saw lean times as opportunities to abandon any practices and products that were either inefficient or unprofitable.

Management has several significant responsibilities to the workers: to invest in new tools and technology; to obtain the orders and develop the markets that are necessary to maintain full employment; and, simultaneously, to improve the efficiency of existing operations. Management also has the responsibility for creating a climate of friendly competition among the workforce. As a former football star at Ohio State, Lincoln compared the friendly competitions that should exist in a company with those that exist on well-functioning athletic teams. The objective is to create an environment in which workers can be "stretched" to develop their talents.

Lincoln's Values and the Customer

Lincoln Electric has applied the golden rule to its customers by providing high quality products, a continuous stream of product innovations, strong customer liaisons resulting in strong customer service, and continuous cost reductions that are passed on to customers in the form of lower prices. Over much of Lincoln's 104-year history, its prices have remained fairly constant in nominal dollars despite inflation, except during those periods when the United States experienced very high levels of inflation. To accomplish this and pay its production workers more than twice the average wage of a similar cohort of workers in the Cleveland area has required significant and continuous improvement in employee productivity. Lincoln's history not only is one of continuously improving productivity but also continuously improving the quality of its products.

To further strengthen Lincoln's long-standing emphasis on cost reduction, the company instituted, in 1986, a *Guaranteed Cost Reduction Program* that has become the principal marketing strategy of the company.

Under this program, Lincoln's sales engineers are put through extensive training in which they are taught to understand customers' problems and to propose solutions that guarantee cost reductions if Lincoln's instructions are followed. If cost reductions do not materialize after following the prescribed procedures, Lincoln pays its customer the difference between what was promised and what was achieved. This customer enrichment accounts for the extraordinary loyalty Lincoln enjoys from both its customers and its distributors.

Lincoln's Values and the Worker

The golden rule's direct implications for the treatment of employees are clearly reflected in the company's operational values. Respect for the *dignity* of the worker is key among them. Lincoln's top management is well aware of the role work plays in contributing to the dignity and self-respect of its production workers.

The company is very selective in its hiring practices; "only one applicant in 75 is hired, and half of them leave within 90 days."[6] Nevertheless, until recently, the company employed anyone, regardless of educational level, if the person was believed to have the motivation and ability to do a specific job. At present, a high school diploma is required for employment in domestic operations.

To further promote the dignity of the worker and to improve the operations of the company, Lincoln encourages genuine *openness and trust between management and the production worker*. To do this, top management has established numerous formal and informal arrangements that facilitate open dialogue with production employees. Most prominent among these arrangements is an employee-elected advisory board that meets biweekly with top management to discuss workplace issues and to resolve problems. Creation of the advisory board in 1914 was one of the first actions taken by James Lincoln as general manager. Lincoln said, "[I]f I could get the people in the Company to want the Company to succeed as badly as I did, there would be no problems we could not solve together" (Lincoln, 1961, p. 8).

This openness contributes to a high level of trust between top management and employees. By being so open to the ideas of production employees, Lincoln has encouraged the development of their *rational, managerial,* and *creative capacities,* which in turn has contributed significantly to the company's agility, competitiveness, and success. "[W]ith very few foremen around, workers must often make decisions on their own."[7]

Application of the golden rule is also seen in the responsibility management assumes for the development of its subordinates. Lincoln seeks to develop the natural capacities of its workers in order for them to assume certain levels of managerial responsibility and accountability. This is in turn reinforced by significant incentives, which focus on production workers' *productivity, cooperation, quality of work,* and *innovation.*

The golden rule has also led Lincoln to adopt a wage and salary structure in which everyone shares fairly in the company's prosperity and adversity. In 1995, for example, the ratio between the salary of the chairman and president of Lincoln Electric and the total compensation of the average factory worker was 15 : 1. The chairman earned approximately $900,000, and the average factory worker earned $60,000. In 1992, the ratio in Japan was 20 : 1 and the overall ratio in the United States was 100 : 1.[8] In 1965, the ratio of salaries of CEOs to the wages of average factory workers was 44 : 1. In 1997, the overall ratio between U.S. CEOs and the average factory worker increased to a ratio 326 : 1.[9] The pay disparity between CEOs and U.S. workers is increasing to alarming levels.

As a result of these salary and wage disparities, the egalitarian pay structure at Lincoln Electric certainly lends substantial credibility to Lincoln's values and contributes to the atmosphere of trust that exists between management and the production workers. It demonstrates that top management is operating equitably in relationship to its employees.

Job security is also a major value of the company toward its employees and that, too, began with James Lincoln (Lincoln, 1961, p. 38). The company *formally* guarantees domestic employees with three or more years' experience at least 30 hours of work per week. In return, employees must be willing to work overtime as required, and if, due to lack of work, an employee is shifted to a position carrying a lesser pay grade, that person must accept the associated adjustment in pay.

The company makes a commitment to the worker, and the worker makes a commitment to the company.

By treating employees with dignity and respect; by providing employees access to top management; by sharing fully with employees the fruits of their labor through salaries, bonuses, and stock purchase plans; and by providing job security, Lincoln is clearly implementing the golden rule with regard to its workers. Through the implementation of these values and the effective development of all its people, Lincoln has developed a skilled and knowledgeable workforce that has allowed the company to build competitive advantage. Lincoln's success is more the result of *the development of its people* than of the company's investment in plant, technology, and materials.

Furthermore, management's strong commitment to employees over the past century has paid dividends in terms of the virtues that have long been observed in the company's workforce. These virtues are presented in Table 1.2.[10] Here is where Lincoln shines: Pride of workmanship is high, and identification with the company is strong. Although the company promotes strong individualistic behavior on the part of Lincoln's employees, it fully recognizes the interdependence of

Table 1.2 Virtues Encouraged by Lincoln's Management Systems

Lincoln's management systems have encouraged the development of these internal virtues, which are consistent with the Judeo-Christian work ethic:

- Honesty
- Trustworthiness
- Openness
- Diligence
- Creativity
- Ability to manage oneself
- Loyalty to company and customers
- Fairness in the treatment of one another
- Hard-working people whose eyes are on the task and not the clock
- Teachability/Humility
- Accountability
- Competence
- Punctuality
- Cooperativeness—ability to get along with others and build community

its workers and, through the implementation of the golden rule, imposes common moral understandings about how these relationships are to be regulated in the workplace. Nevertheless, the interdependence of operations does sometimes cause trouble among production workers when one or more workers fail to perform their duties efficiently.[11] This always occurs under a piecework system in which there is dependency among employees.

Lincoln's Values and the Shareholder— Adapting to Recent Problems

Already an international producer and distributor of arc-welding equipment, Lincoln launched into a very aggressive international acquisition program in Europe, Asia, and Latin America, beginning in 1986. Numerous factors indicated that an aggressive international expansion program was overdue:

1. The mature nature of the domestic market.
2. The shifts to offshore production by U.S. manufacturers, including some of Lincoln's customers.
3. The problem of substitutes for steel, such as plastics, aluminum, and concrete.
4. The impact of foreign competition on Lincoln's need to achieve scale economies and remain a global, low-cost producer of arc-welding equipment and consumables.

Lincoln was acquainted with foreign operations. Under the influence of James Lincoln, the company had opened "greenfield" manufacturing operations in three foreign countries. The first of the three operations was established in Toronto, Canada, in 1925. Next, in 1938, Lincoln built manufacturing facilities and established sales offices in Sydney, Australia, to serve the Australian and Asian markets. The third and last expansion during the era of James F. Lincoln occurred in 1955 when Lincoln was invited to start manufacturing operations in France, under the Marshall Plan.[12]

After the death of James Lincoln on June 23, 1965, William Irrgang, a brilliant engineer who had at one time experienced the terror of Nazi Germany, became president and later chairman of the company. Given his experiences in Europe, he remained skeptical of foreign expansion and sought to serve customers worldwide from Lincoln's plants in Ohio or from the facilities in Canada, Australia, or France. He was firmly opposed to additional foreign expansion. And expansion through acquisitions of domestic competitors was not permissible under antitrust laws in the United States given Lincoln's dominant position in the welding consumables and equipment markets in this country. In 1986, when George Willis became chairman of Lincoln Electric after the death of William Irrgang, Willis immediately signaled the need for Lincoln to begin an aggressive program of international expansion.

Lincoln then began to embark on a program to increase its competitiveness in international markets. To improve economies of scale in its Canadian and U.S. operations, Lincoln acquired, in 1986, the manufacturing assets and product licenses for welding consumables of Airco, US Oxygen's arc-welding operations. These assets were located both in Montreal and in Cleveland. After the purchase of Airco, they were consolidated in Cleveland.[13]

In 1987, Lincoln acquired L'Air Liquide's liquid arc-welding operations in Australia. After the acquisition, Lincoln sold the acquired manufacturing plant and merged its consumable business and sales force with Lincoln's previously established Australian operations. This acquisition resulted in economies of scale in Lincoln's Australian subsidiary.[14]

Lincoln acquired two companies in Brazil—Brasoldas and Torsima—in 1987 and 1988, respectively. They were combined to create one Brazilian subsidiary in Rio de Janeiro. These facilities included a large plant for the production of consumables. Lincoln's purpose in these two acquisitions was to serve Brazil's large market for welding equipment and consumables, an outgrowth of the country's large structural steel fabrication industry. The Brazilian subsidiary also gave Lincoln access to a growing market in Chile.[15]

Construction of a plant in Naraha, Japan (Japan-Nippon Lincoln Electric KK), was completed in 1989. The purpose of this plant was to gain access to the Japanese distribution system, which, at the time, was biased against foreign manufacturers. This, in turn, led Lincoln to sign a contract with 30 welding distributors in Japan. Lincoln was seeking to gain acceptance of its welding products in Japan's huge building-construction market. Lincoln's strategy was to be the lowest-cost and highest-quality producer of welding equipment and consumables in Japan.[16]

Lincoln completed a new plant for the manufacturing of welding consumables in Venezuela (Venezuela-Lincoln Electric CA) in 1989. This plant was consolidated with the full acquisition of a previous joint venture in Carabobo, Venezuela.[17]

Lincoln purchased Harris Calorific from the Emerson Electric Company in 1992. Harris Calorific (calorific means the science of heat), the oldest manufacturer of gas welding and cutting apparatus in the United States,[18] then became a separate division of The Lincoln Electric Company. The division is headquartered and has manufacturing facilities in Gainsville, Georgia: other facilities are in Pianoro and Milano, Italy; Rathnew, Ireland; and Monterey Park, California. The plants in Italy and Ireland were acquired as a part of a deal between Lincoln Electric and Norweld Holding A/S of Norway.

In March 1988, Lincoln purchased the assets of Armco Mexicana in Mexico City. Armco was primarily an electrode manufacturer. In May 1988, Lincoln acquired Industrias Sigma, a welding machine manufacturer. In 1992, Lincoln purchased Champion International, it produced electrodes, welding machines, and welding wire. These three acquisitions were all brought together in Mexico City.[19]

In 1988, Lincoln entered into a joint venture with Norweld Holding A/S of Oslo, Norway. The initial contract called for Lincoln to own approximately one-third of the joint venture. Norweld manufactured welding machines and consumables. In 1989, Norweld sold its British subsidiary to Lincoln (Lincoln Electric UK) as part of the original agreement. In 1989, Lincoln acquired Lincoln KD SA, Spain, and it became part of its Norweld operations. This increased Lincoln's ownership of the joint venture to approximately two-thirds. In 1992, the company purchased the remaining interests, and Norweld became a wholly owned subsidiary of Lincoln Electric.

Lincoln Smitweld bv, a manufacturer of consumables, with a plant located in Nijmegen, the Netherlands, had been owned by Norweld and was acquired by Lincoln as part of its overall deal with Norweld. By 1991, Lincoln Norweld had become Lincoln's major European subsidiary.

Lincoln's next big move was to purchase, in 1991, the welding equipment business of Meser-Griesheim of Germany (renamed Messer-Lincoln Gmbh). The German acquisition was made because the German market for equipment and electrodes was estimated at 40 percent of the entire European market. Lincoln did not have adequate participation in the German welding market and Meser-Griesheim had a 25 percent share.[20] The new company was headquartered in Frankfurt, Germany, and manufactured arc-welding equipment in Volklingen.

Messer-Lincoln Gmbh was the most expensive of all of Lincoln's foreign acquisitions. Although exact costs of the purchase of Meser-Griesheim are not available, the notes (especially Note G) to the financial statements contained in the company's *1991 Annual Report* indicate that the purchase price was in excess of $75 million.

Donald Hastings estimates that the entire foreign acquisition program carried out by George Willis cost $325 million.[21]

Problems of the Rapid Foreign Acquisition Program

The acquisition of manufacturing capacity in Germany, Brazil, Venezuela, and Japan did not prove to be a wise decision, and Lincoln rapidly restructured and divested itself of these operations. Lincoln also streamlined and reduced operations in their other European plants. This resulted in operating losses and restructuring charges in 1992 and 1993. The combination of losses on foreign operations and associated restructuring charges led to overall losses (after taxes) of $23.9 million and $70.1 million in 1992 and 1993 respectively. Estimates of after-tax losses from this rapid foreign expansion program, including restructuring charges, exceeded $100 million. The losses in 1992 and 1993 were the first consolidated losses ever recorded in the company's history.[22]

The company encountered a number of difficulties when it attempted to adapt its culture and management systems to foreign operations. In some countries, such as Mexico, adaptation worked very well; in other countries, Lincoln encountered great resistance and consequently faced operating difficulties and financial losses.

The three companies Lincoln acquired in Mexico were not performing well before the acquisition. Lincoln moved a sales engineer from Cleveland to become general manager of the single consolidated company in Mexico City. The general manager thoroughly believed in the principles of the Lincoln management system, and began implementing principles enunciated by James Lincoln shortly after arriving. In doing so, however, he adapted the practices to the laws and culture of Mexico.

Lincoln's German-made products became noncompetitive as a result of mandated social welfare costs of employment, coupled with rigidities in German work rules and low levels of worker productivity relative to those at Lincoln's U.S. operations. For example, piece rates are not permitted under German law, nor is labor mobility or cross-training of the workforce. Each of these elements plays an important role in creating competitive manufacturing and management systems at Lincoln.

In another oversight, Lincoln was not aware that Brazilian law mandates that bonuses paid to employees for two consecutive years become part of the employees' base wage. This legal mandate severed the link between Lincoln's reward system and the company's productivity in that country. Lincoln also encountered unforeseen and fierce competitive obstacles in Brazil and Venezuela.

Losses encountered in Lincoln's foreign operations threatened the company's loan covenants and, potentially, its financial solvency. The company was in violation of the covenants attached to the loans that were necessary to finance the expansion program.

Shareholder returns were poor for the four-year period from 1990 through 1993. Return on average shareholder equity was a mere *4.4 percent in 1990* and *5.5 percent in 1991,* and then fell drastically to *minus 19.78 percent in 1992* and *minus 22 percent in 1993.* Lincoln, traditionally a low-debt company, increased long-term debt to $250 million and to 63 percent of average stockholder equity.[23]

During these difficult times, Lincoln's workers, particularly those in the Ohio Company (i.e., the two Ohio plants), put forth heroic efforts to further improve domestic operations and thus try to offset the foreign losses that the company had incurred. To boost production it was necessary to identify and eliminate bottlenecks in the Cleveland plants. Once the critical areas were identified "415 people in bottleneck areas gave up 614 weeks of vacation, and some people worked seven days straight for months on end."[24] From 1991 to 1992, productivity of the employees of the Ohio Company, as measured by *sales per employee,* increased by 6 percent; and from 1992 to 1993, productivity increased by 12 percent.

Lincoln's management, in turn, rationalized its foreign acquisitions, and, as a result, foreign operations turned profitable in 1994 and remained so through 1998 and into 1999. The return on equity (ROE) for the average shareholder since 1994 has averaged approximately 20 percent. This is an excellent return, especially for this industry.

It is important to observe that Lincoln Electric responded quite naturally to this adversity—there was no need for change projects or for reengineering of its operations. The *resilient trust* between management and workers led to extraordinary mutual efforts to respond and correct a very serious problem. The *agility* exhibited by Lincoln in solving this problem was a completely natural manifestation of the human values deeply imbedded within the culture of the company.

We turn now to examine and analyze the management systems that are currently in place at Lincoln Electric.

Notes

1. Lincoln Electric Holdings, Inc., Press Release, "Lincoln Electric Posts Record Earnings for 1998," February 3, 1999.

2. See James F. Lincoln, *A New Approach to Industrial Economics* (New York: Devin-Adir Company, 1961). His two other books deal exclusively with the incentive management system instituted at Lincoln Electric. They are *Lincoln's Incentive System* (New York: McGraw-Hill, 1946) and *Incentive Management* (Cleveland, OH: Lincoln Electric Company, 1951). Another book, *The American Century of John C. Lincoln,* by Raymond Moley, is a biography of John C. Lincoln and presents useful background information on the company.

3. New International Version of the Bible (New York: Hawthorne Books, 1962, 1975).

4. This information is adapted, with permission, from James F. Lincoln, *A New Approach to Industrial Economics* (New York: The Devin-Adir Company, 1961).

5. Milton Friedman, *Capitalism and Freedom* (Chicago: University of Chicago Press, 1962), 133.

6. A quote from Richard Sabo of Lincoln Electric, in Section 3, Money & Business, "Royal Blue Collars," p. 12, of *The New York Times* (Sunday, March 22, 1998).

7. Ibid., p. 12.

8. Reported on the *MacNeil/Lehrer News Hour,* June 5, 1992, and reproduced in Kenneth Chilton, "Lincoln Electric Incentive System: Can It Be Transferred Overseas?" *Compensation and Benefits Review* (November–December 1993): 25.

9. *Business Week,* April 21, 1997, and April 20, 1998. Quoted in ExecutivePayWatch, http://www.paywatch.org/paywatch/index.htm.

10. These virtues are strongly related to those identified by Max Weber, *The Protestant Ethic and the Spirit of Capitalism,* trans. Talcott Parsons (New York: Charles Scribner's Sons, 1958); by Michael Novak, *The Spirit of Democratic Capitalism* (New York: Simon and Schuster, 1982); and Michael Novak, *The Catholic Ethic and the Spirit of Capitalism* (New York: Free Press, 1993).

11. Section 3, Money & Business, p. 12, *The New York Times* (Sunday, March 22, 1998).

12. Christopher A. Bartlett and Jamie O'Connell, *Lincoln Electric: Venturing Abroad,* Boston: Harvard Business School, Case 9-398-095 (April 22, 1998): 5.

13. The Lincoln Electric Company, *1987 Annual Report,* p. 2, Cleveland, Ohio; and Scott J. Schraff, "Strategic Management at The Lincoln Electric Company" (master's thesis, Cleveland State University, 1993): 26.

14. *1987 Annual Report,* 2; Schraff, 32.

15. *1987 Annual Report,* 2; Schraff, 34.

16. *1988 Annual Report,* 2; Schraff, 32–33.

17. Ibid.

18. http://www.lincolnelectric.com/corp98/index.htm.

19. The Lincoln Electric Company, *1988 Annual Report,* p. 2, Cleveland, OH; Schraff, "Strategic Management," 34–35.

20. *1990 Annual Report,* 2; Schraff, 29.

21. Donald F. Hastings, "Lincoln Electric's Harsh Lessons from International Expansion," *Harvard Business Review,* May–June 1999, p. 164.

22. Ibid., p. 163.

23. Ibid., p. 168.

24. Ibid., p. 174.

Chapter
2

Management Systems:
Management Style and Philosophy

In this and subsequent chapters, I describe and analyze the current management systems at Lincoln Electric. Following the general approach illustrated by Figures 2.1 and 2.2, the influence of Lincoln Electric's values on the design of the company's *formal* and *informal* management systems is traced. These management systems are used to implement Lincoln's various stakeholder strategies.

FORMAL AND INFORMAL ORGANIZATIONS AND MANAGEMENT SYSTEMS

Formal management systems are used in the formal organization of institutions. A formal organization is defined as the system of coordination authorized by the management of an organization. Barnard defines it as "a system of consciously coordinated activities or forces of two or more persons."[1] Formal organization is also "the planned structure and represents the deliberate attempt to establish patterned relationships among components that will meet the objectives effectively."[2] Formal management systems are designed by management to establish patterns of behavior that will permit the organization to achieve its goals and objectives. These systems are effective if they facilitate the communication of relevant information to the decision makers. Communication is used for carrying out the tasks of planning, measurement, resource allocation, performance reporting, and performance appraisal.

Informal management systems are used by the informal organizations of institutions. As defined by Barnard, "informal organization is the aggregate of the personal contacts and interactions and associated groupings of people. . . . Though common or joint purposes are excluded by definition, common or joint results of important character nevertheless come from such organization."[3] Informal organization is defined as a web of "personal and social relations which is not established or required by formal organization. It arises from the social interaction of people which means that it develops spontaneously as people associate with each other."[4] The informal management systems evolve as a system of interpersonal relationships that are potentially very useful for carrying out the same functions as the formal management systems. Informal management systems are not based on formal authority but rather upon relationships.

Formal and informal organizations and management systems are highly interdependent. In Barnard's words, "They are interdependent aspects of the same phenomena—a society is structured by formal organizations, formal organizations are vitalized and conditioned by informal organization. . . . there cannot be one without the other. If one fails, the other disintegrates."[5] Similarly, Davis believes that management should seek "to integrate closely the long-run interests of the formal and informal systems so that they will operate to evaluate and reward people in about the same way."[6]

In other words, formal and informal management systems should be mutually supportive and aligned with the requirements of the environment in which the company operates. This internal and external alignment is necessary to effectively implement organization strategies. Dysfunction is the result if the interrelated formal and informal systems are misaligned. The resulting dysfunctions lead to poor performance.[7]

GENERAL MODELS FOR THE DESIGN OF MANAGEMENT SYSTEMS

The management systems at Lincoln Electric in relationship to the environment are discussed, as well as the relationships between the entire set of formal and informal management systems.

Lincoln's management systems account for much of the historical success of the company's managerial processes. The combination of management systems and processes in turn produce organizational qualities that explain the long-term success of the company.

Figures 2.1 and 2.2 provide us with an "engine of analysis" to describe and analyze the effects of executive leadership, values, and beliefs on the management systems of Lincoln Electric. This success is difficult to understand without an understanding of the detailed design of their system of management.

If executives of other companies are seeking to duplicate the results achieved by Lincoln, they must understand the interrelated "systemic effects" of their values subsystems and systems.

Agile or Adaptive Management Systems

Agile management systems[8] consist of a set of formal and informal systems designed to assist management in steering an organization toward the achievement of its purpose by bringing unity out of the diverse efforts of subunits and of individuals. These two sets of systems are distinct but highly interrelated, sometimes indistinguishable, subdivisions of management systems. They are considered agile if the two systems are internally consistent with one another and designed to permit learning so as to meet the competitive challenges posed by the environment on a continuous basis.

The Formal Systems

Formal systems (see Figure 2.1) make possible the delegation of authority, by making *explicit* the structure, policies, and procedures to be followed by members of the organization. Formal documentation of these structures, policies, and procedures assist members of the

Figure 2.1   Formal Management Systems.

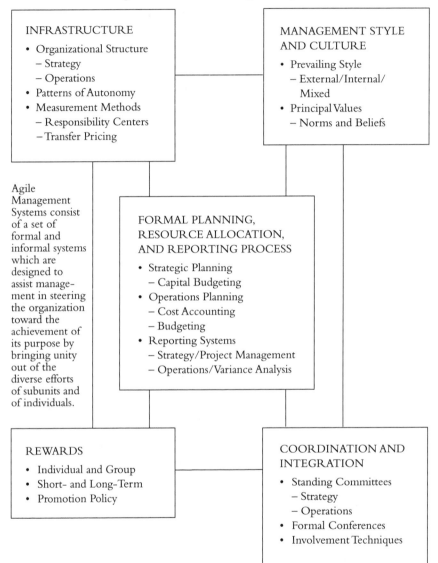

INFRASTRUCTURE

• Organizational Structure
  – Strategy
  – Operations
• Patterns of Autonomy
• Measurement Methods
  – Responsibility Centers
  – Transfer Pricing

MANAGEMENT STYLE
AND CULTURE

• Prevailing Style
  – External/Internal/
    Mixed
• Principal Values
  – Norms and Beliefs

Agile
Management
Systems consist
of a set of
formal and
informal systems
which are
designed to
assist manage-
ment in steering
the organization
toward the
achievement of
its purpose by
bringing unity
out of the
diverse efforts
of subunits and
of individuals.

FORMAL PLANNING,
RESOURCE ALLOCATION,
AND REPORTING PROCESS

• Strategic Planning
  – Capital Budgeting
• Operations Planning
  – Cost Accounting
  – Budgeting
• Reporting Systems
  – Strategy/Project Management
  – Operations/Variance Analysis

REWARDS

• Individual and Group
• Short- and Long-Term
• Promotion Policy

COORDINATION AND
INTEGRATION

• Standing Committees
  – Strategy
  – Operations
• Formal Conferences
• Involvement Techniques

organization in performing their duties. Figure 2.1 is a generic overview set of five mutually supportive management subsystems. This system of structures, procedures, and patterned responses assists management in planning and maintaining strategies to meet organizational goals in routine and stable environments.

The formal subsystems are designed to focus on the needs of customers and markets, to be consistent with the informal systems of the organization, and to be mutually supportive of each other. Moreover, each subsystem is designed to include explicit provision for managing both short-term concerns and the innovations necessary to remain competitive.

The subsystems of the formal management systems, shown in Figure 2.1, are:

- Management style and culture of the organization
- Infrastructure
- Rewards
- Coordination and integration
- Control process

The Informal Systems

As stated earlier, all organizations have informal dimensions that are a companion set of systems to the formal. They complement the formal systems in a manner similar to the way the informal organization complements the formal organization.

Informal systems require of management a mind-set that differs from that required to operate formal structures, policies, and procedures. "Formality" in these systems leads to a pattern of defined and explicit behaviors and expectations; "informality" refers to a pattern of interacting roles.

Figure 2.2 contains a summary of the structure of mutually supportive management subsystems that comprise the informal systems. For the formal infrastructure, the informal counterpart is emergent roles. Emergent roles are the informal relationships and responsibilities based on expertise, experience, and trust; they build cooperative norms and facilitate problem solving and learning through the development of

Figure 2.2   Informal Management Systems.

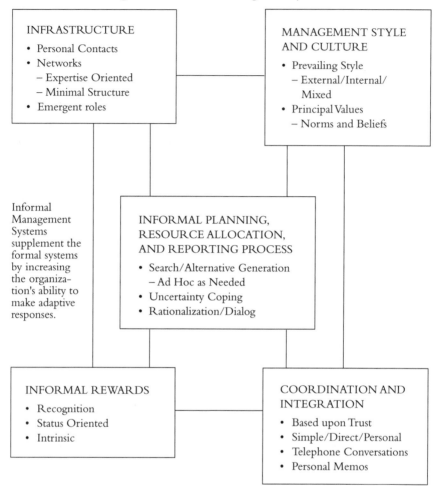

INFRASTRUCTURE

• Personal Contacts
• Networks
  – Expertise Oriented
  – Minimal Structure
• Emergent roles

MANAGEMENT STYLE
AND CULTURE

• Prevailing Style
  – External/Internal/
    Mixed
• Principal Values
  – Norms and Beliefs

Informal
Management
Systems
supplement the
formal systems
by increasing
the organiza-
tion's ability to
make adaptive
responses.

INFORMAL PLANNING,
RESOURCE ALLOCATION,
AND REPORTING PROCESS

• Search/Alternative Generation
  – Ad Hoc as Needed
• Uncertainty Coping
• Rationalization/Dialog

INFORMAL REWARDS

• Recognition
• Status Oriented
• Intrinsic

COORDINATION AND
INTEGRATION

• Based upon Trust
• Simple/Direct/Personal
• Telephone Conversations
• Personal Memos

informal working relationships. Informal contacts promote compatibility among personnel, build community, and encourage the "willingness to serve" organizational purposes. The remaining three outer
boxes are recognition activities, informal coordinating mechanisms, and
style and culture. Recognition activities consist of personal feedback
based on performance; informal coordinating mechanisms are cooperative networks of relationships that emerge as a result of socialization
and mutual adjustment; and style and culture consist of the prevailing
style of management and the principal values of the organization.

Outside of the formal management process, informal management consists of activities engaged in by members of the organization when encountering nonroutine decision making, such as realignment of goals or new information to increase understanding of new opportunities, problem areas, and potential solutions to problems.

These informal systems supplement the formal systems by increasing an organization's ability to learn and to make proactive and adaptive responses. Informal systems usually develop as complex patterns of interpersonal activities or temporary structures controlled by the prevailing culture that supports management in adapting and maintaining the organization in the face of environmental changes. As with the five formal subsystems, each informal subsystem should be designed in a mutually supportive and reinforcing manner.

It is critical to recognize that if the "values espoused" by Lincoln or any other company are to be congruent with those values "in action" in the organization, these values must affect the detailed design and operation of both formal and informal management systems.

MANAGEMENT SYSTEMS: STYLE AND PHILOSOPHY

There have been six chief executive officers over the 104-year history of Lincoln Electric, although the style of management at the top has not been constant for this time period.[9] Yet there have been some aspects that have remained fairly constant.

James F. Lincoln developed Lincoln's management philosophy and its values. His philosophy, thoroughly grounded in Judeo-Christian ethics, has had certain implications as to how the company manages relationships with its employees, customers, and shareholders. That part of the management philosophy at Lincoln has been largely constant during its 104-year history. There have been, however, significant differences in the styles of management of the six CEOs.

James Lincoln was known to be fairly autocratic in that he reserved a great deal of authority for himself as the CEO. He believed "very strongly in his ability to control resources, coordinate activities, and balance the needs better than anyone else."[10]

Lincoln's philosophy of management also reflected a high regard for human beings, consisting of a strong belief in the ability of employees to develop for the good of themselves and the customers of the company. This belief was then and is now backed up by significant effort on management's part to facilitate the process of employee development.

Management's philosophy includes dedication to extensive employee training and development, which involves a commitment to inviting employees to participate in company decisions as long as that involvement is in areas where the employees have expertise. In addition, the philosophy has always recognized human dignity and manifests itself in trust in and respect for employees. Finally, the philosophy embodies a dedication to reward employees according to their productivity, creativity, and dedications. These characteristics have been the hallmark of the management philosophy at Lincoln for its entire history. In return, employees have responded with extraordinary efforts geared toward helping the company succeed.

James Lincoln was, by accounts of those who knew him, a shy person. While maintaining a strong direction of the company from the top, he also established a significant set of collaborative and participative relationships between management and employees. He established an advisory board in 1914. Although extensive, participation was then and is now restricted to areas in which employees have an interest and can demonstrate operational expertise.

William Irrgang, appointed as CEO by James Lincoln in 1965, followed a similar management style. He was very much a controller. He was committed to incentive management, productivity, and cost control, and he was determined to continue the existing management philosophy and perfect the systems. Irrgang firmly opposed global expansion.

George Willis was different. Appointed by William Irrgang in 1986, he sought to break what he perceived as the "insularity" of the company. As a part of this process, he recruited new engineering and marketing talent and broadened Lincoln's product line. Willis maintained the organizational principles established by James Lincoln and perpetuated by Irrgang, such as a flat organization structure with a very large span of control between supervisors and employees, a strong emphasis on productivity and cost control, and an equally strong commitment to incentive management. Still, Willis's practices differed significantly from his two predecessors. Like his two predecessors, Willis pushed productivity and cost reduction very hard and was by all evidence one of the finest manufacturing executives in the nation. He believed that

Lincoln was the best manufacturing company in the world. But he was unlike his predecessors in the amount of attention he gave to the company's customers. Willis spent approximately one week per month out in the field visiting customers. Willis also differed from James Lincoln and William Irrgang in that his managerial style emphasized power sharing. Willis gave significant amounts of autonomy and accountability to subordinates. Although both James Lincoln and William Irrgang appointed their successors when they were close to death, Willis established a more orderly succession planning process. He also began a series of management training programs both to broaden and deepen the management expertise. Recognizing that business was becoming global, he was eager to expand Lincoln's foreign operations.

The management style of Donald Hastings was even more participative and fluid. He emphasized teamwork and he gave significant levels of autonomy to his president and chief operating officer, Fred Mackenbach. He practiced a very "hands-on" management style. Hastings took on the role of increasing sales, and Mackenbach took on the role of reducing costs.[11] The regional vice presidents were also granted more autonomy in overseeing North American and international operations.

Early indications are that Anthony (Tony) Massaro, Lincoln's sixth CEO and chairman, is building a global corporation. He is granting significant autonomy to regional presidents and to country managers. The formal management information systems connecting the parts of the company also have been improved considerably. Commenting on Massaro's approach to restructuring Lincoln's European operations, Jay Elliot, Lincoln's chief financial officer, states:

> Tony did not follow the historical Lincoln practice of imposing a solution from on high. Instead, he created a European Management Team, comprised of the general manager of each facility. . . . We were collectively responsible for gathering comparable data, then analyzing them to determine which plants would close and how production would be shifted around.[12]

Table 2.1 highlights the major characteristics of the prevailing management style at Lincoln Electric. It is characterized by strong formal authority at all management levels and is also typically "hands-on." Historically, top management at Lincoln has always known

Table 2.1   Management Style and Philosophy at Lincoln Electric

- Strong formal authority of each management position is the hallmark of the management style at Lincoln. Each department has complete authority. Significant levels of managerial autonomy have been emerging recently at Lincoln.
- Hands-on operational management style is prevalent.
- Openness and trust characterize relationships between management and labor.
- Status symbols distinguishing management and workers are minimal, but they are increasing as the company becomes public and global.
- Managers are the coaches who must be obeyed—workers are the players, and only the players can win the game.
- Management actively seeks participation in each worker's area of expertise.
- The most important participative technique is to grant significant responsibility and authority to employees, thereby enhancing trust.
- Participation is confined to issues about which employees are knowledgeable.
- No union or work rules exist in domestic operations—harmonious relationships between labor and management is the norm.
- Foreign operations vary significantly and are mostly unionized.

"welding." Even Massaro, the current CEO and chairman, although relatively new to the company, knows the welding business—he was group president for Industries and Environmental Systems in his previous position at Westinghouse. Not only does Massaro understand the business, he has had extensive international experience, which was badly needed at Lincoln.

There has never been a disconnect at Lincoln between strategy formulation at the top and what takes place on the production floor. This linkage between strategy and operations is a characteristic of highly competitive companies.

Lincoln's strong formal authority is balanced by its equally strong commitment to empowering its workforce. In fact, the span of control ratio between production workers and supervisors is approximately 100:1 giving management little choice but to grant significant amounts of autonomy to workers and to listen to their suggestions. Participation, is not blanket; management authority is reserved.

There may be a slight bias against middle management at Lincoln. One hears that "management often tends to be obstructionist. If you have creative people on the production floor, get rid of the people over them." This attitude toward management, together with its huge span of control, has led to real *empowerment* of production-level personnel—another characteristic of highly competitive organizations.

The extensive span of control at Lincoln does create the need for honesty and judgment among production workers. Because there simply are not enough supervisors to monitor productivity levels of individual production workers "honest counts" of output are required to facilitate the piecework system. Commitment to the truth is an operational value.

Lincoln does not use its supervisors to ensure that its people are working—that task is handled by the piecework system, the honor system, and the merit bonus program. Instead, management sees its role as that of coach who is in charge but who clearly recognizes that it is the players (i.e., the workers) who "win or lose the game." Thus, although the management system is directive, it is simultaneously empowering. The most important aspect of the company's empowerment program is the considerable amount of responsibility and trust that is placed in the hands of the workers. The belief is that through education, training, and experience, workers are able to operate as entrepreneurs and managers in order to make decisions within their specific areas of responsibility. These practices encourage workers to develop personal, creative, and managerial mastery.

During Lincoln's history, relationships between management and workers in its domestic operations have been harmonious. Contributing to this is the absence of status symbols within the company. The level of trust and goodwill between management and workers has also allowed Lincoln to operate without unions.

As in most organizations, the quality of first-line supervision at Lincoln varies considerably. Most supervisors at Lincoln perform their intended role of coaching which is widely advocated by management writers as the proper role for middle management in organizations that seek to become learning organizations. The principal proponent for this role of management is Peter Senge. His arguments are made in his influential book, *The Fifth Discipline*.[13]

The management style at Lincoln's foreign operations is more diverse, making it impossible to generalize. Management styles do differ from country to country, and work rules do exist in some foreign operations. Personnel familiar with the cultures of the countries in which Lincoln operates now manage most foreign operations.

Notes

1. Chester I. Barnard, *The Functions of the Executive* (Cambridge: Harvard University Press, 1968), 73.

2. Fremont E. Kast and James E. Rosenzweig, *Organization and Management: A Systems and Contingency Approach,* 4th ed. (New York: McGraw-Hill, 1985), 235.

3. Barnard, 115.

4. Keith Davis, "Informal Organization," in *Human Relations in Business* (New York: McGraw-Hill, 1959), 98–118, and in Harold Koontz and Cyril O'Donnell, *Readings in Management* (New York: McGraw-Hill, 1959), 234.

5. Barnard, 120.

6. Davis, 253.

7. These findings are supported by the works of Peter M. Blau and Richard W. Scott, *Formal Organizations: A Comparative Approach* (San Francisco: Chandler Publishing, 1962); and E. J. Miller and A. K. Rice, *Systems of Organization: The Control of Task and Sentiment Boundaries* (London: Tavistock Publications, 1967).

8. This section, especially Figures 2.1 and 2.2, reflect the overall approach to the design of management systems taken in Joseph A. Maciariello and Calvin J. Kirby, *Management Control Systems: Using Adaptive Systems to Attain Control* (Englewood Cliffs, NJ: Prentice-Hall, 1994). The general approach is repeated in Calvin J. Kirby and Joseph A. Maciariello, "Integrated Product Development and Adaptive Management Systems," *Drucker Management* (fall 1994); in Joseph A. Maciariello, "Management Systems at ServiceMaster: A Theocentric Approach," *Drucker Management* (spring 1996); and in "Management Systems at Lincoln Electric: A Century of Agility," *Journal of Agility and Global Competition,* Vol. I, No. 4 (New York: John Wiley & Sons, 1997), 46–61. The two *Drucker Management* issues were published by the Peter F. Drucker Graduate School of Management, Claremont Graduate University, Claremont, CA 91711.

9. James Lincoln's book entitled *A New Approach to Industrial Economics* contained the most comprehensive discussion of his philosophy of management.

10. Scott J. Schraff, "Strategic Management at The Lincoln Electric Company" (Master's thesis, Cleveland State University, 1993): 17.

11. Schraff, 59.

12. This quote appears on page 9 of Christopher A. Bartlett and Jamie O'Connell, *Lincoln Electric: Venturing Abroad,* Case 9-398-095, Boston: Harvard Business School (April 22, 1998).

13. Peter Senge, *The Fifth Discipline* (New York: Doubleday/Currency, 1990).

Chapter 3

Management Systems: Infrastructure, Coordination, and Integration

The infrastructure at Lincoln Electric is quite unusual. For most of the history of the company, for example, no formal organization chart existed. Today, Lincoln does have a formal organization chart, but it is downplayed to eliminate strong distinctions in status between employees and executives. This aids in promoting the company's egalitarian values.

The informal organization at Lincoln remains strong and is supportive of the formal organization. Nonbureaucratic behavior is encouraged and expected, as is openness and free-flowing communications. Table 3.1 summarizes the characteristics of the infrastructure.

Strong formal authority does exist, however, and there is indeed a formal, hierarchical structure. Although the company has not had more than three levels of management throughout its history, the recent rapid international expansion has altered that structure. Now Lincoln has a chairman, president, and CEO; regional presidents; vice presidents; superintendents; and forepersons. Country Managers have been appointed to manage manufacturing and sales in foreign countries. Distribution operations have been reorganized into six international distribution centers.

Table 3.1   Infrastructure at Lincoln Electric

Organization Structure

- Formal organization charts exist but not widely displayed or used.
- Strong formal authority.
- Established structures and hierarchies.
- Semidecentralized historically; more decentralized at present.
    - —Five Regional International Presidents: Europe, Latin America, Asia, Russia/Africa/Middle East, and North America. Each regional president is a vice president of Lincoln Electric. The five meet bimonthly with the CEO to discuss global strategy.★
    - —Each president has regional sales responsibility. Also responsible for manufacturing if facilities exist in their region. International presidents are responsible for planning, budgeting, and all integrated operations—marketing, manufacturing, and distributions. If manufacturing facilities do not exist in a country, country managers are responsible for making recommendations if these facilities are warranted.
- Six international regional distribution centers have been established. Distribution is now run from these large regional distribution centers.
- High levels of autonomy given to workers—traditionally a flat organization structure, but that has changed recently with foreign acquisitions.
- High span of control (100 workers for 1 supervisor); routine supervision is nonexistent.
- Very selective recruiting standards.
- Six thousand four hundred employees worldwide—three thousand five hundred in the Ohio Company.

Responsibility-Measurement Methods

- High degree of personal responsibility and accountability.
- Detailed measurement methods on each position.
- Balanced emphasis on internal competition and teamwork.

Informal Organizational Relationships

- Nonbureaucratic behavior.
- Workers encouraged to assume new roles as needed to solve problems.
- No work rules.
- High level of informal interactions because of open communications.
- Not status oriented—few status symbols.

★ The reorganization of international operations is described in Christopher A. Bartlett and Jamie O'Connell, *Lincoln Electric: Venturing Abroad,* Boston: Harvard Business School, Case 9-398-095 (rev. April 22, 1998), 10.

Thus, Lincoln has gone from two-to-three layers to five-to-six layers. As a result, the company's organization structure is not as flat as it once was. Nevertheless, there is still the 100 : 1 span of control between production employees and supervisors—enormous by any standard.

Routine supervision is uncommon. Problems are handled at their source, *quickly and without fanfare.* Only major problems get passed up to management. The high levels of autonomy are matched by detailed measurement of performance on each position. That is, high production worker *autonomy* is backed up by high production worker *accountability.*

The high span of control contributes significantly to high levels of productivity computed on a unit-cost basis. It results in replacing middle-level managers with factory workers who take on many chores that are considered managerial. Employees become managers and entrepreneurs and in the process the company reaps huge savings in supervisory costs. These savings in turn provide the funds to pay employee bonuses (to be discussed in Chapter 4). To obtain this quality of workforce, high levels of selectivity are applied in recruiting. On average, 75 people are interviewed to fill one production job. Recruiting criteria include motivation, as well as the potential capacity of an individual to develop and grow in a factory environment. Although it hasn't always been the case, current practice in hiring is the requirement of a high-school diploma.

There is internal competition among employees under the Lincoln System, but it doesn't prohibit teamwork. In order for employees to operate effectively under the reward system, they must be internally competitive with one another *but within an environment characterized by teamwork.* This is because the total value of the bonus pool available to employees under the Lincoln reward system is directly dependent on the overall profitability of the company.

As a result, if an individual's performance is evaluated way above average under the measurement system but there is no bonus pool because of overall company performance then that individual doesn't receive a bonus! Therefore, the measurement and reward system creates both competitive individual and teamwork incentives. The criteria that are used in measurement also create incentives for employees to meet short- and long-term company goals.

The piece rate and bonus merit system contribute to very low absenteeism and turnover at Lincoln. Absentee rates have averaged between 1.5 and 2.5 percent per year. The labor turnover rate, after the initial probationary period, and excluding employees who retire, averages approximately 3 percent annually.[1]

CHRONOLOGY OF TOP EXECUTIVE SUCCESSION

Table 3.2 is a chronology of top executive succession at Lincoln Electric since its founding. Figure 3.1 provides a time-line of executive succession over the entire history of the company.

What is most notable about chief executive succession at Lincoln Electric is the orderliness of that succession. During 100 years in business, the company had only five CEOs. Each of these five served long tenures and four had direct connections with the Lincoln family—particularly with James F. Lincoln—thus helping to perpetuate the values, ethical underpinnings, and management systems of the company.

Each of the three CEOs who succeeded James F. Lincoln had direct connections with him; he was instrumental in either hiring or mentoring them in the "ways" of the company. Each CEO served a long tenure. Because of the connections with James F. Lincoln, each CEO was instrumental in perpetuating the values, ethical underpinnings, and management systems of the company. *As a result, the values and ethical underpinnings of their management systems were intact, more or less, for a century!*

Anthony Massaro became Lincoln's sixth president and CEO on November 1, 1996, while Hastings continued as chairman. He was the first "outsider" named to the CEO position. Massaro, who came from Westinghouse, and Jay Elliot, the current CFO who came from Goodyear, were brought into the top management's ranks to shore up Lincoln's lack of global experience and to help the company deal with the realities of managing foreign operations and foreign expansion. It is Massaro's task to make Lincoln a successful global company.

Massaro's assessment of the foreign expansion program of the late 1980s lends credence to this explanation for the break in internal succession. He suggests that "the timing [of the foreign acquisitions] was ill-advised because the economies of the world went into recession

Table 3.2   Chronology of Executive Succession at Lincoln Electric

- John C. Lincoln founded Lincoln Electric in 1895 as a motor business.
- John C. Lincoln was president of Lincoln Electric from 1885–1929 and chairman until his death in 1954.★
- James F. Lincoln joined Lincoln Electric in 1907.
- James became general manager in 1914 and had the title vice president and general manager until 1929.
- James F. Lincoln became president officially, in 1929, then moved up from president to CEO and chairman in 1954 when John died; James was chairman until his death in 1965 at the age of 82.
- William Irrgang became president in 1954. He was a brilliant German engineer who joined the company in 1928. He became CEO and chairman in 1972, a position he held until his death in 1986. The positions of CEO and chairman were left vacant from 1965 to 1972 in deference to the legacy of James F. Lincoln.
- George Willis became president under Irrgang in 1972 and CEO and chairman in 1986—at which time Lincoln began its expansion into foreign operations.
- Donald Hastings became president under Willis in 1986; he succeeded Willis as CEO and chairman in 1992. John F. Lincoln hired Donald Hastings and Hastings spent 44 years at Lincoln before retiring in May of 1997.
- Frederick Mackenbach became president and chief operating officer under Hastings in 1992.
- Anthony A. Massaro became president and chief operating officer under Hastings on April 1, 1996.† He became president and CEO on November 1, 1996, and chairman, president, and CEO on May 27, 1996 at the company's annual meeting.

★ As James got more involved in the business, John got involved in a number of other business ventures; he also worked as an inventor. John's other ventures were outside of welding. He purchased a great deal of land in Scottsdale, Arizona, and developed it. He started the Camelback Inn, and he owned real estate in Cleveland and Columbus.

† He was formerly group president and executive vice president of Westinghouse Electric Corporation and joined Lincoln in 1993.

Figure 3.1   Executive Succession at Lincoln Electric.

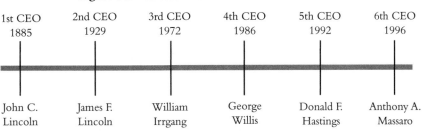

1st CEO	2nd CEO	3rd CEO	4th CEO	5th CEO	6th CEO
1885	1929	1972	1986	1992	1996
John C. Lincoln	James F. Lincoln	William Irrgang	George Willis	Donald F. Hastings	Anthony A. Massaro

shortly after the acquisitions" and that "some of the acquisitions were in areas where there was no growth and we paid for that subsequently." However, Massaro says the policy of global growth will continue, but "[w]e are doing our global expansion on a much more selective basis, in areas where the markets are growing and in areas where our products are in demand."[2]

The potential downside to this break in the continuity of executive succession, however, lies in the threat it may pose to a culture and set of management systems that have proven to be very effective for over a century.

MANAGEMENT SYSTEMS: COORDINATION AND INTEGRATION

Table 3.3 provides a list of the various practices employed by the management of Lincoln Electric to coordinate and integrate the company's operations. Lincoln uses both its extensive formal and informal networks to share information with all of its employees regarding the company's operations and financial performance.

Among Lincoln's numerous formal liaison committees and boards, its advisory board is particularly noteworthy. All nonmanagerial personnel elect the advisory board and it meets with top management on a biweekly basis to discuss work-related issues. The advisory board also has the responsibility for evaluating suggestions made by employees through the company's suggestion system. It recommends which suggestions to implement and estimates probable savings, if any, that result from their implementation.

In writing the preface to James Lincoln's book, *Towards a New Industrial Economics,* Charles G. Herbruck states:

> Realizing that he was relatively young and inexperienced, yet desiring desperately to succeed in business and personally, he called together the people of the company and asked them to elect representatives from each department who would sit with him and advise him on the company's operations. The group was to be purely advisory in function, but was to have no limits on the scope of its interests and concerns. Mr. Lincoln in writing later about this group said, "I knew that if I could get the people in the company to want the company to succeed as badly as I did, there would be no problems that we could not solve together."[3]

Table 3.3   Coordination and Integration

- Advisory board elected by employees meets biweekly with top management to discuss and address employee concerns.
- A junior board of directors, consisting of middle and top managers approved by the chairman and elected by peers, discusses a wide range of topics with the chairman on a monthly basis. Each manager serves for one year and is then subject to reelection every six months.
- Top management also has regular meetings with middle managers to discuss their concerns.
- International presidents meet with the CEO every 60 days to review progress and improvements.
- Open-door policy of top officers to production employees and to middle managers.
- Suggestion system.
- High level of trust—span of control is one of the manifestations and proof of trust.
- Management-by-walking around.
- Fair amount of job rotation.
- Nonbureaucratic personal communications.
- Candor is emphasized in performance evaluations.
- The piecework system results in identifying production bottlenecks quickly because of their implications for lower pay and productivity.
- Numerous training programs.
- Training in sales for production employees with potential aptitude.

This was the birth of the advisory board. It has met bimonthly since its inception in 1914. Numerous suggestions and innovations have contributed to making Lincoln the company it is today. In addition, and perhaps as important, it has been one of the key formal vehicles for building unity out of the diverse efforts of the company, and the vehicle where management and labor relations have been worked out without strikes and without frequent work stoppages.

The advisory board was a remarkable innovation at a very early stage in the development of the company. Moreover, it was without equal in the United States as a mechanism for peacefully resolving conflicts between labor and management.

The informal communication system at Lincoln is also quite extensive: The open door policy, candor in communications and feedback, and the visibility of top and middle management on the factory floor enhance coordination and integration.

Information regarding the operations and the financial performance is shared with everyone through Lincoln's extensive formal and informal network of coordination and integration. This helps to create identity on the part of production workers with the company's overall economic performance. Sharing financial information is also very important because most employees are owners of Lincoln stock.

Not only does the advisory board meet biweekly with top management to discuss work-related issues, but it also has the responsibility for evaluating suggestions. The board then makes recommendations as to which suggestions should be implemented and prepares estimates of probable savings.

The numerous internal coordinating mechanisms established at Lincoln go a long way toward developing trust and identification with company goals and objectives. Putnam has put forth a notion of social capital for public entities (i.e., cities, states, and nations) that emphasizes associational membership and public trust.[4] Such a concept is truly imbedded into the design of Lincoln's management systems, although no such quantitative index exists for companies. Because Lincoln's social capital is very high, its cost of coordination and control is very low, thus contributing to low cost, high productivity, and agility.

Lincoln facilitates coordination and integration of its operations through cross-training and job rotation. The absence of work rules and the ability to cross-train factory employees have made it possible to place factory personnel in sales positions when the company has encountered periods of recession. For example, Lincoln has trained certain of its production workers in the sale of arc-welding equipment, and this has led to the development of a profitable operation directed toward small business establishments.

Here again we see that Lincoln has very naturally put in place an agile solution—this time to meet the threat to continuous employment associated with the cyclicality of its business and with its own very successful efforts to continuously improve total productivity.

Training and job rotation also give employees a "sense of the whole," so that their work may be identified with the work of the entire company. It thus serves as a very effective device for coordinating and integrating company activities. In turn, this further enhances identification with the company interests.

SOME LESSONS LEARNED

After surveying the degree of participation that exists in Lincoln's system of coordination and integration, together with the power of the company's incentive system and the very high growth rates in productivity, Lincoln provides a compelling example of the following conclusions of Robert N. Bellah, et al.:

> The recovery of a high rate of productivity necessarily requires various forms of worker participation—whether in involvement in decisions about what happens on the work floor, or in ownership of shares in the company, or in bonuses for increased profitability.[5]

The Lincoln system of rewards and recognition is reviewed next.

NOTES

1. Donald F. Hastings, "Lincoln Electric's Harsh Lessons from International Expansion," *Harvard Business Review* (May–June 1999): 170.

2. These quotes from Massaro were taken from an interview conducted by Thomas W. Gerdel, a reporter from the *Plain Dealer,* Cleveland, which appeared on Sunday, September 29, 1996.

3. James F. Lincoln, *A New Approach to Industrial Economics* (New York: Devon-Adir Company, 1961), 7.

4. Robert D. Putnam, "The Prosperous Community: Social Capital and Public Life," *American Prospect* 13 (spring 1993): 35.

5. Robert N. Bellah, Richard Madsen, William Sullivan, Ann Swindler, and Steven M. Tipton, *The Good Society* (New York: Vintage Books, Random House, 1991), 101. In this particular reflection, the authors refer to similar findings in *The Cumo Commission Report,* The Cumo Commission on Trade and Competitiveness (New York: Simon & Shuster, 1988).

Chapter
4

Management Systems:
Rewards and Recognition

THE PIECE-RATE SYSTEM

Over 90 percent of Lincoln's production workers are covered by the piece-rate system—the centerpiece of the reward system—which is intended to distribute the results of the output of the company among the people who produced that output.[1] Using time and motion studies, the company's industrial engineers set piece rates according to the level of productivity required at planned levels to yield the base wage level appropriate for each particular job. Lincoln has established over 70,000 piece rates.[2]

The setting of piece rates requires substantial effort on the part of the industrial engineers. Piece rates have to be updated to reflect technological change. In the absence of technological change, rates are only modified in response to cost-of-living changes or in response to other significant changes in the production process.

There is one exception to these three reasons for changing established piece rates. If workers are able to convince management that rates for a particular job are unfair, rates can be changed. Such challenges are very rare, however, because it is the management's desire to establish a piece-rate system to distribute rewards according to genuine merit.

The 70,000 piece rates are set and revised by three industrial engineers in the Machine Division and three to four such personnel in the Electrodes Division. Typically time-and-motion work is done only when jobs are established. If a job to be added is a standard job on which historical productivity data exist, methods personnel do not break the new job down into motions. If a job is established for which no historical data exist, then the job is broken down into motions, and the piece rate is set accordingly.

Piece rates work well in a production environment for two reasons. The first reason is economic. Piece rates turn production workers into entrepreneurs—pay depends on output that, in turn, depends on learning and creativity. A less obvious reason for the effectiveness of piece rates is that they provide an efficient *information-flow mechanism.*

To understand the information-flow mechanism provided by a piece-rate system, consider a Just-in-Time inventory system. JIT relies on each input to a process arriving at each step of the manufacturing process just in time for further processing. If the material does not arrive on time, work stoppages occur. When a work stoppage occurs, production workers and production managers must identify the problem quickly to resume production. Under JIT, work stoppages may occur because of a problem created by a supplier or because of a problem with the quality of the input. Management then determines the cause of the problem. This information would not be available as quickly if the company held buffer stocks of inventory.

Similarly, under piece rates, problems and their causes are quickly identified. This happens because workers do not get paid unless they produce. When production is interrupted, workers are motivated to identify and solve the problem quickly. Therefore, piece rates create an information flow that is triggered when people aren't making money. People complain, information flow is immediate, and motivation is high to locate the source of the problem.

Piece rates thus accomplish the same thing as JIT—they both lead to the identification of bottlenecks.

Table 4.1 summarizes the entire rewards and recognition system at Lincoln.

THE BONUS SYSTEM

In addition to the piece-rate system, all employees (including white-collar employees[3]) are eligible for annual bonuses. These bonuses are

Table 4.1   Rewards and Recognition

- Piece-rate wages plus a bonus based on performance.
- Performance evaluation semiannual ratings based on four measures contained on a merit-rating card: output, quality, dependability, and ideas and cooperation.
- Bonuses are tied to performance, but bonus component has been weakened recently.
- For the ten years ending in 1998, bonus pool has averaged approximately 61 percent of the wage base. The average has been trending down. In the 30-year period from 1955 to 1984, the net bonus pool averaged 92.25 of the wage base. The percentage is down from where it has been historically—at or above 1.0—and the emphasis has been shifting to total compensation. Lincoln wants employees to understand that the company is incurring costs for their benefits package, including retirement costs.
- The retirement plan is a defined benefits plan that has been in existence for many years.
- Although employees pay their health care premiums, the premiums come out of the employee's gross bonus pool. The company pays these premiums so that they may come out of employee wages on a pretax basis.
- Promotions from within are typical, but this is changing somewhat as the firm becomes global. However, the numbers of executives who have been brought in from the outside are only about a dozen.
- Total compensation, based on piece-rate wages, is still considerably above average for the Cleveland area. The average composite wage for comparable manufacturing/governmental personnel in the Cleveland area in 1996 was $26,000; the average Lincoln piece worker earned $60,000.
- Egalitarian pay structure from top to bottom of organization at Lincoln, historically averaging 15-1.
- Employee stock purchase plan. Purchases are at market but without commission. The other way to purchase the stock is through the 401-(k) program on a pretax basis.
- Job security—guaranteed continuous employment after a probation period. Employment is guaranteed at a minimum level of 30 hours per week by management policy
- Pride of workmanship.
- Advisory Board allows for participation.
- Feeling of ownership. Sixty percent of Lincoln's common shares are owned by the Lincoln family, employees, and retirees; institutional ownership is only 17.9 percent of total shares outstanding.
- Strong bonding with coworkers is promoted by merit score bonus system. Healthy competition—bonus system is zero sum—100 points multiplied by the number of employees, *but* there exists a non-zero sum dimension to the bonus system for performers who are exceptional.
- The size of the overall bonus pool is based on total company profits. No profits, no bonus!

calculated according to semiannual assessments based on the following four criteria: output, quality, dependability, and ideas and cooperation. The form used for assessment is called the Merit Score Card.

Only the top five officers of the company are excluded from this bonus system. Instead, they are paid a modest salary plus a bonus based on company profits. This contributes to an egalitarian wage and salary structure, because the officers' total salary package fluctuates in the same direction as the employees' bonus plan.

Let us consider how the bonus process works.[4] Lincoln's management allocates each department 100 points (25 for each of the four criteria) for each production employee. Thus, each department manager has a fixed number of points to allocate among production employees—providing the competitive dimension of the rating system. An employee can earn well above or well below 25 points for each criterion during the bonus period.

Each employee is evaluated semiannually on each of the following four criteria:

1. *Output.* This is a quantitative assessment of output produced.

2. *Quality.* This is a quantitative assessment determined by appraising the number and seriousness of the defects produced during a six-month period and by subtracting points from the 25 that are allotted to quality. The quality assurance department determines who in the organization produced the parts that turned out to be defective. The department manager then makes the adjustment to the employee's quality score. The merit score system is significantly objective in its assessment of quality in that charges are made directly to the worker for poor quality. Quality defects not only result in deduction of quality points (somewhat subjective), but employees must also make the necessary corrections to their defects on their own time (very objective). The number of points lost (5 versus 10) for defects depends on whether the defect is found by the quality assurance department or whether it is discovered by the customer.[5]

3. *Dependability.* This is a quantitative and qualitative measure. Absenteeism is the only quantitative measure taken; it results in a deduction of points—approximately .4 per day absent.[6] After that, dependability is a judgment call made by the department manager for each employee. Absenteeism does affect output

ratings, making it objective. But what if an employee is truly sick? Employees are not allowed sick days, but a pay allowance is granted to employees who do have a confirmed illness. This allowance is taken from contributions made by employees into a "sick pool" which is replenished as needed. The subjective dimension has to do with just what constitutes a "confirmed illness," and is subject to manipulation.

4. *Ideas and Cooperation.* Here the department manager looks at the overall cooperativeness of each employee as well as the employee's contribution to the suggestion system for the period of evaluation. If an employee makes a suggestion that is implemented as a result of the recommendation of the advisory board, this may influence the merit score, depending on the significance of the suggestion.[7] Suggestions are therefore quite objective and may be reduced to dollar savings. Everything else in this category is subjective.

Once each employee has been rated on the four criteria, supervisors proceed to rank employee cards on each criterion. They look at the highest performer on output, for example, and rank that employee number 1. Then they place each person from top to bottom—without allocating points at this stage. Finally they go to the middle-most card (the median), and that's where they apply the 25 points—half above and half below.

The Merit Rating Cards

Figures 4.1 through 4.4 provide sample rating cards for each of the four factors in the Lincoln Incentive System. They have been prepared based on discussions with the management of Lincoln Electric in October 1996. The overall box format is adapted by permission from the case "Lincoln Electric Company, 1989," written in 1989 and copyrighted by Arthur Sharplin, McNeese State, Lake Charles, LA.

Arriving at the Bonus Fraction, Calculations, and Performance Rankings

Actual results of the merit rating process have ranged from "as low as 45 to as high as 160 points. About 75 percent of the scores tend to

Figure 4.1 Lincoln Electric Merit Rating Card: Output.

OUTPUT

POOR			NORMAL			EXCEPTIONAL

LOWER OUTPUT ←————————————→ HIGHER OUTPUT

THIS CARD WILL BE USED TO ASSESS HOW *PRODUCTIVE YOU HAVE BEEN* DURING THE PAST SIX MONTHS. THE RATING WILL BE DETERMINED BY YOUR SUPERVISOR IN CONJUNCTION WITH THE PRODUCTION CONTROL DEPARTMENT AND THE ENGINEERING DEPARTMENT. ABSENCES WILL NEGATIVELY INFLUENCE THESE RATINGS.

range between 90 and 110."[8] Points earned by employees in excess of 110 must be approved by upper management and are added to the total number of points allotted to a department. In the past, "less than 1 percent of employees earned 140 points or more."[9] All "excess bonus points," above 110 are not taken away from the pool of bonus points available to other employees of the department. As a result, the

Figure 4.2 Lincoln Electric Merit Rating Card: Quality.

QUALITY

POOR			NORMAL			EXCEPTIONAL

LOWER QUALITY ←————————————→ HIGHER QUALITY

THIS CARD WILL BE USED TO ASSESS THE *QUALITY OF YOUR WORK* ON BOTH A QUANTITATIVE AND QUALITATIVE BASIS BY APPRAISING THE NUMBER AND THE SERIOUSNESS OF THE DEFECTS YOU HAVE PRODUCED. DEFECTS DETERMINED WITHIN THE SHOP ARE MUCH LESS SERIOUS THAN DEFECTS DETERMINED BY THE CUSTOMER. QUALITY ALSO RELATES TO EFFICIENCY IN THE USE OF MATERIALS AND THE ELIMINATION OF WASTE AND TO YOUR SUGGESTIONS FOR IMPROVING THE PRODUCT. THIS RATING IS DONE BY YOUR SUPERVISOR IN CONJUNCTION WITH THE QUALITY ASSURANCE AND ENGINEERING DEPARTMENTS.

Figure 4.3   Lincoln Electric Merit Rating Card: Dependability.

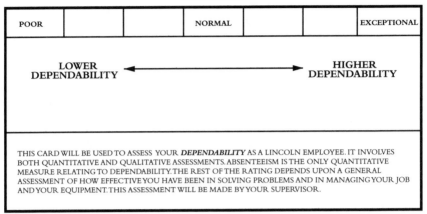

merit point system creates healthy competition among employees, but not the kind of competition that is ruinous to cooperation among coworkers.

The board of directors sets the size of the bonus pool to be paid to workers each year. This sum is then divided by the total wages of employees eligible for the bonus to create a fraction referred to as the

Figure 4.4   Lincoln Electric Merit Rating Card: Ideas and Cooperation.

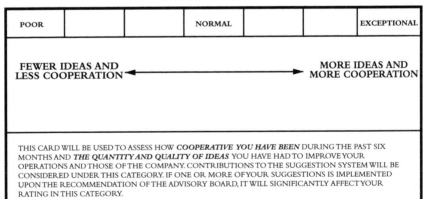

bonus fraction. That fraction averaged near 1.0 from 1955 through 1981. For the past 12 years, it has ranged between .52 and .77. From 1992 to 1998, it ranged between .5 and .6.

In the past, employees have used 1.0 as a benchmark. The fraction actually reached 1.23 in 1965 but has since drifted down. It was .56 in 1998.

Top management reduced the bonus fraction to cover losses associated with the international expansion program. The employees thought that the reductions should have ended after a year or two, but they failed to realize that if a company loses $100 million and starts replacing it at the rate of $10 to $15 million per year, it takes a number of years to make up those losses.

It should be noted, however, that even in the two worst years of the company's history, 1992 and 1993, the bonus fraction exceeded .6. This demonstrates the company's commitment to incentive management. It also reflects a recognition by the board of directors of the tremendous productivity of the workers in the Ohio company, especially during those very difficult years.

Although employee unrest increased as the bonus fraction decreased, by 1996 the employees had lowered their expectations. Will Lincoln's bonus fraction ever go up to 1.0 again? Because of the need for retained earnings to finance expansion, top management doubts that it will. Here again, the solution to a thorny problem—one that could have seriously damaged the company—is being resolved because of Lincoln's unique management system that is laced with trust and instilled with human values.

There probably is a point below 1.0 that is acceptable to employees, but the board is not sure where that point is.[10]

Exactly how is an employee's bonus calculated? The bonus for each employee is determined by multiplying the employee's base wages from the piece-rate system by that employee's merit rating score for the year (normally between .8 and 1.2). The result—a figure that we might call *earnings subject to merit*—is then multiplied by the bonus fraction to arrive at the bonus for a specific employee. For example, suppose an employee's total base wage for 1998 is $40,000, and that her merit rating is 1.1. Earnings subject to merit would then be $40,000 multiplied by 1.1, or $44,000. Now suppose the bonus pool is 75 percent of the wage pool creating a bonus factor of .75. This particular employee therefore earns a bonus for 1998 of .75 multiplied by $44,000 or $33,000. Her total compensation for the year is $77,000 out of which she must pay, on a pretax basis, the cost of her health care insurance.[11]

The piece-rate system is set up to allow an employee of normal productivity to earn a competitive base wage. (The average total base wages at Lincoln have always been above average for the Cleveland area.) The bonus system has allowed diligent workers to earn bonuses equal to or in excess of their base pay. So strong is the bonus plan that in the past, factory workers have been known to earn over $100,000 per year! (Why would anyone want to be a manager at Lincoln?) Lincoln's compensation program has created what *The New York Times*[12] calls "Royal Blue Collars," production workers who earn over $100,000 per year.

The most striking factor of the Lincoln piece-rate and bonus system is the variance of the results with the norm in the United States. One becomes convinced that we as a nation can do much better. Lester Thurow, professor of economics at MIT and former dean of the Sloan School of Management, has addressed the sharp shift in earnings in the United States. The sharp shift in the distribution of earnings that occurred between 1973 and 1993, and the potential implications of this trend, which intensified in 1994 and 1995, have led him to the following conclusions:

> On Labor Day this year, as with a lot of Labor Days, most laborers don't have a lot to celebrate. The median real wage for full-time male workers has fallen from $34,048 in 1973 to $30,407 in 1993 [in 1992 dollars]. . . .
> The tide rose (the real per capita gross domestic product went up 29 percent between 1973 and 1993), but 80 percent of the boats sank.[13]

More confirming evidence of the long-term decline in real wages by workers in the United States is cited by Richard B. Freeman, professor of economics at Harvard University and program director for labor economics at the National Bureau of Economic Research. He found that the rate of growth of real wages from 1973 to the mid-1990s was negative.[14] This according to "the most widely used statistical measures of real wages—hourly earnings reported by workers on the U.S. Current Population Survey of households divided by the consumer price index, and earnings reported by employers on the U.S. National Employer Survey, also divided by the CPI."

Freeman reports that according to the first survey, the decline of real median wages of male workers was 13 percent. And according to the second survey, "the average weekly earnings of nonsupervisory private sector workers declined by 12 percent."

Lincoln has faced the same forces that have put pressure on median wages in the United States—globalization and automation. Yet its management systems, although severely tested, have produced more equitable results for their workers. The company and its employees have thrived while many other companies and their employees have been sent reeling into processes of reengineering, downsizing, and rightsizing to compete effectively in this new environment.

Lincoln's practices regarding adjustments to the labor force are at odds with the practices of many U.S. companies. In the first 10 months of 1998, U.S. companies cut their workforce by 523,000 mostly domestic employees. This number of employees involuntarily separated from employment was 200,000 more than was eliminated in the first 10 months of 1997, despite the fact that through October 1998, the rate of unemployment in the United States had remained below 5 percent for 16 consecutive months.[15]

In the same article, Jeffrey Pfeffer, professor of organizational behavior at Stanford's Graduate School of Business, states: "There are some companies that wouldn't hold workers one minute longer than they needed. They will hold inventories of goods for a longer time, but they don't want to hold inventories of people."[16]

Pfeffer refers to this policy as just-in-time employment, akin to just-in-time inventory methods used for commodities. Just-in-time employment has the effect of treating people as *commodities,* which violates our basic nature and has repercussions on the companies that follow such a policy. The most tangible repercussions felt by such companies is that they will probably find that the skills and talents of people cannot be as easily acquired.

In contrast, Lincoln has not laid off a single worker in its domestic operations in six decades.[17] The result has been "a loyal and talented workforce that requires little supervision,"[18] according to Richard S. Sabo, a spokesman for the company.

Lincoln's example is powerful proof that human values that are deeply and *genuinely imbedded* in the management systems of a company produce agility and continuous adaptation without massive technological reengineering or financial restructuring. This is the power of an agile organization! Moreover, agility at Lincoln extends beyond manufacturing into service and engineering functions.

Although the piece-rate system may have limited applicability to certain service and knowledge-related activities, the merit card system (or similar performance rating systems) used for the bonus portion of the compensation program at Lincoln has widespread use in other organizations.

OTHER ASPECTS OF REWARDS AND RECOGNITION

Job security is surely a major reward at Lincoln. At least 30 hours per week of work are guaranteed for employees with three or more years' experience. In return, employees must be willing to work overtime as required. If an employee is shifted into a position carrying a lesser pay grade due to lack of work, that person must accept the associated adjustment in pay.

Lincoln uses many techniques to maintain a policy of continuous employment. The company is in a very cyclical business. In boom times, it tries to meet demand by first using overtime; in lean times, it halts all hiring and reduces work hours across the board. As of February 1999, Lincoln was not hiring production workers in Cleveland.

In past periods of downturn, Lincoln has trained certain of its production workers to market and sell arc-welding equipment to small business establishments. This led to the development of a very profitable business. The absence of work rules allows this cross-training to take place in an unrestrained way.

PARTIAL REVISIONS TO THE MERIT SYSTEM

A management consulting firm was engaged by Lincoln during 1996 to review the use of the merit rating system for all hourly and salaried nonproduction personnel. The consultant conducted focus group meetings with employees who had previously expressed some dissatisfaction with the way merit rating cards were being used to evaluate nonproduction personnel. They felt that the structure of their positions was not being evaluated properly. The result of these focus group meetings led to recommendations to management that the merit rating system be changed, but just for nonproduction employees.

As a result of this study, a new system called the Performance Development System (PDS)[19] was introduced on October 1, 1997. This introduction was preceded by three months of training for the affected personnel, including salaried and hourly nonproduction employees, the supervisors of these employees, and personnel in Lincoln's Human Resources Department.

The new system is comprised of four steps:

1. Performance planning,
2. Performance coaching,
3. Interim review, and
4. Performance evaluation and performance rating.

These four steps constitute a *cybernetic management process* for planning, evaluation, and development of Lincoln's personnel who are not devoted directly to production. This category of personnel includes employees from sales, engineering, human resources, plant maintenance, and the office support functions.

Figure 4.5 is an overview of the cybernetic dimensions of the PDS. PDS begins with employee performance planning. Each supervisor shares the content of the overall business plan with each employee as it relates to that employee's function. This then becomes the basis for each individual's annual performance planning process. The supervisor works in consultation with the employee to develop a performance plan for the next year, but ultimate approval of the plan rests with the supervisor.

At this point, there is a difference between the ingredients of a performance plan for hourly and salaried personnel. For hourly personnel, the emphasis is on identifying the competencies that are critical to the performance of a particular position in light of the needs of the department and the company. The six general competencies applicable to all employees are:

1. Leadership/ownership
2. Decision making/judgment

Figure 4.5 The Performance Development System.

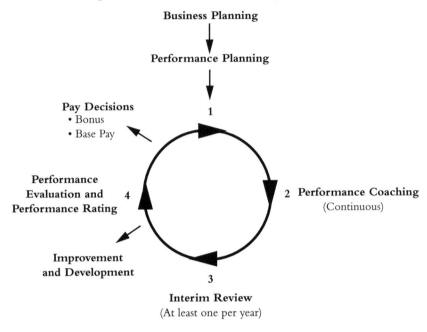

Business Planning

Performance Planning

1

Pay Decisions
• Bonus
• Base Pay

Performance
Evaluation and   4
Performance Rating

2 **Performance Coaching**
(Continuous)

Improvement
and Development

3

Interim Review
(At least one per year)

3. Results orientation

4. Teamwork/communications

5. Quality/customer focus

6. Creativity/innovation

If the employee or supervisor believes that any of the six competencies do not apply to a particular position or that other competencies are required, appropriate changes are made. In case other competencies are required, Specific Performance Expectations (SPEs) are identified.

For salaried personnel, each supervisor works with the employee to establish specific goals and competencies for the position that will help the department and the company achieve its strategic goals. Goals are expected to be challenging but attainable, and they should be coupled with specific steps each individual employee should take to further develop themselves.

Goals are expected to be *S*pecific, *M*easurable, *A*ttainable, *R*elevant, and *T*ime-based. These five specifications form the easily remembered acronym SMART. They are self-explanatory, except to note that a goal may be either quantitative or qualitative.

Once goals and competencies are formulated for salaried employees, each is weighted according to the priorities of the department and the company. For salaried employees, goals and competencies must total 100 points. Goals must range from 40 to 60 points, and competencies must range from 40 to 60 points. No single competency should be assigned more than 20 points.

Only competencies, not goals, are developed for hourly employees. As in the case of salaried employees, the weightings must equal 100 points, and no competency should exceed 30 points.

Once performance planning is complete, performance coaching begins. Performance coaching is an ongoing process throughout the year which provides employees help in meeting their performance targets. In this process, employees get feedback and recognition from supervisors. They may seek help in removing any impediments to achieving their targets. Progress is noted, as are problems. This is both a formal and informal review process. Employees are encouraged to continuously self-assess their progress during the year against their performance targets and goals.

The third step in the PDS is the interim review. Each employee meets with his or her supervisor at least one time during the year. At this point, there is discussion of progress and the employee's annual performance evaluation. The next steps for improving performance and competencies are also discussed.

This leads to the final step in the annual PDS process—performance evaluation and performance rating. A formal meeting is held once a year by each supervisor to discuss and assess the progress employees have made in improving skills, developing themselves, and, in the case of salaried employees, achieving their goals. This in turn leads the supervisor to rate each employee according to five criteria:

Criteria	*Performance Rating*
1. Exceeds expectations	1.2
2. Meets all expectations	1.0
3. Meets most expectations	0.8
4. Meets some expectations	0.6
5. Does not meet expectations	0.2

The point value assigned to each competency and goal (for salaried employees) is then multiplied by the appropriate performance rating that applies. The number of points for *each* competency and goal is totaled. Points for *all* competencies and goals are then totaled. The total points are used for adjustments to base wages and salaries, as well as for bonus determination.

Unlike the merit rating system for production employees, the total number of points for a department under PDS may not average 100 per employee. To remedy this situation, total performance ratings are normalized mathematically so that PDS ratings will average 100 points per covered employee. In effect, this results in converting PDS points to merit points so that production and nonproduction employees are put on equal footings for the purpose of determining the appropriate bonus.

Nonproduction employees who are ranked over 110 points have the opportunity for outstanding contributions. Points in excess of 110 are added to the department total. As with production employees who are rated over 110 points, this rating of nonproduction employees requires the approval of senior management.

The goal of the revised performance planning, development, and evaluation system is to bring alignment between the interests of Lincoln and those of its employees. Its purpose is to provide value to customers, employees, and shareholders. It seeks to distribute the rewards of the firm justly to those who produce the output.

Figure 4.6 depicts an overview of the performance development cycle as it was implemented in 1997.

THE DIFFICULTIES INVOLVED IN PAY-FOR-PERFORMANCE SYSTEMS

We have now completed our discussion of Lincoln's piece-rate and bonus system. The bonus system is applied to all but a handful of people at Lincoln Electric whereas the piece-rate system is limited to production/operations-type jobs. Both piece rate and bonus components of Lincoln's reward system are examples of Pay-for-Performance Systems where compensation is directly linked to individual performance.

Figure 4.6 The Performance Development Cycle—1997.

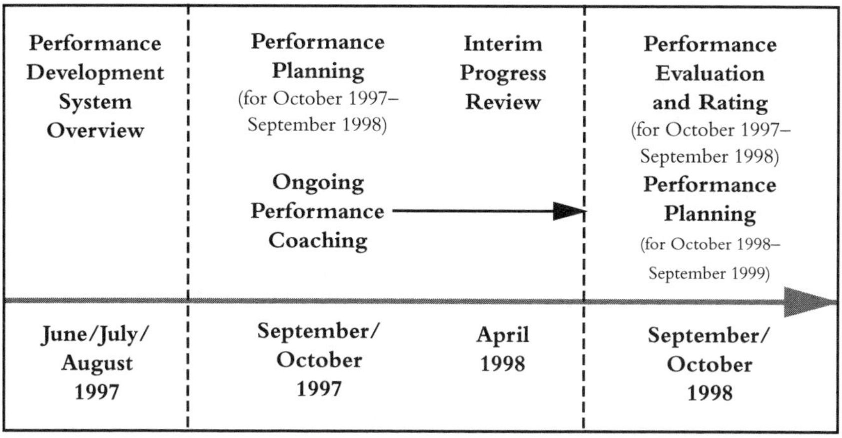

Performance Development System Overview	Performance Planning (for October 1997– September 1998) Ongoing Performance Coaching	Interim Progress Review	Performance Evaluation and Rating (for October 1997– September 1998) Performance Planning (for October 1998– September 1999)
June/July/ August 1997	September/ October 1997	April 1998	September/ October 1998

It has been recognized that such pay-for-performance systems *cannot be effective* unless supported by other aspects of a company's management systems. Michael Jensen provides an insightful analysis as to why companies tend to avoid pay-for-performance reward systems like those found at Lincoln and described in this chapter. His central argument is:

> Although not well understood, the forces leading organizations to avoid strong monetary incentives fall into two categories. The lack of trust between employees and supervisors and their distaste for conflict lead organizations to avoid pay-for-performance systems based on *subjective* performance evaluation. Similarly, problems associated with determining and modifying objective performance measures, and the dysfunctional behavior induced by resourceful employees faced with such measures, lead organizations to avoid pay-for-performance systems based on *objective* performance evaluation. The compensation system that results from this set of forces appears to be one with little or no pay for performance.[20]

As we have seen, Lincoln's reward system contains both objective and subjective dimensions. Given the real difficulties revealed by Jensen, how has Lincoln been able to avoid the conflict and gamesmanship that result from pay-for-performance systems?

Pay-for-performance at Lincoln is part of the overall organizational culture and is supported by other aspects of the company's management systems such as the open-door policy and the advisory board. Moreover, enormous effort has gone into the development of piece rates and the performance measures in the bonus system. Many safeguards have been built into the reward system to minimize the difficulties that Jensen specifies. As a result, the "lack of trust" that Jensen refers to is not a problem at Lincoln. Moreover, any conflict emanating from the piece-rate and bonus system can be resolved through the coordination and integration system at Lincoln.

Nevertheless, the critique of pay-for-performance systems made by Jensen is valid and only a company with a high trust culture and a reinforcing set of management systems, including an egalitarian style of management, can minimize the potential problems associated with pay-for-performance and reap the enormous motivational benefits. Lincoln is such a company and so are the two other companies whose culture and management systems are described in Chapters 10 and 11 of this book.

Notes

1. Kenneth Chilton, "Lincoln Electric's Incentive System: Can It Be Transferred Overseas?" *Compensation and Benefits Review* (November–December 1993): 22. In a conversation with a company official the author has learned that the percentage of production workers covered by piece rates is now lower than it was in 1993.

2. Carolyn Wiley, "Incentive Plan Pushes Production," *Personnel Journal* (August 1993): 89.

3. This is very important in light of the growth of the service sector in the U.S. economy. These four criteria may be used broadly although probably more subjectively than at Lincoln and companies like Lincoln.

4. This description is based on the article by Carolyn Wiley, "Incentive Plan Pushes Production," *Personnel Journal* (August 1993): 86–91, as modified by comments from Richard Sabo.

5. Kenneth Chilton, "Lincoln Electric's Incentive System: Can It Be Transferred Overseas?" *Compensation and Benefits Review* (November–December 1993): 23.

6. Ibid.

7. One of the potential dangers of the piece-rate pay system is its negative influence on quality and its negative influence on cooperation and innovation. The two measures, quality and ideas and cooperation, work against the potential negative incentives of piece-rate pay.

8. Chilton, p. 23.

9. Ibid.

10. The board of directors has recently changed the mechanism it uses to determine the bonus pool. The bonus pool is now determined by a formula established at the beginning of each year that relates the size of the bonus pool to overall corporate profitability as defined by earnings before interest and taxes. This eliminates any surprises and reduces potential conflict.

11. Asking employees to pay health care insurance out of their bonuses creates an incentive to choose health care coverage wisely. Because health care costs are such a large portion of the fringe benefits offered employees in the United States, this strategy makes abundant sense as a cost and quality control measure. It should be noted that the bonus fraction used in this example is the "gross bonus fraction" which contains provision for health care premiums. In all the other citations of the bonus fraction, I have used the "net bonus fraction" after provision for health care premiums.

12. *New York Times* (Sunday, March 22, 1998): Sec. 3, p. 1.

13. Lester C. Thurow, "Companies Merge; Families Break Up," *New York Times* (Sunday, September 3, 1995): Sec. 4, p. 11, Late Edition.

14. Richard B. Freeman, "Towards an Apartheid Economy?" *Harvard Business Review* (September–October, 1996): 116.

15. "Downsizing Is Common Plan That May Not Work," *The Plain Dealer,* Sunday edition, Cleveland, OH, December 20, 1998. The data in the article are taken from those produced by the outplacement firm of Challenger, Gray & Christmas, located in Chicago, which tracks reductions in the labor force in the United States.

16. Ibid.

17. Ibid.

18. Ibid.

19. The discussion of PDS in this section is based on materials supplied to the author by the Human Resource Department of The Lincoln Electric Company for use in this book.

20. Michael C. Jensen, *Foundations of Organizational Strategy* (Cambridge, MA: Harvard University Press, 1998), 208.

Chapter
5

Planning, Resource Allocation, and Reporting

Strong product technology planning and marketing drive the numerous elements involved in Lincoln Electric's formal planning, resource allocation, and reporting processes. Sales engineers, trained to assist customers in the understanding and use of Lincoln's products, carry out marketing programs. This in turn leads to cost reductions in customer operations, an important aspect of the company's guaranteed cost reduction program. This program is another example of how Lincoln attempts to enrich its customers by tailoring its products and services to meet specific customer needs. This strong focus on solutions to real customer problems is one of the most effective vehicles used by the company to produce continuous business adaptation and expansion.

Historically, the company has brought costs down through productivity improvements while raising quality through skill and innovation. These cost savings, quality improvements, and innovations have led to price reductions which in turn have increased product demand. Lincoln's market strategy is a productivity-cost-quality-innovation strategy, focusing on the customer needs and market expansion.

This emphasis on the customer first has led to enormous attention to the production process and other internal business processes. First, the process has been streamlined recently by *Rhythm,* a software program designed to enhance the flow of goods and materials in the production planning and control process. Next, product planning, development, and marketing, and periodic product and market evaluations use empowered, cross-functional teams. These teams seek to meet or exceed customer expectations while abandoning products and markets that are no longer productive.[1] Then, strict accountability standards for productivity, quality, and innovation are applied, thus focusing employees on customer interests.

A formal measurement process that is applied to all positions in the organization then strengthens accountability. Table 5.1 summarizes all the elements in the formal planning, resource allocation, and reporting process. Table 5.2 summarizes all the elements in the informal planning, resource allocation, and reporting process. All these elements work toward serving customer needs.

Table 5.1   Formal Planning, Resource Allocation, and Reporting Process

Operations

- Strong product and technology R&D—industry leader.
- Strong marketing using technically trained people to make sales and service calls.
- New computer software—Rhythm—for scheduling production work through plants.
- Strong emphasis upon process controls.

Planning, Resource Allocation, and Reporting Process

- Decentralized planning and budgeting systems involving international presidents.
- Pricing based on productivity improvements and reductions in cost.
- Guaranteed cost-reduction program for customers.
- Periodic review process for products and markets.
- Internal financing for growth through the use of retained earnings gave way to external debt and equity financing in order to finance global expansion between 1989–1993.

Evaluation and Rewards Process

- Supervisors plan and keep detailed performance records based on employee dependability, output, quality (meet ISO quality 9000 requirements), innovation, ideas (suggestions), and cooperation.
- Merit pay scheme for nonproduction employees.

Table 5.2   Informal Planning, Resource Allocation, and Reporting Process

Operations
- R&D, engineering, purchasing, and manufacturing work closely to implement innovations—cross-functional teams are common. In each division, the engineers are located on the factory floor and routinely check out ideas with production personnel.

Planning, Resource Allocation, and Reporting Process
- High level of employee empowerment.
- Problem solving done participatively for domestic operations.
- Flexibility to adapt to changing situations—problems in international expansion, recessions, product changes, and so on.
- Supervision and coaching—not close monitoring in the management process.
- Flexibility during crisis time.
  —Domestic workers were willing to give up vacations and holidays to assist the company.
  —High levels of cooperation exist between labor and management.
- International operations are more formal, but there is still a degree of informal planning and reporting in international operations. Recent acquisitions have brought the total number back up to 15 foreign countries.

Evaluation and Rewards Process
- Workers willing to give up some of the bonus to offset losses from international operations.

Strong customer orientation is clearly illustrated by the pricing practices of Lincoln. From 1933 to 1973, the company kept prices fairly constant in nominal dollars. In 1973, however, Lincoln experienced double-digit inflation in raw material prices, and started to increase prices by 3.5 percent to 4.5 percent. Nevertheless, Lincoln is still the low-cost producer in the industry.

Despite having a clear customer focus, Lincoln did not have a well-developed strategic planning or resource allocation process. The responsibility for strategic planning was placed at the senior vice president level, and strategic decisions, such as those involving foreign acquisitions during the period between 1986 and 1993, were made on an ad hoc, opportunistic basis. A more formal strategic planning, resource allocation, budgeting, and reporting process is now in place (see Table 5.2).

In the past, strategic decisions have been made as follows: the vice president actively sought acquisition possibilities and then submitted the report to the chairman and president, although any officer could have come up with a potential acquisition.

The absence of a formal strategic planning and resource allocation process that penetrated the ranks and was "owned" by operating management hampered the effective allocation of financial resources in the past. As we have seen in the last chapter, however, the company now drives its PDS with a formal and informal strategic and business planning process.

Despite any weakness in Lincoln's formal planning and resource allocation process, in the past the company has used their informal processes to avert and solve many serious problems. For example, by voluntarily giving up vacations and agreeing to a reduction in their annual merit bonuses, Lincoln's domestic employees helped the company to solve the financial problems caused by the initial international expansion program. "Key employees gave up a total of 614 weeks of vacation time on both July 4th and Labor Day weekends to meet production and shipping goals"[2] to help overcome losses that were incurred in foreign operations in 1992 and 1993. These losses were the first ever incurred by the company in its 104-year history.

In fairness to the employees of Lincoln USA and to holders of Lincoln debt, top management agreed early in 1994 to shut down its operations in Brazil, Germany, Venezuela, and Japan. This began a process of rationalization of Lincoln's foreign operations that restored both Lincoln and its foreign operations to profitability.

In 1992, Lincoln earned a profit of $24.9 million in the United States but lost over $60 million in its foreign operations, although sales of foreign operations amounted to 39 percent of the company's total sales. In 1993, Lincoln earned a profit of $42.6 million in the United States but lost over $91 million in its foreign operations, although sales of foreign operations amounted to 37 percent of the company's total sales.[3]

In 1994, on the other hand, foreign operations were profitable, yet only 11 percent of the profits were derived from foreign operations, whereas foreign operations accounted for 25 percent of the company's total sales. Nevertheless, the turnaround began. In 1995, 26 percent of company sales came from its foreign operations, and 20 percent of its profits came from foreign operations. The sales and profit percentages in 1996 were about the same as 1995. Because of adverse currency fluctuations, 26 percent of the company's dollar sales came from foreign operations in 1997, but only 17 percent of its profits. In 1998, 85 percent of the company's profits were derived from the U.S. operations, whereas U.S. sales accounted for 75 percent of the total.

Most of the risk to the company remains in the foreign operations. High current risk and modest to good returns is the current status of the company's foreign operations. Nevertheless, foreign markets are growing in terms of sales at rates faster than the U.S. market, so management continues to expand Lincoln's foreign operations, but now on a more selective and rational basis.

Lincoln engaged in a major joint venture to build a plant in Jakarta, Indonesia, and that plant became operational in 1998. The company now has offices in Singapore to serve and manage its businesses in Asia, and a plant in the Philippines became operational in 1999. Lincoln has also recently acquired an Italian company, Electronic Welding Systems (EWS), that manufactures welding machines that are smaller than traditional machines.[4]

Production employees in the Ohio Company generally believe that the risks of foreign operations are enormous and that the profits are still modest. The political instability in Asia and Latin America plays havoc with currency values and markets, which threatens the income from the bonus plan because the entire company is financially interlocked.

Employees at the Ohio Company see that the foreign piece of Lincoln's operations is "chewing" at their bonuses. In the process, Lincoln may be eroding trust among production workers, which gets at the core of the effectiveness of their management systems. The company must proceed very carefully here.

Lincoln continues to proceed to expand its business both domestically and internationally. One of the key reasons for the continued global expansion is that some of Lincoln's largest customers—Caterpillar and General Motors—are global. Still, global expansion is being planned much more carefully so as to capitalize on growth markets in areas of the world where Lincoln's products are in demand. Lincoln's goal is to achieve an annual 10 percent growth rate in sales for the next five years, which, if successful, will bring total sales to $1.5 billion by the year 2002.[5]

Finally, the planning, resource allocation, and reporting process at Lincoln is undergirded by a long-term view of what makes sense for its customers and employees. This is not common in most publicly owned companies in the United States, where management is under constant pressure from investors to produce consistent, good, short-term earnings, as well as growth.

Often these two objectives conflict—what is good for the long-term often penalizes short-term performance. Lincoln can take the long view because it is in its culture to do so and because the "Lincoln Family" closely holds its stock. Figure 5.1 presents a diagram of the company's return on average shareholder's equity over a 31-year period from 1968 to 1998. Weighted average return on equity (ROE) has been positive for all but two of those 31 years.

Weighted ROE has averaged 13 percent over this entire period. But if we remove the ROEs for the two years (1992 and 1993) in which the foreign acquisitions were restructured, we find that the 28-year average moves up to 16 percent. This compares very favorably

Figure 5.1 The Lincoln Electric Company Return on Equity 1968–1998.

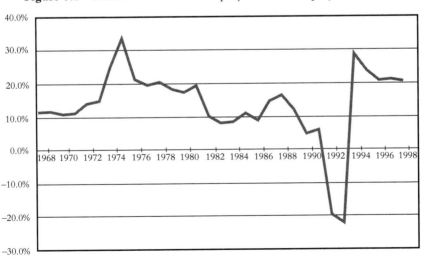

to other firms in the metalworking, machinery, and equipment industry (SIC code 3540). For example, the average ROE for the entire
industry for the five-year period of 1993 to 1997 was a mere 7.2 percent. Lincoln's ROE for the past five years through 1998 was 22.7
percent, clearly indicating that Lincoln's performance for its shareholders has been very good.

Figure 5.2 presents the dividend yield on Lincoln stock from 1974
to 1998. Figure 5.3 presents the rate of growth in the share price of
Lincoln stock from 1974 to 1978. Finally, Figure 5.4 presents the total
yield received by the shareholders of Lincoln Electric from 1974 to
1998. The average annual return to the shareholders of Lincoln Electric for the 25-year period from 1974 to 1998 has been 16 percent.
The average annual return for the five-year period from 1994 to 1998
has been 39 percent, reflecting the results of the restructuring of foreign operations. Lincoln's historical share price data, adjusted for stock
splits, appears in Table 5.3.

Figure 5.2   The Lincoln Electric Company Dividend Yield 1974–1998.

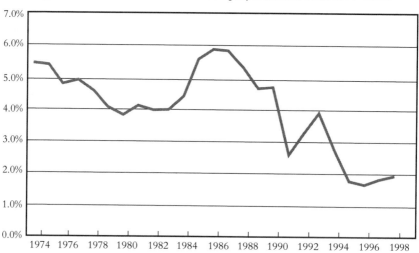

Figure 5.3 The Lincoln Electric Company Rate of Growth of Share Price 1974–1998.

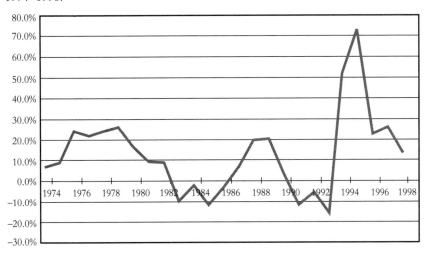

Figure 5.4 The Lincoln Electric Company Total Yield to Lincoln Shareholders 1973–1998.

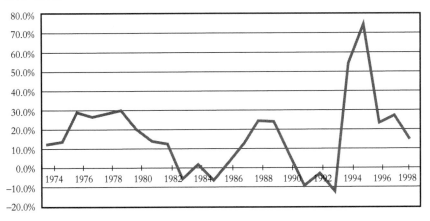

Table 5.3 Lincoln Electric Historical Share Price Data

	Share Price Restated	Splits	Dividend on Original	Dividends Restated	Dividends Restated	Dividends Yield	Dividends Growth	Dividends Yield
1965	n/a		2.90					
1966	n/a		3.20					
1967	n/a		3.10					
1968	n/a		3.30					
1969	n/a		3.50					
1970	n/a		3.50					
1971	n/a		3.50					
1972	n/a		3.50					
1973	$ 65.00		3.64			6%		
1974	$ 69.00		3.75			5%	6%	12%
1975	$ 74.50		4.00			5%	8%	13%
1976	$ 92.00		4.40			5%	23%	28%
1977	$111.50		5.45			5%	21%	26%
1978	$137.50		6.30			5%	23%	28%
1979	$172.50		7.00			4%	25%	30%
1980	$200.00		7.60			4%	16%	20%
1981	$217.50		8.90			4%	9%	13%
1982	$235.00		9.30			4%	8%	12%
1983	$211.00		8.40			4%	-10%	-6%
1984	$205.00		9.00			4%	-3%	2%
1985	$180.00		10.00			6%	-12%	-7%

Year							
1986	$174.00		10.20	1.08		6%	-3%	3%
1987	$185.00		10.80	1.17		6%	6%	12%
1988	$220.00		11.65	1.20		5%	19%	24%
1989	$262.50		12.20	1.26		5%	19%	24%
1990	$270.00		12.60	1.26		5%	3%	8%
1991	$237.50		6.05	0.61	0.30	3%	-12%	-9%
1992	$222.50		7.20	0.72	0.36	3%	-6%	-3%
1993	$186.13	June 1993–10 = 1	7.20	0.72	0.36	4%	-16%	-12%
1994	$281.25		7.60	0.76	0.38	3%	51%	54%
1995	$485.00	June 1995–2-1	8.40	0.84	0.42	2%	72%	74%
1996	$590.00		9.60	0.96	0.48	2%	22%	23%
1997	$738.80		13.00	1.30	0.65	2%	25%	27%
1998	$832.40	June 1998–2-1	16.00	1.60	0.40	2%	13%	15%

NOTES

1. Lincoln Electric has institutionalized a process to abandon products and markets that are no longer profitable and productive. The "Abandonment Decision" is one of the most difficult to make and implement in organizations, yet Lincoln seems to do it in a very natural way, again illustrating an agility built into the management systems of the company.

2. Kenneth Chilton, "Lincoln Electric's Incentive System: Can It Be Transferred Overseas?" *Compensation and Benefits Review* (November–December 1994): 33.

3. Information on company sales and profits by region of the world was derived from the company's Annual Reports and 10K statements.

4. *The Plain Dealer* (Sunday edition, Cleveland, OH, September 29, 1996).

5. Ibid.

Chapter
6

Agility and Adaptability at Lincoln Electric

A detailed review of each subsystem of the formal and informal management systems at Lincoln Electric is now complete. Figures 6.1 and 6.2 are replications of Figures 2.1 and 2.2 but now contain a summary of the formal and informal management systems in place at the company.

Figures 6.1 and 6.2 reveal the interrelationships of the five subsystems that comprise the formal and informal management systems at Lincoln. Each subsystem follows the values and management style of the organization and boosts each other in a mutually supportive way. Furthermore, the formal management systems support the informal systems, making for more effectiveness, thus further boosting potential performance.

In general, whether the formal and informal management systems result in boosting performance depends on how well both sets of systems are aligned with the realities of the specific and general environments faced by the company. This is a subject to which I now turn.

AGILITY AND ADAPTABILITY OF LINCOLN ELECTRIC

The management systems of an organization "cradle" or support the basic managerial processes of that organization. Executives operate

Figure 6.1   Lincoln Electric Formal Management Systems.

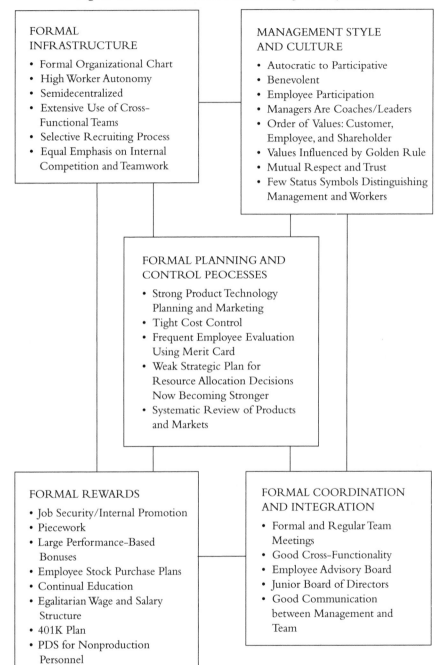

FORMAL
INFRASTRUCTURE

- Formal Organizational Chart
- High Worker Autonomy
- Semidecentralized
- Extensive Use of Cross-
  Functional Teams
- Selective Recruiting Process
- Equal Emphasis on Internal
  Competition and Teamwork

MANAGEMENT STYLE
AND CULTURE

- Autocratic to Participative
- Benevolent
- Employee Participation
- Managers Are Coaches/Leaders
- Order of Values: Customer,
  Employee, and Shareholder
- Values Influenced by Golden Rule
- Mutual Respect and Trust
- Few Status Symbols Distinguishing
  Management and Workers

FORMAL PLANNING AND
CONTROL PEOCESSES

- Strong Product Technology
  Planning and Marketing
- Tight Cost Control
- Frequent Employee Evaluation
  Using Merit Card
- Weak Strategic Plan for
  Resource Allocation Decisions
  Now Becoming Stronger
- Systematic Review of Products
  and Markets

FORMAL REWARDS

- Job Security/Internal Promotion
- Piecework
- Large Performance-Based
  Bonuses
- Employee Stock Purchase Plans
- Continual Education
- Egalitarian Wage and Salary
  Structure
- 401K Plan
- PDS for Nonproduction
  Personnel

FORMAL COORDINATION
AND INTEGRATION

- Formal and Regular Team
  Meetings
- Good Cross-Functionality
- Employee Advisory Board
- Junior Board of Directors
- Good Communication
  between Management and
  Team

Figure 6.2   Lincoln Electric Informal Management Systems.

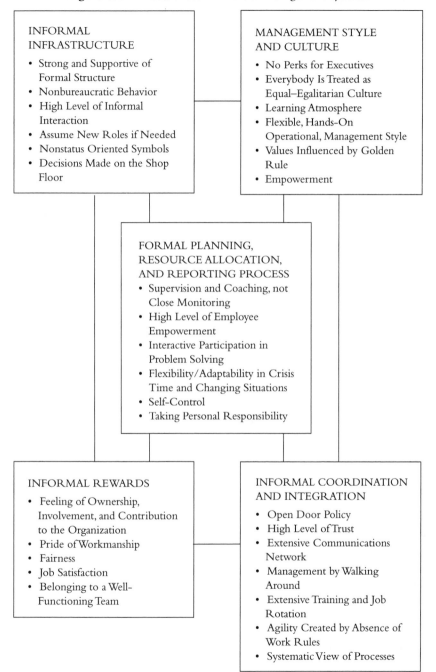

INFORMAL
INFRASTRUCTURE

- Strong and Supportive of
  Formal Structure
- Nonbureaucratic Behavior
- High Level of Informal
  Interaction
- Assume New Roles if Needed
- Nonstatus Oriented Symbols
- Decisions Made on the Shop
  Floor

MANAGEMENT STYLE
AND CULTURE

- No Perks for Executives
- Everybody Is Treated as
  Equal–Egalitarian Culture
- Learning Atmosphere
- Flexible, Hands-On
  Operational, Management Style
- Values Influenced by Golden
  Rule
- Empowerment

FORMAL PLANNING,
RESOURCE ALLOCATION,
AND REPORTING PROCESS

- Supervision and Coaching, not
  Close Monitoring
- High Level of Employee
  Empowerment
- Interactive Participation in
  Problem Solving
- Flexibility/Adaptability in Crisis
  Time and Changing Situations
- Self-Control
- Taking Personal Responsibility

INFORMAL REWARDS

- Feeling of Ownership,
  Involvement, and Contribution
  to the Organization
- Pride of Workmanship
- Fairness
- Job Satisfaction
- Belonging to a Well-
  Functioning Team

INFORMAL COORDINATION
AND INTEGRATION

- Open Door Policy
- High Level of Trust
- Extensive Communications
  Network
- Management by Walking
  Around
- Extensive Training and Job
  Rotation
- Agility Created by Absence of
  Work Rules
- Systematic View of Processes

through managerial processes to acquire, allocate, and expend physical, financial, and human resources. In this process, they react *to* and proactively act *on* both the specific business environment and the general economic, technological, political, and social environments in which a company operates. The overall agile management model that will be used in this chapter to summarize these management processes as they apply to Lincoln Electric is shown in Figure 6.3.[1]

Each part of the model is described in terms of its impact on the company. The management process at Lincoln Electric places primary emphasis on meeting or exceeding the needs of the company's customers. Customer satisfaction is sought through the application of a set of management systems that seeks to capitalize fully on those aspects of human nature which bring forth maximum motivation from employees and which lead to high levels of productivity, quality, innovation,

Figure 6.3   The Agile Management Model for Lincoln Electric.

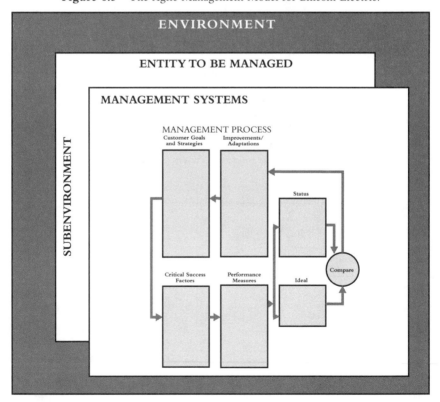

and customer satisfaction. Our primary attention in this section is on the way in which Lincoln's management systems assist the company's executives in this process. The management process is presented in the center of Figure 6.3 and enlarged in Figures 6.5 and 6.6.

The Macro Environment Faced by Lincoln Electric[2]

Figure 6.4 highlights the macro environment faced by Lincoln Electric. The company is a major competitor in the global market for welding products, electric motors, and environmental systems. It is a worldwide manufacturer of arc-welding products and a major producer of premium quality electric motors, robotic welding systems, environmental systems, and plasma and oxyfuel cutting equipment.

As discussed previously, the company continues to strengthen its business in North America, and it has recognized excellent growth opportunities in international markets, especially in the developing regions of Asia, Latin America, and Eastern Europe. The company also seeks to become an international supplier to its major domestic customers as they continue to expand abroad.

The environmental uncertainty faced by Lincoln comes from domestic forces, including cyclicality of the business of its major customers as well as substitution away from metals to plastics and concrete

Figure 6.4 The Macro Environment at Lincoln Electric.

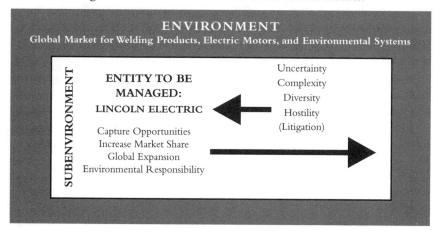

in products and structures that have traditionally used steel and arc-welding equipment and consumables. In addition, many domestic steel producers are shifting production facilities offshore. This uncertainty also arises both from the currency risk and the political risk of doing business abroad. Management also faces major environmental complexity as it seeks to cope with the challenges of managing a global company. Lincoln currently has manufacturing operations in 15 countries and a sales and distribution network covering 160 countries.[3]

The company has been facing extreme environmental diversity in trying to adapt its very successful domestic management systems to its operations in foreign countries. Finally, Lincoln is currently facing environmental hostility stemming from litigation resulting from the 1994 Northridge, California, earthquake affecting the Los Angeles area. A class action lawsuit was filled by owners of 1,500 buildings who alleged that the E70T-4 category of welding electrodes manufactured by Lincoln and by other companies were defective for use in the effected buildings. The dollar value attached to the lawsuit was over $1 billion. It was the company's belief that the lawsuit is groundless because E70T-4 electrodes performed well in the Northridge earthquake, as well as in more severe earthquakes in other parts of the world. Moreover, E70T-4 met the building code that was in force in the Los Angeles area at the time of the 1994 earthquake. The company was recently dismissed by the Superior Court of California from the $1 billion class action lawsuit.[4]

The Implications of Environmental Contingency Theory on the Design of Lincoln's Management Systems

The literature on contingency theory, as well as management practice, suggests that the design of management systems, including organizational structures and management processes, should be adjusted to match various environmental contingencies to increase the probability of achieving success.[5] The management systems of organizations that harmonize with the characteristics of the environments they face are more likely to be successful. Specifically, more *organic,* or informal, organization structures and processes are believed to be more effective in highly uncertain, complex, and dynamic environments than more rigid structures and processes.[6] This occurs because uncertain, complex, and dynamic environments increase the need for rapid information processing. Informal integration and coordination devices within organizations facing such environments facilitate this rapid information processing. As we have discovered, the management systems of Lincoln are balanced with the required highly informal elements.

The Subenvironment at Lincoln: Products, Markets, and Technology

Lincoln is a dominant competitor in the arc welding business. It has three or four major competitors plus a number of smaller niche competitors. A major domestic competitor in the welding machines market is Miller Electric of Wisconsin.

In addition to its domestic competitors, Lincoln competes on a worldwide basis with ESAB, a major firm in Sweden that was established in 1906 and is slightly larger than Lincoln with over 7,600 employees. ESAB competes in all of Lincoln's markets. ESAB manufactures welding generators, automatic machines for submerged arc welding, wires, electrodes, and fluxes. The company also constructs turnkey plants for the manufacture of welding electrodes.[7] A second major international competitor in the welding and gas cutting market is L'Air Liquide, located in France.

The basis of market competition in the arc-welding business is price (cost), brand preference, product performance, quality, warranties, service, and technical support. As a result, Lincoln has established strong research and development activity and strong technical sales and service activity directed toward meeting its customers' needs.

Although estimates of global market shares are not available, Lincoln believes it currently has a 42 percent share of the U.S. market for welding consumables. The company estimates that the size of the market for consumables in the United States is $750 million per year.

Lincoln also produces a full range of arc-welding machines. The market for welding equipment in the United States is estimated at $620 million. Estimates of market share are not available for the equipment market, but the company believes itself to be in the top bracket of arc-welding equipment producers in the United States. In 1998 the company derived 93 percent of its revenues from its arc-welding business with the remaining 7 percent of its revenues coming from its motor business. It now derives 100% of its revenues from arc welding since it sold its electric motor business to Regat-Beloit, Inc. on May 28, 1999.[8]

The technology of arc welding involves the joining together of metal by the use of welding machines to generate an electric arc so as to create a molten deposit from a consumable electrode which in turn is used to fuse metal together. Often the welding process involves metal cutting so Lincoln's equipment includes all kinds of metal cutters. The company's welding equipment includes power sources, welding machines, and welding equipment. This automated equipment is used in light manufacturing, maintenance, and high-production welding environments. These latter environments often use Lincoln's robotics welding equipment. The company's products are used in auto manufacturing, shipbuilding, rail car manufacturing, pipeline assembly, and building construction. Small portable welding machines are also sold in the do–it–yourself (DIY) market through retail chains such as Wal-Mart (Sam's Club), Sears Hardware, Loews, and Home Depot.

The arc-welding industry is cyclical, tied to the production and sale of major durables such as automobiles, heavy industrial and agricultural equipment, and commercial construction buildings. In up-cycles, it has not been unusual for Lincoln to experience double-digit growth rates in sales and profits, whereas in down-cycles, its growth rates have become negative. The average annual growth rate in Lincoln's markets in the United States for the five-year period from 1990 to 1995 was approximately 3.4 percent, in nominal dollars, virtually flat in real terms.

Although Lincoln was already an international distributor of arc-welding equipment and was manufacturing electrodes and equipment in Canada, Australia, and France, the nature of the domestic market, its cyclicality and substitutes, caused Lincoln to embark on an aggressive international acquisition program in the late 1980s.

Lincoln acquired nine plants in Europe and Latin America and in addition built two plants, one in Japan and the second in Venezuela. In 1996, 32 percent of the company's sales, including export sales from the United States, were to customers located in foreign nations. Export sales from the United States in 1996 were 16 percent of total foreign sales and 5 percent of total sales. Approximately 80 percent of operating income, however, was derived from U.S. operations in 1996.

Lincoln's motor business had also been evolving. In 1992, the company acquired the motor business of the Delco Division of General Motors, increasing its presence in the industrial motors market. The company continued prior to the sale of the business, to design, manufacture, and market a broad line of motors used in industrial applications. Aluminum-framed motors range in power from $\frac{1}{3}$ hp to 250 hp, whereas iron-frame motors range from approximately 250 hp all the way up to 1,250 hp.

The Subenvironment: Competition

Lincoln is one of the few broad-based suppliers of arc-welding equipment and consumables in the world, but in each business, the company competes with other broad-line producers, as well as with specialized niche market companies. Foreign competition is especially intense from low-cost imports of commodity-type electrode consumables. The current (1997–1999) strong dollar makes foreign imports very attractive to U.S. customers.

U.S. steel manufacturers tend not to be competitors in the business of arc-welding consumables. However, integrated steel producers in Japan do produce consumables and compete with Lincoln in domestic and foreign markets. The worldwide steel industry is always a real and potentially powerful competitive threat.

Lincoln believes that the worldwide market for welding equipment and consumables is in excess of $8 billion annually. The United States, Japan, and Western Europe account for over 45 percent of the total market. Developing markets pose major opportunities. For example, it is believed that the welding market in China is currently close in size to the U.S. market. Moreover, developing countries have huge infrastructure needs generating substantial current and potential demand for welding equipment and technology.

The company's motor division participated in a $1.3 billion segment of the U.S. motor market. This market is adjusting rapidly to new U.S. regulations regarding fuel efficiency requirements that went into effect in late 1997. Companies in this industry are required to completely redesign their products to meet these mandated efficiency requirements. The market for industrial motors is very competitive. Domestically, the company competed with nine other manufacturers, four of which—Baldor, Emerson Electric, General Electric, and Reliance Electric—control 60 percent of the domestic market. Six companies divided the remaining 40 percent, of which one was Lincoln Electric. Lincoln was a relatively small competitor in this market, and its future in this business was uncertain thus making its sale of the business logical at this point.

Figure 6.5   The Cybernetic Management Process.

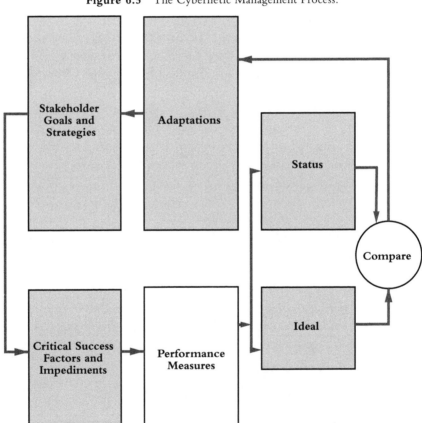

The Management Process—Focus on the Customer

Figure 6.5 is a generic representation of the cybernetic management process. Lincoln has goals and strategies for each stakeholder so as to provide *inducements* to each of its stakeholders in order to bring forth the *contributions* from each that the company requires to survive and prosper. The management systems of the company are designed to provide the information, communications, and support necessary to furnish these inducements.

Once goals and strategies are established for each stakeholder, the company proceeds to establish critical success factors. Next, the firm attempts to devise performance measures to assess performance with regard to each critical success factor. Then it proceeds to collect status on each performance measure and compares that status to an ideal that the company has established. If the comparisons are favorable, all is well. If the comparisons are unfavorable, management intercedes through its management systems with adaptations that may be operational or strategic in nature. This cybernetic process is repeated in a never-ending process for each stakeholder.

Figure 6.6 fills in Figure 6.5 to represent a *composite cybernetic management process* for Lincoln Electric to meet customer needs through employee performance. Figure 6.5 may be specified for each of the stakeholders separately, as well as for the internal business processes that are necessary for meeting all stakeholders needs, following the pattern suggested by Kaplan and Norton.[9]

Analysis of Each Variable in Lincoln's Composite Cybernetic Management Process

Each variable in Figures 6.5 and 6.6 has a precise meaning. Figure 6.6 contains an enormous amount of information for Lincoln's composite management processes which focus on the customer. Each variable should be interpreted carefully. Explanations for each of the variables summarized in the management process in Figure 6.6 are described, one variable at a time, in succeeding sections of this chapter.[10] The logic of each of the variables in the model is depicted graphically in Figures 6.7 to 6.13.

Figure 6.6   Lincoln Electric Company Composite Cybernetic Management Process Focusing on Customer Needs.

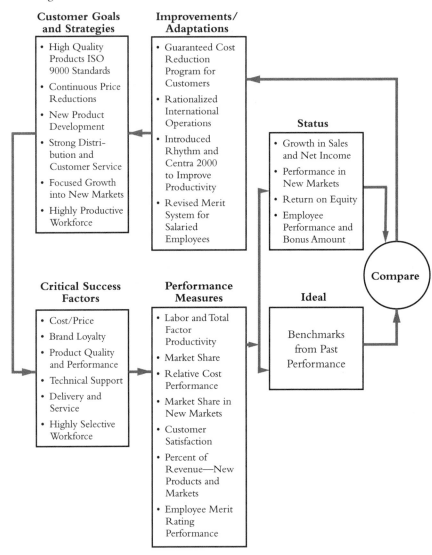

Figure 6.7   Customer Goals and Strategies.

<table>
<tr><td></td><td>Customer Goals
and Strategies</td></tr>
<tr>
<td>Whose interests are we
seeking to fulfill?

How are we seeking to
fulfill these interests?</td>
<td>

• High Quality Products
ISO 9000 Standards

• Continuous Price
Reductions

• New Product
Development

• Strong Distribution
and Customer Service

• Focused Growth into
New Markets

• Highly Productive
Workforce

</td>
</tr>
</table>

Figure 6.7 depicts the strategies pursued by Lincoln to attain the goal of meeting or exceeding customer expectations. Given the critical importance of meeting customer expectations, each of these strategies is described in detail. The cybernetic management process illustrates the importance of specifying goals and strategies carefully, because the goals and strategies for each stakeholder drive the entire management process. A mistake in specifying goals will distort the entire management process for that stakeholder.

Lincoln's Market Strategies

High Quality Products–ISO 9000 Standards

Implementation of this strategy starts with a very high degree of vertical integration, which means that Lincoln Electric controls the quality of all the parts that go into their products. All of its consumable and machine facilities meet ISO 9002 standards.

Implementation of this strategy continues by making each individual employee accountable for the quality of the products produced. This accountability is maintained through performance tracking that is able to trace defective products to specific plants and specific employees.

Research and Development

The company maintains a research and development department in the Electrodes Division consisting of 57 engineers which enables the company to continuously improve its welding technology. This helps the company to bring forth innovations leading to cost reductions, value-added solutions to customer problems, and novel solutions to welding problems associated with difficult welding operations, such as those associated with nuclear submarines, oil and gas pipelines, and off-shore drilling platforms.

Strong Distribution Networks

Lincoln believes it has the strongest domestic distribution network for welding products in the United States. The company has 950 welding distributors and six international regional distribution centers located strategically across the United States and the world so Lincoln's standard products can reach 95 percent of its customers within a two-day period. In addition, the company has two distribution centers in Canada that are integrated with the distribution centers in the United States. Although the company began to restructure its foreign acquisitions in 1992, it maintained broad international distribution capability. Through its various foreign subsidiaries and its domestic operations, it supports in excess of 1,200 distributors outside of the United States.

Large, Technically Trained Salesforce

The domestic salesforce consists of engineers, experienced in welding, who, with the support of the research and development department, can help Lincoln's customers achieve cost-saving solutions to their problems. The salesforce is located in 34 district offices throughout the United States and consists of approximately 260 trained personnel. Each salesperson can assist distributors or customers with welding demonstrations that show them how to use Lincoln's equipment to solve their welding problems. The company uses this capability to implement its guaranteed cost reduction program. It also uses this program to keep in close touch with its customers and their needs. It allows the company to stay in close contact with distributors. Distributors are glad to handle Lincoln's products because of the support they received from the company's trained salesforce.

The company's foreign operations have a salesforce of about the same number—with half of the 260 operating out of Lincoln's various international subsidiaries. The company maintains 20 sales offices in 17 foreign countries. In addition, the company has an export salesforce in over 85 countries, primarily where the company does not have foreign subsidiaries.

Highly Productive Workforce

The overall set of management systems creates a highly empowered workforce which allows the company to tap the highest nature of employees for the good of customers, employees, and shareholders. The empowered workforce is further energized by a powerful incentive management system. High levels of cross-utilization of employees and widespread encouragement of suggestions to reduce costs and improve operations are additional dimensions of the implementation of strategy with regards to the workforce. An absenteeism rate of 2 percent and a turnover rate of 4 percent per year are astonishing and attest to a highly motivated, loyal, and productive workforce and to the effectiveness of the company management systems.

Focused Growth into New Markets

Part of the company's strategy for future growth is to focus on developing countries where infrastructure needs are greatest, especially in Central Europe, Latin America, and Asia. Consolidated operations in Europe are expected to provide a launching pad for the company's expansion into Central Europe. Although Lincoln maintains a sales office in Brazil, it uses its presence in North America—United States, Canada, and Mexico—as its main base for penetrating all of Latin America. The company plans to leverage its long presence in Australia to increase exports to Southeast Asia.

Strategies of licensing, joint venturing, and private labeling are being employed in countries in which the company does not have manufacturing capacity to develop markets and market potential before embarking on expensive capacity expansion projects.

Critical Success Factors for Meeting Customer Expectations in Arc-Welding

The company believes that the values of eight factors are crucial for attaining the desired goals through the strategies it has selected for its arc-welding customers. The critical success variables are:

- Cost/price
- Brand loyalty
- Product quality and performance
- Technical support
- Delivery and service
- Highly selective and trained workforce

Figure 6.8 depicts these variables whose value management believes to be important for meeting or exceeding customer satisfaction.

Key success variables are crucial for attaining the goals and strategies being pursued by management. Their value is at least partially out

Figure 6.8 Customer Critical Success Factors.

Which variables are important to measure?	Critical Success Factors
	• Cost/Price • Brand Loyalty • Product Quality and Performance • Technical Support • Delivery and Service • Highly Selective and Trained Workforce

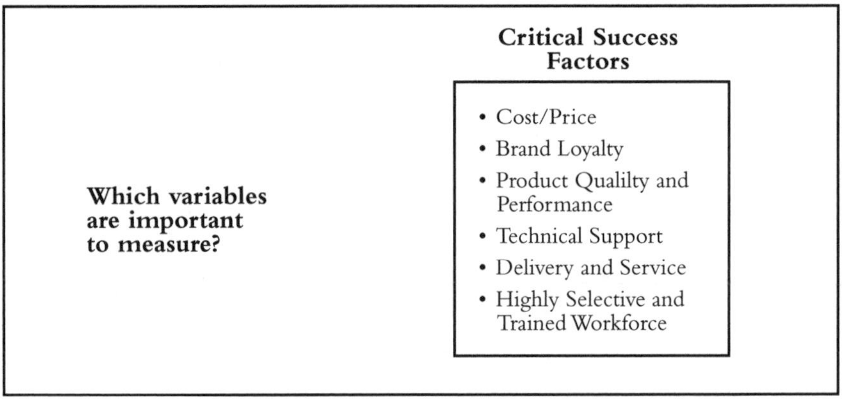

of managements control, otherwise they would be management decision variables, which could be set by management, not key success variables.

For example, Lincoln wishes to continue to be the low-cost producer in the industry. This will allow Lincoln to provide customers with high-quality products at the lowest cost possible. Yet the cost variable is only partially within the control of management. It is influenced by raw material prices and by the productivity of labor. Both of these variables are partially within the control of Lincoln's management. It is the management process as supported by the management systems that assists executives in achieving cost targets. In a similar way, this is the situation for each variable that management identifies as a key success variable.

Once key success variables are identified, the management process then turns to measurement. Figure 6.9 illustrates the measurements made in the merit rating system. The variables in the merit rating system are important for almost all of the key success variables in Figure 6.8 although the measurements in Figure 6.9 do not cover all the measurements that are necessary at Lincoln.

Figure 6.9 illustrates how we arrive at performance measures that attempt to accurately represent one or more key success variables. We do so by deciding how to measure the value of each key success

Figure 6.9 Employee Performance Measures.

	Customer Performance Measures
How to measure? **What is the unit of measure?** **Requesting method or vehicle?**	• Labor and Total Factor Productivity • Market Share • Relative Cost Performance • Market Share in New Markets • Customer Satisfaction • Percent of Revenue— New Products and Markets • Employee Merit Rating Performance

variable. Often, it is not possible to measure each success variable directly, but rather it is only possible to assess the value of each variable through the use of a proxy variable.

Quantitative and qualitative measures are used in the performance measurement system at Lincoln Electric to ensure that critical success factors have structurally valid performance measures which indicate the extent to which strategies are being implemented successfully. Lincoln's performance measures include output, quality (ISO 9002 certification), dependability, and cooperation. Lincoln assesses quality through the quality variable in the merit rating process. Although quality is really "in the eyes of the customer" and defects and departures from ISO standards certainly indicate the lack of quality, neither is a direct measure of quality.

In the measurement process, we must specify the measure whose value we seek to assess and decide how we are going to collect and present the data. Figure 6.10 then goes through the mechanics of making the calculations and reporting results.

The calculation of status is then compared with the ideal. The ideal levels for the performance measures at Lincoln have been established over a 50-year period. These levels for performance measures have been set by time-and-motion studies, by interactions with customers, and by knowledge of the competition. Here Lincoln has accumulated a great deal of data on the historical performance of employees with regard to the merit rating system. These ideals then

Figure 6.10   Employee Status Reports.

	Status
What do we do with the results? • **Calculations** • **Ratios** • **Representation** • **Reporting**	• Growth in Sales and Net Income • Performance in New Markets • Return on Equity • Employee Performance and Bonus Amount

Figure 6.11   Ideal Employee Performance Levels.

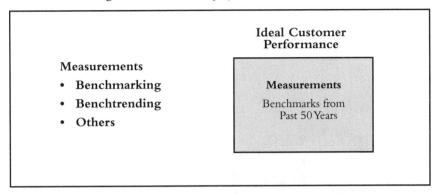

may be compared with actual semiannual performance measures. Figure 6.11 shows the calculations of ideal performance measures in the cybernetic management process.

Status assessments and comparisons are made for each position. This is shown in Figure 6.12. Adaptations are decisions that result from this comparison process. The specific adaptation depicted in Figure 6.13 are

Figure 6.12   Differences between Employee Performance and Ideals.

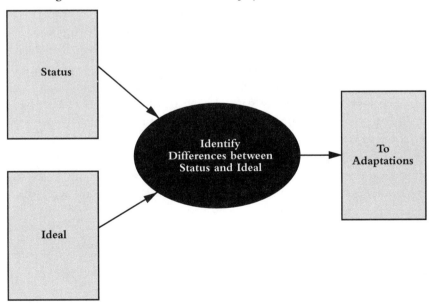

Figure 6.13   Adaptations by Lincoln to Meet Customer Goals and Strategies.

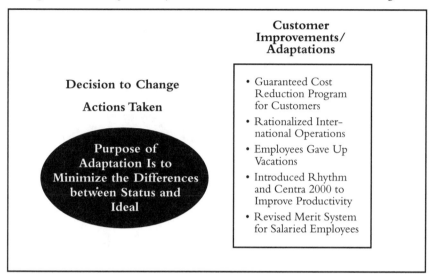

actual examples of how management has adapted to competitive conditions. It displays a number of improvements made by management to improve business processes to better meet customer needs.

Figure 6.13 also depicts how employees in the Ohio Company reacted to the setbacks the company experienced in the early 1990s. Lincoln's domestic employees cooperated in solving financial problems caused by the acquisition of international firms by giving up vacations and by agreeing to a reduction in their annual merit bonus.

The seven diagrams illustrated each of the variables of the management process contained in Figure 6.6. Figures 6.7 to 6.13 are representative examples of the management process variables at Lincoln, as the company seeks to meet and exceed customer expectations. The culture and management systems support and facilitate the functioning of this management process as the company responds to, and proactively attempts to influence, its environments.

Notes

1. I am indebted to Doug Stahl, research engineer at The Bechman Research Institute of the City of Hope, Duarte, California, and to Emily T. Papadopoulos, systems engineer, Anixter, Inc., Anaheim, California, for their assistance in the preparation of Figure 6.3. These graphics are specific applications of the general graphics that appear in the monograph by Joseph A. Maciariello, Calvin J. Kirby, and Nathaniel N. Kelly, *The Design of Adaptive Control Systems,* The Agility Forum, Bethlehem, PA (http://www.agilenet.org), 1996.

2. The material in this section is based on public information. Specifically, it is based on the 1996 10K report filed by Lincoln with the Securities and Exchange Commission on March 21, 1997. The 10K report may be accessed on the Internet as follows: www.sec.gov./Archives/edgar/data/59527.

3. Lincoln Electric Holdings, Inc., Press Release, "Lincoln Electric Posts Record Earnings for 1998," February 3, 1999. Since this press release, Lincoln has entered into a joint manufacturing venture in Istanbul, Turkey. The company now manufactures products in 16 countries.

4. Page 12, Form 10-Q, Lincoln Electric Holdings, Inc., filed with the Securities and Exchange Commission for the three months ended March 31, 1999.

5. For example, Henry Mintzberg, *The Structuring of Organizations* (Englewood Cliffs, NJ: Prentice-Hall, 1979); and Raymond E. Miles and Charles C. Snow, *Organizational Strategy, Structure and Process* (New York: McGraw-Hill, 1978).

6. Tom Burns and G.M. Stalker, *The Management of Innovation* (London: Tavistock Publications, 1961); Fremont E. Kast and James E. Rosenzweig, *Organization and Management: A Systems Contingency Approach* (New York: McGraw-Hill, 1985); Paul R. Lawrence and Jay W. Lorch, *Organization and Environment* (Boston: Harvard Business School Press, 1986); and Jay Galbraith, *Designing Complex Organizations* (Reading, MA: Addison-Wesley, 1973).

7. This information was obtained from the ESAB's Internet site www.esab.se. ESAB is owned by the holding company Charter PLC Internet site www.charter.com.

8. Page 12, Form 10-Q, Lincoln Electric Holdings, Inc., filed with the Securities and Exchange Commission for the three months ended June 30, 1999.

9. Robert S. Kaplan and David P. Norton, *The Balanced Scorecard: Translating Strategy into Action* (Boston: Harvard Business School Press, 1996).

10. The material in this section is also based on public information. Specifically, it is based on the 1996 10K report filed by Lincoln Electric with the Securities and Exchange Commission on March 21, 1997 as referenced in note 2 of this chapter.

Chapter
7

Management Systems Dynamics and Stakeholder Management at Lincoln

L incoln Electric clearly has been successful in terms of surviving for over a century and adapting continuously to the requirements of its key stakeholders: customers (in particular), employees, and shareholders. Figure 7.1 is a diagram summarizing the dynamic process at Lincoln Electric, along with the qualities of the systems that have made the company an agile, global competitor. Reading the diagram from left to right, one can see that Lincoln's executives (agility source 1) have designed formal management systems and have been proactive in influencing the direction of informal systems (agility sources 2) so as to produce relational variables. These relational variables have been identified in the literature on motivation as being crucial to organizational success.[1]

Although the six relational variables in Figure 7.1 are highly interdependent, trust is the key to successful dynamics in the management systems and processes of organizations. Once high levels of trust exist in an organization, it is relatively easy to gain employee commitment, which in turn enhances the ability of an organization to manage conflict in a way that is constructive without destroying the fabric of human relations. Learning is a by-product of employees

Figure 7.1 Sources of Agility, the Agile Management Model, Relational Variables and Outcomes.

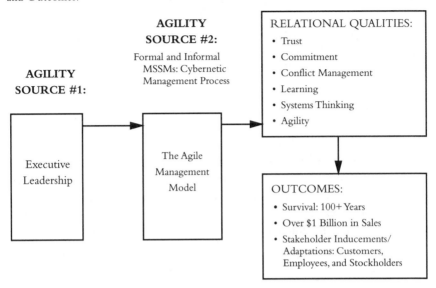

interacting in problem-solving situations within the context of cross-functional teams and within the context of their general organizational responsibilities. Systems thinking is encouraged by these same cross-functional teams, as well as by job rotation and extensive communication between management and employees. These five relational qualities have much to do with producing the attribute of agility/adaptability/speed.

The next question in terms of dynamics is how do these two sources of agility—executive leadership and formal and informal management systems—depicted in Figure 7.1 produce the six relational variables? I'll now discuss the sources of each relational variable.

RELATIONAL QUALITIES

At the highest level, the overall key to producing relational qualities in the management systems and processes of the company is leadership and the values established by both the words and deeds of that leadership—by leaders who "walk the talk." Values that produce the results we have seen at Lincoln are those viewed by its people as just and moral, that is the golden rule, and these values historically have been both stated and demonstrated by top management.

I proceed by identifying aspects of Lincoln's management systems and management process that contribute to the creation of each of the relational variables.

Relational Variable: Trust

Achieving company-directed behavior on the part of executives and workers is the objective behind the design of any set of management systems. Many authorities in management believe that trust among participants is the key to facilitating this goal-congruent behavior. McAllister has found that trust is a crucial factor in creating cooperation between individuals and an organization.[2] Trust is viewed as a factor which, if present among individuals in an organization, can lead to cost reduction, competitiveness, and successful adaptation to the changing needs of stakeholders.[3]

Trust is facilitated at Lincoln through genuine, open communications between management and production workers and through genuine employee participation in the governance of the company. This occurs in numerous ways but the biweekly meetings of the advisory board are especially noteworthy. Communications are also enhanced by the access of employees to top management. This access is accomplished in multiple ways, including the visibility of top management on the production floor, the biweekly meetings of the advisory board, the suggestion system, and the open-door policy at the company.

High levels of autonomy and empowerment as represented by the span of authority and responsibility at the worker level implies trust and respect. With a span of control between workers and supervisors of 100:1, management is in effect saying to the production worker that each worker must use his or her own judgment. Supervisors are simply unable to manage each task of each worker. This high level of empowerment results in production workers taking responsibility and making suggestions. The net result not only is trust but also suggestions by employees for improving operations and productivity. The sense of fairness created by the egalitarian pay structure at Lincoln, including the absence of elaborate executive perks, creates a sense of fairness and distributive justice. This sense of distributive justice removes any notion of worker exploitation and contributes to building trust in the company. The absence of bureaucratic behavior permits unimpeded dialogue between workers and middle and top management. This dialogue can clear up misunderstandings that are constantly present in all organizations, and it thus contributes toward eliminating suspicion among organizational participants. The extensive training that goes on at Lincoln, together with the company's attempts to provide workers with the most technologically advanced tools, also builds workers' confidence. The "honest weights and measures" at Lincoln in the performance measurement and reward system builds trust, which includes prompt and reliable feedback on performance.

Trust-inducing behaviors are found in both the formal and informal management systems of the company. In fact, a lack of consistency between major formal and informal subsystems will likely cause *erosion of trust*. This could occur at Lincoln if, for example, the company were to discharge major segments of the workforce in violation of its agreement to maintain continuous employment after a three-year probationary period.

The performance measurement and reward system, the advisory board, the degree of empowerment, training programs, the egalitarian pay structure, and the suggestion system are all part of the formal management systems. On the other hand, the values ("walking the talk") of the company, the absence of bureaucratic behavior, and the open-door policy are parts of the informal system of management. The formal reinforces the informal. For example, if the reward system were seen as unfair, the attitude of employees toward management would become strained, and the level of participation of employees in informal dialogue to improve operations would very likely diminish.

The trust created by the culture of the organization and the resultant open communications allows employees to actively voice disagreement with the policies of management without fear of reprisal. Because each party shares a common interest in the success of the company, management should feel less defensive and threatened by employee criticism of current policies.

Relational Variable: Commitment

Commitment has to do with the degree to which the individual shares with other individuals the goals and objectives of an organization. Commitment and trust are closely related. Virtually all aspects of trust build commitment.

Commitment at the first level comes from an individual's self-regulation system. Dalton and Lawrence describe, in terms of a cybernetic-feedback system, the potential self-regulatory aspects of commitment of an individual to the work of an organization:

> Individuals become committed to certain objectives and often work tirelessly to accomplish them. The direction for this control derives from individual goals and aspirations. The standards become expectations about one's own performance and certain intermediate targets we set for ourselves. The signal for corrective action is any indication that we may not achieve our goal or meet the deadline to which we have psychologically committed ourselves. The rewards for compliance to these self-administered controls include satisfaction, elation, and a sense of self-mastery. The sanctions in this system for noncompliance range from a mild sense of disappointment to a deep sense of inadequacy.[4]

An individual's self-commitment can be reinforced by formal and informal management systems. For example, the information provided through the formal and informal management system regarding progress toward individual and organizational goals can make personal commitment more efficient. Likewise, formal rewards and informal recognition of accomplishment can reinforce commitment to organizational goals.[5]

To the degree that commitment exists in an organization, it becomes instrumental in aligning individual and organizational goals and in attaining those goals. Moreover, the greater the commitment an individual has to an organization, the more loyal that person will be to the organization and the less likely that person will be to resign. On these facts management literature is clear.[6]

Lincoln's management systems are full of devices that build commitment, beginning with the high degree of selectivity in the recruiting process. In recruiting production workers, the company selects one in 75 applicants. Clearly, the company is seeking highly motivated people who bring with them the strong desire to succeed. There are numerous additional mechanisms in Lincoln's management systems that facilitate the process of building commitment.

The promise of continuous employment after a probationary period gives employees a sense of permanence with the company. It is difficult for employees to develop a commitment to Lincoln or any other organization if a great deal of insecurity exists as to employment.

Permanence is reinforced by widespread ownership of employees of company stock through various stock purchase and 401K plans. Employee ownership of shares in Lincoln provides employees with a long-term personal interest in the economic welfare of the company.

Participation builds commitment and Lincoln's employees are completely involved in decisions that affect their work at the company. The advisory board is crucial here but so are all the other informal arrangements, such as nonbureaucratic behavior, management by walking around, and the open-door policy of top executives.

The company's performance measurement and reward systems provide accurate and timely feedback that helps to build commitment. The high span of control and the resultant autonomy of the worker help develop the creativity and self-mastery talents of the employees. The entire culture of the company and its management systems encourage the growth and development of the employee.

The company's performance appraisal, compensation, and bonus system increases commitment by equitably distributing the outcomes of production. Employees know they will receive their fair share of the work they do and that the results of their labor will not be distributed disproportionately to top management and to shareholders. This knowledge increases the cooperative attitude of labor toward management and results in enhanced commitment of employees to the organization.

The attitudes of the company toward employee development, encouraging each employee to use his or her full talents at the workplace, enhance commitment of employees to the company. As employees develop, their human capital, self-worth, and economic productivity increase.

Relational Variable: Conflict Management

One source of conflict is the difference that exists between individual and organizational goals. In the design of management systems, we seek to bring congruence between individual and organizational goals, but this is a very difficult task. Yet different subunits of an organization see different realities, creating inevitable—perhaps desirable—conflicts in order to arrive at decisions that are in the best overall interest of the organization.

Conflict is prevalent in all organizations and has many sources. In a recent book dealing with systems to reduce the cost of conflict, the authors, consultants in conflict management, discuss the widespread presence and causes of conflict:

> Sometimes it results from conflicting interests, other times from poor communication, evil intent on the part of one party, selfishness, personality disorders, or scarce resources. Look in on the workings of any business, even a thriving one, and you are likely to see one or more of these causes operating.[7]

The presence of conflict can affect variables that are crucial to organizational success. Conflict can ultimately tear apart an organization by reducing cooperation through its influence on other relational variables such as trust and commitment. Although decision processes often use conflicting points of view to arrive at effective decisions, conflict must be managed less it destroy the organization through its affects on both the informal and formal management systems.

The challenge to executives is not to eliminate conflict but to reduce the dysfunctional variety and to develop mechanisms for dealing with conflict within the organization's management systems. Lincoln has done this particularly well.

The employee-management communication system at Lincoln puts all parties in constant problem-solving modes. The high level of trust that exists among employees and management allows disagreements to surface in a candid manner. Commitment and trust create the motivation to solve problems in a manner that is in the best interest of the company as a whole.

The performance measurement and incentive systems place a significant value on cooperation, thus working toward the management of conflict. Nevertheless, some dysfunctional conflict is present at Lincoln, as it always will be in organizations. Lincoln's piece-rate system does at times cause conflict. When new technology is introduced on a production line, piece rates change, and this can cause conflict. Also, the very interdependence of the production process at Lincoln can create bottlenecks that affect performance of workers downstream, thus causing conflict. "People know each other's warts and bumps, and they don't always talk about them politely" at meetings.[8]

Relational Variable: Learning

All learning requires feedback. The quicker and more accurate the feedback, the greater the learning. An open and trusting environment is recognized in the literature as well as in practice as being a prerequisite to individual and organizational learning.[9]

Management provides the environment for learning through extensive training and development followed by empowerment and accountability. Learning, growth, and development are further encouraged by the piece-rate and bonus systems, which provide quick feedback on success and failure, giving employees significant incentives for being more productive and more innovative. The bonus system also rewards cooperation, further contributing to sharing ideas and to learning.

Cross-functional teams permit rapid information flow that in turn facilitates learning. The absence of work rules permits job flexibility and job rotation that encourage learning.

Relational Variable: Systems Thinking

Systems thinking at Lincoln starts with a clear focus on the customer and on how to create value for that customer. This leads to questions about how to motivate employees to attain customer values. The management systems at Lincoln are then designed to appeal to all of the higher level qualities in the workforce—morality, dignity, rationality, creativity, mastery, and community—in order to satisfy customers on a continuous basis.

The production system is then brought to focus on advanced technology and sophisticated software systems to facilitate production planning and cost control, functionality, quality, and the schedule requirements of the customer. Marketing focuses on solutions to customer problems, including reducing customer costs and improving customer service. The salesforce is technically trained to solve customer problems. Relations with distributors are well developed and nurtured.

The management system as a whole creates competitive advantage because it lines up with customer interests and with important attributes of human nature. The management systems are designed to operate in a systematic and mutually reinforcing manner.

As so eloquently stated by David LeBlanc, managing director of Lincoln Mexicana, in personal communications with the author on February 5, 1999, when referring to the culture, operations, and management systems at Lincoln:

> The Lincoln System is a "whole, tightly coupled system." The U.S. operation is a well-honed system, engineering, manufacturing, and management. This takes time to develop.

Relational Variable: Agility/Speed/Adaptability

Focusing on the customer and on feedback from the customer provides incentives for the company. This moves against human and organizational tendencies toward inertia.

The relatively flat organization structure has in the past allowed for quick reaction to changes in the market and to changes in technology. These high levels of autonomy have encouraged new thinking, including thinking "outside of the box." Moreover, the absence of work rules allows workers to function in cross-functional problem-solving teams and to emerge as experts in problem-solving situations as situations demand. These cross-functional teams are allowed considerable latitude in problem solving, thus contributing to agility and adaptability.

The strong sense of community makes the company open to each other's problem-solving abilities, thus contributing to adaptability. The high-trust environment aids this because there are fewer questions about intentions, resulting in drastic reductions in transaction costs and agency problems (opportunism). This enhances the company's ability to adapt and increases the speed of adaptation, while reducing the transaction costs of doing so.

Summary: Relational Qualities Yielding Agility and Adaptability

Lincoln illustrates that the key to producing these qualities is leadership and the words and deeds of that leadership. Values that produce the results at Lincoln are those viewed by its people as *just and moral*.

Believing that the company's leaders have the best interest of the organization and its people—customers, employees, and shareholders—in mind, contributes to trust. Moreover, it makes it much easier to openly disagree with such leaders. It is easier to say: "Time out—what is right here?" Lincoln's advisory board and open-door policies make it easy for all levels of management and factory employees to challenge a given practice. Everyone is on the same team, sharing the same vision, under the umbrella of a trust level that can only be called *resilient*. Commitment, the ability to manage conflict, learning, and systems thinking require high levels of trust in an organization.

Executive Leadership, The Agile Management Model, and Performance at Lincoln

The Lincoln management system has succeeded where others have failed because its operating values have been based on the strong ethical underpinnings of the golden rule—the cornerstone of the company's overall management systems and process. It is this fundamental component that empowers each of the company's subsystems and unites them into a mutually reinforcing whole. This mutually reinforcing set of management systems creates goal and vision alignment in the work environment that encourages trust, commitment, conflict management, learning, and systems thinking. This in turn makes the organization *naturally* agile. Chapter 12 provides two short case example of how this natural agility works out in practice.

The point must be stressed, however, that Lincoln has created a *mutually reinforcing system*. The merit and reward system is part of a total value system that seeks equitable distributions of outcomes and a culture of openness and trust that is supported by a well-developed communication process and high levels of empowerment.

In other words, it is the entire Lincoln system that makes the company agile and successful and not merely the measurement and rewards subsystem—as many in the management and academic communities have assumed. This is the reason other companies have failed to duplicate Lincoln's success. It is not possible simply to change the measurement and rewards system and get the results that Lincoln has!

Lincoln's values focus on customers and their enrichment, and on employees and their development. These values, grounded in the golden rule, are infused throughout Lincoln's management systems and for a century have provided the ethical underpinnings for a company that has been naturally agile and truly remarkable—one that deserves to be emulated!

It is striking to note that in an academic article, Milgrom and Roberts propose the advanced mathematical technique of "supermodular optimization" to show the reason it is difficult for companies to copy the rewards and recognition systems of Lincoln.[10] They propose that the difficulty in duplication results from one aspect of the company's system reinforcing the other to boost overall performance. Although their concern is much more limited to the complementarity of the various aspects of the rewards and recognition subsystem, they nevertheless come to a striking conclusion which I believe this book supports faithfully. They state:

> The complementarity perspective suggests a quite different answer. Other explanations focus on piece rates almost exclusively. Our discussion suggests that Lincoln's piece rates are a part of a system of mutually enhancing elements, and that one cannot simply pick out a single element, graft it onto a different system without the complementary features and expect positive results. Analyses of Lincoln that focus on the piece rates and fail to appreciate that their value is dependent on their being supported by the bonus scheme, the ownership structure, the inventory policy, and so on, cannot explain the failures of other companies to mimic Lincoln's system successfully. (p. 204)

I believe the century-long support of Lincoln's executive leadership for moral human values and the strong focus of their managerial processes on the customer and employees is at the heart of the success experienced at the company. These values have impacted the design of the management process and of the subsystems of the formal management systems and have influenced the evolution of the informal management systems as well. The values, the focus on customers and employees, and the formal and informal management systems explain why the management systems at Lincoln have been so successful and why other companies have had difficulty copying them, and, more importantly for Lincoln, why Lincoln has had difficulty adapting these systems in *some* of its acquired foreign companies.

STAKEHOLDER INDUCEMENTS AND CONTRIBUTIONS AT LINCOLN

A company's principal stakeholders—its customers, employers, and stockholders—must be satisfied if a company is to be viable and remain competitive in the long run. The function of the executive is to pursue its purpose—to fill a need that society has while also continuously providing inducements to its stakeholders that will encourage them to continuously make contributions to the company. Because purpose is always directed toward society, it is absolutely correct for Lincoln to rank its customers first among its stakeholders, employees second, and shareholders third. It is the correct thing to do to ensure survival and success. James Lincoln in *A New Approach to Industrial Economics* stated his views on the three stakeholders very clearly:

> How each of these groups should be rewarded is a problem that management must resolve. It must be done in such a way that labor, management, and the customer feel that a proper distribution has been made. Only so will they cooperate. (p. 39)

> In the final analysis, the *purpose of industry* is to supply the public with the products it needs and wants. (p. 44)

> The last group to be considered is the stockholders who own stock because they think it will be more profitable than investing money in any other way. (p. 38)

> The stockholder, as listed here, is not the man who is the owner or who founded the business or supplied the original capital. Such founding owners usually are actual producers and should also be considered. But the absentee stockholder is not of any value to the customer or to the worker, since he has no knowledge of nor interest in the company other than greater dividends and an advance in the price of his stock. (pp. 38–39)

As we have examined the management systems and management process at Lincoln, it may seem like customers and employees are given primary attention at Lincoln Electric at the expense of shareholders. The data on stockholder returns presented in Chapter 5 clearly dispel this notion. If anything is true, shareholder returns at Lincoln have been significantly above average over a long period of time. As shown in Figure 5.4 and discussed in Chapter 5, total yield to shareholders, while varying from period to period, has averaged above 16 percent per year for the 25-year period from 1974 to 1998 and 39 percent for the five-year period from 1994 to 1998.

Lincoln's superior inducements to employees in the form of very high bonus payments can only be justified through equally superior performance on the part of employees. As for customers, Lincoln has historically provided superior products and services. In return for these inducements, customers have been extremely loyal to Lincoln.

At first glance, the guaranteed cost reduction program appears to provide more inducements to Lincoln's customers than contributions to the company. But on further reflection, Lincoln's sales engineers are unlikely to make a guaranteed cost reduction offer to customer firms where the promised cost reductions cannot be realized. Having trained sales engineers to represent the company to customers is likely to prevent the sales department from making commitments to customers that cannot be met by production personnel, a problem endemic to sales organizations.

As far as investors are concerned, a former and retired director of investor relations at Lincoln told me that he has never had an institutional investor call him and say that the culture and management systems at Lincoln will have to change in order to improve shareholder returns. But the converse has happened.

A number of institutional holders have called to say that they are not interested in extra dividends but want the company to reinvest those funds into the employee bonus program. These investors believe a good and loyal workforce is far more critical to their long-term investment than a few percent increase in dividends. How could it be said any better! The "Lincoln Family," broadly defined, has always felt that the bonus program was and is a good investment in a loyal workforce. And in the time of the company's greatest crisis, it was the production worker and salesforce in the Ohio Company that "pulled Lincoln through."

Although I believe James Lincoln's attitude is extreme with regard to the role of the shareholder, I do believe he established an order of priority that *properly reflects the purpose of a business.* The long-term interests of the shareholder are represented very effectively with the correct purpose in place, and with cooperation between labor and management properly established. Moreover, by making executives and workers owners in the company, the interests of executives and workers and of the shareholders of Lincoln are united. Figure 7.2 represents graphically the equilibrium in each stakeholder market discussed in this chapter.

In the long-term, there is no final conflict among customers, employees, and society. Once that is established, executives must establish cooperation among the three stakeholders to ensure that customer needs are met on a continuous basis and that labor and management are engaged in a cooperative relationship in meeting those needs. Finally, it is essential that labor and management realize that each group, and the shareholders, should be paid according to their contribution to the success in meeting customer needs.

Shareholders should be better off under this arrangement than if the purpose of the business is defined in terms of maximizing profits, and labor, management, and stockholders battle each other for their "proper" share of the proceeds. This is illogical. *The customer pays all of the bills, including profits.* Therefore, it is in the interests of all stakeholders to

Figure 7.2 Equilibrium in Stakeholder Markets.

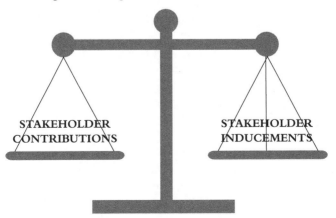

cooperate in a mutually satisfying relationship with the customer. Executives have the responsibility of so managing stakeholder relationships.

Notes

1. Karen L. Higgins, *Management Coordination Systems for an Interorganizational Network,* (Ph.D. diss., Executive Management Program, Drucker Center, The Claremont Graduate School, Claremont, CA, 1997), pp. 24–38.

2. Daniel J. McAllister, "Affect and Cognition-Based Trust as Foundations for Interpersonal Cooperation in Organizations," *Academy of Management Journal* 38, no. 1 (February 1995): 24–59.

3. John O. Whitney, *The Trust Factor* (New York: McGraw-Hill, 1994); and Bromiley and Cummings, "Transaction Costs in Organizations with Trust," Discussion Paper #128, Strategic Management Research Center, University of Minnesota, July 1992, pp. 1–33.

4. Gene W. Dalton and Paul R. Lawrence, *Motivation and Control in Organizations* (Homewood, IL: Richard D. Irwin, 1971), 14.

5. On these issues, see Edwin A. Locke, Garry P. Latham, and Miriam Erez, "The Determinants of Goal Commitment," *Academy of Management Review* 13 (1988): 23–39.

6. See Steven L. Fink, *High Commitment Workplaces* (New York: Quorum Books, 1992).

7. Karl A. Slaikeu and Ralph H. Hasson, *Controlling the Cost of Conflict* (San Francisco: Jossey-Bass, 1998), 6.

8. Richard Sabo of Lincoln Electric, quoted in Section 3, Money & Business, "Royal Blue Collars," page 12 of the *New York Times,* Sunday, March 22, 1998.

9. J. Maciariello and C. Kirby, *Management Control Systems: Using Adaptive Systems to Attain Control* (Englewood Cliffs, NJ: Prentice Hall, 1994), 93–97; and "The Evolution of Organizational Environments," *Administrative Science Quarterly* 12 (1968): 590–613.

10. Paul Milgrom and John Roberts, "Complementarities and Fit: Strategy, Structure and Organizational Change in Manufacturing," *Journal of Accounting and Economics* (1995): 179–208.

Chapter
8

Transplanting Lincoln's Culture and Systems Abroad: Success and Failure

The general reaction of executives and academics reading about Lincoln's experiences with foreign acquisitions is that the Lincoln culture and management systems cannot be transferred to other companies. This may be argued from Lincoln's experiences in attempting to transfer its culture and management systems to its acquisitions and international subsidiaries. My investigation and analysis of the ability of Lincoln to transfer its culture and management systems to its acquisitions is somewhat different and more complex than what has been routinely argued by non–Lincoln executives and academics.

WHERE LINCOLN SUCCEEDED

First, in Lincoln's own international start-up (or greenfield) operations in Canada, Australia, and France, Lincoln has been able to transfer a *substantial part* of its culture and management systems. Lincoln began manufacturing operations in Canada in 1925. "[T]he operation quickly adopted *most* [emphasis mine] of the U.S. incentive system, including an annual bonus starting in 1940 and piecework beginning in 1946. . . . Executives' open-door policy and the worker advisory council ensured communication among the subsidiary's 200 employees. These workers like those in United States, resisted unionization, turning it down in a vote in the 1970s."[1]

The presidents of Lincoln Electric Company of Canada, including Richard J. Seif, the current president, have always been committed to the Lincoln philosophy of management. As a result, major portions of the culture and management systems of Lincoln have been transferred to the company's Canadian operations. It should be noted, however, that Lincoln's workers in Canada have never had a formal guarantee of continuous employment.

Lincoln built a manufacturing facility in Australia in 1938 to serve the Australian and Asia markets. Piece work was introduced "for most production jobs and an annual bonus that usually amounted to between 25 percent and 35 percent of pre-bonus compensation" was also introduced. "Australia was one of the most highly unionized societies in the world, but Lincoln workers rebuffed organizing attempts on several occasions."[2] An advisory board is also in place at the Australian plant.

William (Bill) Miskoe was hand picked by James Lincoln to start the Australian operations. He not only put the Lincoln System into operation in Australia but he became somewhat of a legend in business circles in that country. Miskoe's career at Lincoln Electric spanned a period of almost 50 years. He was energetic and thoroughly immersed in the culture and management systems of Lincoln. He trained Robert J. Lee who is currently managing director of Australian operations.

As stated previously, Lincoln was invited into France and began manufacturing operations in 1955. "Expatriates from Cleveland helped implement the incentive system, including piece work, merit ratings, and a bonus that averaged 10 percent to 15 percent of pre-bonus compensation—in the late 1950s. A formal guaranteed employment policy was in effect from then until its repeal in the early 1970s."[3]

Lincoln purchased Harris Calorific from the Emerson Electric Company in 1990, and Harris then became a separate division. Although the division is headquartered in Gainesville, Georgia, and has manufacturing facilities in Gainesville, it also has plants in Pianoro and Milano, Italy; Rathnew, Ireland; and Monterey Park, California. The plants in Italy and Ireland were acquired as part of a deal between Lincoln Electric and Norweld Holding of Norway.

Harris has implemented many of the features of the Lincoln management system throughout its divisions, domestic and international. These features include piece work, merit rating, a bonus plan, and an advisory board, but not guaranteed continuous employment.

The real success story, however, in transplanting Lincoln's culture and management systems abroad is Mexico.[4] As we have seen, Lincoln Electric Mexicana S.A. de C.V. was formed between 1988 and 1992 by an amalgamation of three separate acquisitions. The Mexico City plant supplies Mexico and customers in South and Central America with commodity welding products.

The subsidiary enjoys the trade benefits of being located in Latin America. As a result, they do a considerable amount of business with customers in Central America, Venezuela, and Colombia, and they trade with customers in all other Central and South American Countries.[5]

When the Lincoln Mexicana subsidiary opens up markets for commodity type products, it creates opportunities for exports from the Cleveland plant. Complementary and upscale products, such as welding machines and equipment, are then supplied from Cleveland to customers in South and Central America.

Lincoln Mexicana S.A. was organized for Lincoln in 1988 by Frederick Mackenbach who was then manager of the Los Angeles sales office for Lincoln Electric. Mackenbach worked with James Delaney in developing the Mexican operations and later turned over management of Lincoln Mexicana to him. Delaney instituted the piece-work and piece-rate system in the Mexican plant initially by recruiting a few workers who volunteered to try it on an experimental basis. Once other workers saw that piece-workers were earning much more money than they were, they became convinced of the merits of piece work and piece rates. Delaney also convinced the union leadership to go along with piece work and piece rates demonstrating that it was a win–win situation—the more workers earned, the more dues they would pay to the union.

Delaney recruited David LeBlanc at the Harvard Business School where Delaney was attending Harvard's Advanced Management Program. David LeBlanc then assumed the management of operations at

Lincoln Mexicana. Ralph Fernandez, located in Miami, is currently the president of Lincoln Mexicana. Frederick Mackenbach went on to become the president and chief operating officer of Lincoln Electric from 1992 to 1996.

David M. LeBlanc, current managing director, is a former member of the sales organization in the Ohio Company. He is a graduate engineer and a Harvard MBA. Lincoln Mexicana uses piece work, has a merit rating program, offers a bonus program, and has a genuine open-door policy. It does not have guaranteed full employment, and the piece-rate workers in the Mexico City plant are unionized.

LeBlanc began implementing piece rates (*destajo* in Spanish) on an expanded basis in Lincoln Mexicana in 1991. Productivity has risen dramatically since that time. Whether measured as *output per labor hour* or *output per machine hour,* the results have been the same. Productivity at the plant has tripled since 1991.

The use of piece rates does, however, pose formidable challenges according to LeBlanc. The piece-rate system is difficult to manage. Each time there is a change in technology, each of the affected piece rates must be changed to reflect the output potential of the new technology. This requires an enormous amount of work on the part of industrial engineers. And this is a recurring process. Every time the company changes technology it must also change piece rates.

The experience in Mexico illustrates the approach that must be taken if the company is to successfully implement the Lincoln culture and management systems in its own international acquisitions. Moreover, it is also instructive for other companies seeking to implement a "Lincoln-like" system.

The principles of the Lincoln system at Lincoln Mexicana, as communicated to the author and summarized by David LeBlanc, are those enunciated by James F. Lincoln:

> They consist of a belief in the dignity of people and a commitment to the development of people. The belief in people is a belief that they are potentially very capable and as a result, they are able to grow and develop to a very high level of creativity and ingenuity. The principles include a commitment to distributing rewards justly—according to output. As a result, workers are paid based upon productivity through the piece-rate system.

The bonus at Lincoln Mexicana is based on the profits of the subsidiary and the merit rating scores of individual employees. Under the merit rating system, workers are rated on the following five factors: Group Goal Achievement, Self-Improvement/Initiative, Discipline/Quality, Teamwork/Responsibility, and Leadership.

Practices regarding the bonus in the Mexican subsidiary are different. The law in Mexico mandates profit sharing among workers. All companies must distribute 10 percent of pretax income as employee bonuses. A number of companies operating in Mexico seek to avoid paying the 10 percent bonus by establishing "shell companies" without employees, and they accrue profits of their operations in Mexico to these phantom companies.

The Lincoln principles include a respect for the dignity of each individual and for their abilities, actual and potential. As a result, Lincoln Mexicana is committed to being "an open company." Employee involvement in making suggestions and improvements to their operations is sought.

James Lincoln was also committed to guaranteed employment. Moreover, he believed that there should be no need for a union if a company provides all and more of what employees seek when they join a union.

LeBlanc is firmly committed to these principles. He went through the key socialization processes in Cleveland, and he fully understands the Lincoln system. He wanted to take over the plant in Mexico because he wanted to transplant the Lincoln system.

How these principles are applied depends on the particular circumstances faced in Mexico, and the speed at which one is able to apply these principles in a foreign acquisition such as Mexico depends on the history of the acquired companies. The three businesses that Lincoln acquired and consolidated in Mexico City were already failing. Employees saw that their firms were now coming under the management of a very successful U.S. firm, and they knew changes were necessary to make the Mexican subsidiary succeed. So it was easier to implement major portions of the Lincoln System in Mexico than in Spain where Lincoln acquired a very successful company.

Although LeBlanc is fully committed to the "Lincoln Way," he believes the actual practices he follows have to be adapted to the existing context in which the company is operating in Mexico. As a result, the practices he follows in Lincoln Mexicana are not exactly those that are followed in Cleveland even though there is *no disagreement over principles.*

As another example, Mexico is a highly unionized country. Any company without a union risks that "corrupt" organizers will approach the company's workers and organize its members in a harmful way. Therefore, LeBlanc set out to build very positive relationships with the union at Lincoln Mexicana. This is clearly a practice that is different from what is practiced in Cleveland, but one that is consistent with how the principles must be applied in Mexico. The leader of the union in Mexico is an attorney. A constructive relationship developed between the union leader and Lincoln Mexicana. While fully representing his workers, the union leader became a "believer" in the Lincoln System.

LeBlanc describes relationships with the union as "terrific." He has negotiated a deal so that only the piece-rate portion of the workforce is in the union. To work in a piece-rate job at Lincoln Mexicana, you must join the union. Twenty-five to 35 percent of employees at Lincoln Mexicana are not in piece-rate positions, and, as a result, they are not members of the union. Nonunion workers include those in maintenance functions and forktruck drivers. Piece rates do not make a lot of sense for these positions. To employ piece rates effectively, a company must have an almost unlimited volume of work. Following the principles of the Lincoln Way, LeBlanc believes that piece work builds on the dignity and talent of the personnel at Lincoln Mexicana. So, piece work and piece rates have been implemented according to Lincoln principles within the context of its plant in Mexico City.

Similarly, the management of Lincoln Mexicana has followed the Lincoln principle of providing labor with more than the wages and benefits they would receive from organizing into a collective bargaining unit. The average annual wage of the cohort workforce from which Lincoln hires its piece-rate workers is approximately $2,000. The average compensation of the production workers at Lincoln Mexicana is between $5,000 and $7,000 per year.

Guaranteed employment not only works in growing markets but in the long run it is contingent on growing markets. However, guaranteed employment is *not compatible* with the chaotic and fiercely competitive markets in South America. If the supervisors see poor performance at Lincoln Mexicana, they do not hesitate in letting people go. Yet the bias is toward growing the business and toward continuous employment whenever possible. Again, hold the Lincoln *principle* but adapt the *practice*.

The same pattern follows as far as establishing an advisory board. James Lincoln established the advisory board in 1914 to mediate disputes with employees and to seek their advice as to how to improve operations. LeBlanc at first established weekly lunch meetings with workers at Lincoln Mexicana, but he found that most of the issues brought up during these sessions were trivial, such as complaints about the food in the cafeteria. As a result, he has established a genuine open-door policy and has made a deliberate attempt to keep in touch with all of the employees at the subsidiary. He estimates that he knows approximately 350 of the 420 employees. So by "walking around" and by maintaining an open door, he believes the subsidiary is accomplishing the same thing as the Cleveland operation does with a formal advisory board.

Periodic major meetings take place with representatives of the union and with Lincoln employees. As a result, strong communications exist among union representatives, the company, and its employees—again, follow the principle and adapt the practice to the realities of the host country. Union-company relations are so constructive that the union leader and David LeBlanc are encouraging other companies in Mexico City to consider the system in place at Lincoln Mexicana.

The merit rating system used in Lincoln Mexicana is like the merit rating system used in Cleveland in that it has four ranking criteria. The criteria are not exactly the same.[6] Moreover, a more formal goal setting process exists in the merit rating procedure. Upper management establishes annual written goals for each major work unit within the plant. Based on these group goals, key managers assign goals to individual workers. Employees are then evaluated based on their performance according to the four criteria. These four criteria as they relate to the original merit rating criteria are:

Lincoln Mexicana Merit Criteria	Original Lincoln Criteria
Group Goal Achievement	Output
Self Improvement/Initiative	Dependability
Discipline/Quality	Quality
Teamwork/Responsibility/ Leadership	Ideas and Cooperation

As a result, the merit rating system used at Lincoln Mexicana is both more formal and less individualistic. Yet the bonus fraction (i.e., the size of the bonus pool divided by the total wages of those subjected to the bonus) has been rising. Here are the bonus fractions over the past five years in Lincoln Mexicana:

Year	Bonus Fraction
1994	0%
1995	19
1996	38
1997	55
1998	60

As a point of comparison, the bonus fraction in the Ohio Company for 1998 was 56 percent. Therefore, the piece-rate system and the merit rating system are contributing to significant growth in the productivity and profits of Lincoln Mexicana. This increased productivity and profit show up in the bonus fraction. The bonus is paid twice a year at Lincoln Mexicana. The government-mandated bonus is paid in May of each year. The merit bonus is paid on December 12, which is the day on which Mexico's patron saint, the Virgin of Guadalupe, is honored and celebrated (Día de Nuestra Señora de Guadalupe). Thus, the merit bonus is paid as a celebration bonus.

Finally, because of the relatively high levels of total compensation, the Mexican subsidiary can be and is very selective in its hiring practices. Entry-level educational qualifications in Mexico are the equivalent of the junior high level in the United States.

When the managing director of Lincoln Mexicana was asked how long it would take to transfer Lincoln's culture and management system to a newly acquired foreign firm, he said that he thought it depended first on the history of the acquired firm. He believes that it would take a manager who is dedicated to transferring the system somewhere between five and ten years. It takes that long for the new management to recruit and train a highly motivated workforce, and to make the specific adaptations to the culture and the laws of the host country.

WHERE LINCOLN FAILED

Lincoln, in 1986, was clearly playing catch-up to the realities of globalization. From 1965 to 1986, William Irrgang was determined to retain the company's domestic focus. Yet in his last letter to shareholders in 1985, he appeared to begin recognizing the imperatives of globalization. He stated:

> The changing structure of the national economy continues to be a challenge to the welding industry in this country. Some of the companies in the basic heavy metal manufacturing industries have relocated their manufacturing facilities outside the United States in an attempt to reduce cost[s] and become more price competitive in international markets.[7]

To see the difficulty confronting Lincoln that Irrgang was alluding to, we only have to examine the stagnation of sales that preceded Lincoln's international expansion program. If you remove the "boom year" of 1981, sales were basically flat at approximately $375 million from 1978 to 1986. After the international expansion program, from 1987 to 1998, sales revenue grew at a compounded rate of growth of approximately 9 percent. Moreover, for the year 1998, nonexport, international sales were approximately $370 million, which is close to the level of domestic sales when the international expansion began. Sales of foreign operations including exports from the United States were 32 percent of total sales in 1998.

Although Lincoln's foreign expansion program has been fraught with problems, there is little doubt that the company's growth in sales over the past 11 years has been dramatically affected by foreign operations. Sales growth has been almost equally divided between growth in domestic sales on the one hand, and growth in international sales of foreign operations and exports on the other. Exports of $92.5 million in 1998 are partly the result of "feeder" exports from the United States that are derived from Lincoln's foreign operations.

Lincoln's management, before beginning the acquisition program in 1986, was fully committed to transferring Lincoln's culture and systems to its newly acquired foreign acquisitions. Yet, the foreign acquisition program was hampered because it was executed very quickly. *Nine acquisitions were made and two new plants were built in a period of about five years in the latter 1980s and early 1990s.* There was no plan to transfer the management systems and too many acquisitions for it to be done systematically.

Moreover, most of the acquisition program was executed during a period of global recession. Massive redundancies in production capability were created in Lincoln's foreign operations. To make matters worse, premium prices were paid for acquisitions in Europe, because of the excessive demand for these assets created by the desire on the part of multinational companies to have a manufacturing presence in Europe before the elimination of all internal European tariffs.

In making foreign acquisitions during the 1988–1992 period, Lincoln looked first at being compatible with the acquired firm's core business. They did not look at compatibility with the values and management systems of the acquired organizations. Perhaps even more important, they did not look deeply at the compatibility of their operations with the culture and laws of the host countries in which their acquisitions were located.

In my view this was a mistake but not one that would permanently limit Lincoln's management from transferring their systems and their values. Transfer depends on the compatibility of Lincoln's systems with the laws of the host country.

As a result of the company's initial experiences in globalization and the resultant traumatic process of fully rationalizing and restructuring its acquisitions, it has evolved a new approach to globalization. This new approach to foreign acquisitions involves adapting Lincoln's culture and management systems to the acquired firm and host country. It means accepting differences caused by unions, customs, and regulations of host countries. And in the process, it often means becoming more like other firms.

The example of Lincoln Mexicana is quite instructive. There is difficulty in transferring a culture and management system that has been developed over a century in Ohio, and one that is significantly different than normal among U.S. companies.

The mere presence of unions and work rules and intrusive labor laws in place in acquired foreign companies, such as in Germany, should have been enough for management to anticipate problems in transferring these values and management practices. A much different situation no doubt would have prevailed if Lincoln's foreign operations consisted of start-up companies in countries without mandatory work rules and other restrictive labor practices.

On the other hand, a closer look at the Lincoln experience of absorbing foreign operations, greenfield, and acquisitions shows that the truth is not one-sided. The Lincoln system can and has been transferred very effectively in many parts of the world. Not only is the system alive and well in Europe (it is in operation in France), but also in Canada, and in Mexico. It has been operating very well in Australia for many years. Modified versions of the piece-rate and merit system also are in use in Lincoln operations in England, Ireland, Italy, and Spain.

So Lincoln has proven that the system can be transferred to foreign operations, but can it be transferred intact and implemented successfully in 18 months? And can it be transferred everywhere? The answer is no. It cannot overcome the economic and political problems that the company experienced in Germany, for example. It cannot tolerate the labor legislation that it found in Brazil. The Lincoln system, which relies on piece rates, merit ratings, cross-training, and bonuses was clearly unworkable in Germany and Brazil. As a result, the company sold its manufacturing operations in these two countries at significant losses.

Furthermore, top management at Lincoln believes that the situation is going to change in Germany—that the work rules and the unions are not going to be as restrictive in the future as a result of the reunification with and the competition from East Germany. The East Germans are competing for jobs in West Germany which will lead to a change in the German culture toward business—the unions are going to have to be less restrictive.

It is interesting to speculate some about Latin America, especially in light of Lincoln's failures in Brazil and Venezuela, although it has been successful in Mexico. Clearly, the ethical virtues enumerated in Table 1.2 are closely associated with those identified by Weber in his work on *Capitalism and the Protestant Work Ethic*. The origins of Lincoln's values, religiously speaking, are Protestant, not Catholic. Latin America is strongly Catholic. The Catholic Church historically has been hostile to capitalism, and Latin America has been the breeding ground for liberation theology, seeking to unite principles of marxism with those of Christianity. The hostility toward capitalism from the Catholic Church has always been based on the very uneven distribution of income resulting from capitalistic economic systems. There is now, however, a growing amount of Catholic scholarship which recognizes that although the distribution of incomes in certain capitalistic societies is very badly skewed, there is no better engine for lifting the income standards of the poor than capitalism, especially if other institutions of democratic capitalism also are used to assist the poor.

Catholic scholarship is increasingly recognizing capitalism as being capable of fully tapping human potential in a way that goes beyond the so-called "Protestant work ethic." Here is the logic of the argument from some Catholic scholars: Capitalism is a process of *creative destruction. It requires entrepreneurship.* It therefore requires an appeal to innovation that people created in the image of God are capable of and that the Lincoln management system attempts to promote. The Catholic hierarchy, before the pope's latest encyclicals, never saw the power of capitalism to raise the standard of living of the poor through creativity and entrepreneurship. In fact, Weber never included creativity in his discussion of the *Protestant Work Ethic*.

The attitude of the Catholic hierarchy toward capitalism is now changing. The social encyclicals of the current pope and work of Catholic scholars, such as Michael Novak, have brought the issue of entrepreneurship to the forefront. The Catholic hierarchy now sees capitalism as a major force in providing a vehicle for uplifting the poor. In fact, Lincoln Electric is a company that has, for the past century, proven that capitalism can provide powerful incentives to significantly uplift the economic levels of people who would otherwise remain in lower income categories. But Lincoln's workers in Cleveland have been selected carefully and have possessed minimum educational skills (high school or equivalent) and high levels of motivation. There is no doubt, as the experience in Mexico illustrates, that a workforce with similar characteristics can be selected out of the population of any country.

The bottom-line answer to the question about transferability of the Lincoln culture and management systems is if you are going to experience the types of restrictions that exist in Germany or in Brazil, or in similar countries, you cannot apply the Lincoln system.

In summary, to successfully transplant the Lincoln system, certain ingredients should be in place. It takes leadership; belief in the Lincoln system; a plan to implement the Lincoln principles while adapting the practices to local conditions; the right people in place in various positions; and time. But, there is no question that it is feasible to transfer the system if these preconditions are met.

To What Extent Is the Historic Culture and Management Systems of Lincoln Electric in Place in the Company's Operations Today?

With the appointment of Massaro as Lincoln's sixth CEO and chairman, the company promoted a person who was not absorbed in the Lincoln culture. They did this because the company needed international experience if it was to become a global company. Anthony Massaro has succeeded in doing the job. But what about perpetuation of the Lincoln culture as the company becomes increasingly global?

The company has a good possibility of retaining and adapting its culture as it becomes global. What is the source of this optimism? First, John Stropki, is currently president of North American Operations. He managed the salesforce in the United States during the 1992–1993 crisis. He was instrumental in boosting sales during this recession period and in helping the company recover from its losses incurred as a result of the poor performance of its foreign operations. He is steeped in the Lincoln culture.

Richard J. Seif, president and CEO of Canadian Operations, is committed to the Lincoln system. Joseph Doria, who Seif replaced in Canada, is now president of Lincoln Electric, Europe. Doria has extensive experience with the Lincoln system and with foreign operations. David LeBlanc in Mexico has demonstrated his success in implementing major aspects of the Lincoln system.

Michael Gillespie, before becoming president of Lincoln Electric in Asia, was a 13-year veteran from one of Lincoln's global competitor's. The people running operations in the Far East are all people without backgrounds at Lincoln Electric, with the exception of Robert J. Lee, managing director of Australia.

Massaro earned his promotion by turning around operations in Europe and by reshaping the company into a global company. He is educating key Lincoln executives around the world in global operations. But the education is two-way—Stropki, Doria, Seif, LeBlanc, Lee, and many other people like them have an opportunity to educate Massaro in various aspects of the Lincoln culture and system.

The "best of both worlds" could result. Recent performance of the company indicates that it is at least a strong possibility that Lincoln will have made the transition to global operations without losing what has made it such a remarkable company for over a century. At least that is the hope.

NOTES

1. Christopher A. Bartlett and Jamie O'Connell, *Lincoln Electric: Venturing Abroad,* Boston: Harvard Business School, Case 9-398-095 (Rev. April 22, 1998): 5.

2. Ibid.

3. Ibid.

4. This section on the operations of Lincoln Mexicana is based on information provided the author in personal communications by David M. LeBlanc, managing director of Lincoln Mexicana, on February 5, 1999 and by Frederick Mackenbach on June 15, 1999.

5. Other Lincoln plants may also supply Latin American markets. Lincoln's policy is to supply customers in Latin America and in other markets at what the company refers to as "Lowest Landed Cost" in the market.

6. This description of the merit rating criteria at Lincoln Mexicana is based on the description provided by Scott J. Schraff, "Strategic Management at The Lincoln Electric Company" (masters thesis, Cleveland State University, 1993), 38.

7. The Lincoln Electric Company, *1985 Annual Report,* p. 2, Cleveland, OH.

Chapter
9

Does Lincoln Electric Offer U.S. Companies Lessons of Lasting Value?

D oes Lincoln offer any help to the majority of U.S. companies at the beginning of the twentieth-first century? Or is Lincoln an example of a company whose legacy has little to offer executives of today? Is the advice of James Lincoln and his successors of any value in this era of global competition and rapid technological change? Obviously, I think so.

To address the question of the value of the Lincoln experience for today's economic realities, I would like to quote extensively and then comment on the issues raised by Donald F. Hastings, the recently retired chairman and chief executive officer of Lincoln Electric. Hastings raised these issues in an address he delivered to the Cleveland City Club on June 21, 1996. The title of the address was "Guaranteed Employment: A Practical Solution for Today's Corporations."[1] Portions of the talk are reproduced here by permission:

> I have been involved with a company where open communication has been a key to our success. Not just one-way communication, where someone in senior management gives an order and it gets delivered in some fashion to employees. But real back-and-forth, give-and-take interaction often heated, but always productive where employees have a genuine voice in the decisions that affect them.

To succeed, communication must be based upon *trust* between management and labor.

You'll find that kind of *trust* if you visit the factory floor at Lincoln Electric. I'm sure you'll hear some complaints too, also about working conditions, management, me, or any number of other things. I hear them when I'm there.

But the criticism is healthy for the company. The people doing the complaining do so because they care.

So I've been looking forward to coming here today to discuss the ideas of guaranteed employment and incentive pay, and to tell you a little bit about what goes on at Lincoln Electric, and why I was recently invited to join President Clinton for a conference on Corporate Citizenship.

There is a national debate going on about the wisdom of downsizing as a major element of business strategy. The invitation letter from the White House said, "This conference will bring together the President, and his key economic team with a diverse group of business leaders from all across the country, to discuss what American business can do to increase economic opportunity and security for their employees and their families, in a way that is good for business and for economic growth."

There were many good things that happened at the conference. He also announced the formation of a corporate citizenship award named for Secretary Ron Brown. And we heard many good stories about the value of things like onsite day care, health care benefits, flexible work schedules, and training programs designed to improve employability.

And these are certainly worthwhile goals. But I left with a feeling that none of them came close to being a recipe for relieving the stress, the uncertainty, the anxiety that plague so many people today. Let's not kid ourselves: Those stresses and uncertainties can be a major drain on productivity as well as a force undermining families and communities.

The real issue is how to give people some guarantee that their good work today will result in their having a job tomorrow. When I raised this issue with President Clinton, he said he did not fully agree. "People make mistakes," he said, adding that sometimes when senior management has diversified too much, a division or two might have to be cut off, resulting in layoffs.

I can understand why the President feels this way after reading some of last year's media reports. One news magazine described some of our nation's costcutting executives as "corporate killers." The reference is to top managers who have dropped the downsizing "bomb" annihilating hundreds of thousands of jobs: 11,000 at Scott Paper, 15,000 at Delta Airlines, 40,000 at AT&T, 60,000 at IBM.

Based on my 42-year experience at the Lincoln Electric Company, I believe massive layoffs generally are a sign of catastrophic failure on the part of management. When past and present management miscalculations have led a company into severe financial troubles, it's not fair to make workers pay with their jobs for the mistakes of others. Senior executives at such corporations are reminiscent of the unfortunate military commander who announced that he "had to destroy the village in order to save it." It's a sad commentary indeed when the *Boston Globe* reports that "saying good-bye (to employees) is a science." In their article they quote a vice president of an outplacement service as follows: "Companies also cut down on accidents if the affair is well planned. In my entire career I have only had one person have a heart attack," he proudly declared.

Further in the article many quotes are taken from a key text on the subject by William J. Morin, "Successful Termination." In it, Morin gives step-by-step instructions on how to terminate employees. Morin said, "Corporations used to feel guilty about laying off people. Now they've got accustomed to terminating people. Their conscience is going away. That's a way of life."

In November, Morin himself was out of a job after a dispute with his employer.

During the past decade, Lincoln Electric and its employees have watched in amazement as millions of people have lost jobs that once seemed secure, as Wall Street has saluted the downsizers by bidding up their stocks. In many cases it's greed more than need. . . .

We're especially proud that 1995 marked Lincoln's forty-eighth year of operating without laying off a single employee for lack of work. . . .

A company suffers in many ways when it responds to an economic downturn by turning people out the door in large numbers. When large numbers of people are let go, there is an inevitable drain of talent and experience. As some have said, corporate memory is lost. Think of the loss of investment that is incurred when people are trained and then cut loose.

Most important, the loss of *trust* and security, the human suffering, the devastated families and communities. . . .

Now, we need to forget the accusing rhetoric we hear so often from labor leaders, corporate heads, government officials, and media sources. After all, management and shareholders are really on the same side—

they all have a stake in their company doing well. So we should get together on what will serve all our interests, rather than focusing on what we think will help one particular group at the expense of the others— a tactic that serves none of us in the long run.

We don't need layoffs, we need creativity.

We don't need fatalism, we need flexibility.

Even though the world has changed tremendously since the 1880s, the same physical, mental, and attitudinal strengths that made a good farmer, blacksmith, or carriage maker in those days would also make a good employee today. The tasks the employee does today might be completely different, but the basic human strengths necessary to do the job well are the same. Management needs to be creative enough and flexible enough to find those strengths in the people they hire, and develop them to their greatest potential.

And that's where guaranteed employment comes in. Not as a right or entitlement, but as a reward, a mutually beneficial agreement that tightens the bond between the company and the employee, recognizing the value of good hard work and loyalty, and advancing the prospect for further contributions in the future.

Guaranteed employment does not mean rewarding the lazy or the incompetent. It means providing security to the person who gives all for the job and the company, who works well, who continually improves through better skills and knowledge, who comes up with new and fruitful ideas but who in today's world might see an entire career chopped down, along with hundreds or thousands of others, by an indiscriminate corporate axe.

Now, which seems right and natural to you? An atmosphere of mutual *trust* and loyalty, or one in which everyone is just a step away from the guillotine?

A company should offer employees more than just a job. It can offer them a real opportunity to build better lives for themselves and for their families. Isn't that one of the primary objectives of corporate citizenship? Based on those principles, employees will work hard, efficiently and enthusiastically. And since customer service is the ultimate test of success in business, employees at such a company will always keep their focus on satisfying the customer.

Even the notion of improving "employability" which, I guess, means training people so they're prepared for the eventuality of being fired, is like handing the football to a running back without any blockers for protection. Employees, who devote a large portion of their lives and themselves to their work, need and deserve protection in the form of job security. Lincoln Electric currently has 94 different training programs in place not to prepare people for termination, but to do a better job for themselves and the company.

I think it's time we take a hard look at what's going on. We need to find creative solutions to replace the notion that downsizing is a cure-all for a company's problems. It's management's responsibility to find these solutions, to plan ahead, to be flexible enough to respond to any new situation. That's what management is all about.

But while I think corporations are too quick to correct their mistakes by slashing their workforce, I don't think the entire responsibility for a company's success or failure should lie with management. You also need the productivity, talent, and loyalty of the workforce.

To be sure, there are a lot of things management can do to bring out the strengths of their workers. But when it comes down to performing, only the worker can do the job.

That's why it makes sense for everyone at a company to share in the profit when times are good, and to feel the burden when times are bad. When you lay people off, their share of the failure is almost always disproportionate to what they contributed to it.

At Lincoln, we've found that incentive bonuses, piecework pay and guaranteed employment help to ensure that compensation is fair and all efforts are rewarded. Compensation depends on the results produced. Those workers who are more productive than average are generally paid higher-than-average rates.

We know we can't provide a 100-percent guarantee of lifetime employment. I'm not aware of any business that can. Only satisfied customers can.

What we do guarantee is that employees with three years of service or more will work at least 30 hours per week, no matter how slow business might be.

During peak times we demand more from our people. This is not only fair, but necessary.

The early 1980s were a good example of the lengths our company will go to avoid layoffs. For Lincoln, those years were a time of hardship. Skyrocketing inflation, sharply higher energy costs and a national recession all affected demand for our products. Our sales, which had been strong and steady, dropped 40 percent during an 18-month period.

How did we respond? We transferred many of our production workers into sales. The very same people who successfully worked to satisfy high levels of demand in earlier years were now working to generate new demand. With their product knowledge, they were good at selling. They brought us new customers, which allowed us eventually to increase production and to weather the recession.

Again, the keys were creativity and flexibility. It was a creative solution by management, and our people had to be flexible to carry it out.

Job security should not be considered a right or a bargaining chip, but it also should not be thrown out completely as a casualty of increased competition. If we agree that job security is something that must be earned, everyone should have the chance to earn it. It should not be given as a gift, nor should it be stolen away.

The only way we'll have any kind of widespread job security in today's business environment is if we change our thinking as to what makes good management. Instead of praising corporations that downsize, we need to look at their actions as admissions of failure, which is what they really are.

A previous City Club speaker, representing a major union, eloquently suggested the following:

> Recognize basic human rights. Rebuild America's strength. Demand product quality and competitiveness. Train all employees. Give them a voice in making business decisions. Avoid conflict, don't promote it. Provide information and education. Respect the worker, and give workers their fair share of the profit.

How can anyone fault these recommendations? At Lincoln Electric, they have been at the cornerstone of our success. Guaranteed employment is just another important part of an overall compensation program that is fair, efficient, productive, and profitable. It requires *trust,* cooperation, loyalty, and creativity to work. It's good common sense. And it does work.

THE ISSUES RAISED BY DONALD HASTINGS

Donald Hastings was the fifth CEO at Lincoln Electric and was initially recruited from the Harvard Business School by James Lincoln. His tenure as CEO ended in 1996 when Anthony Massaro became the company's sixth CEO. It was during Hastings's tenure that Lincoln passed the century mark, rationalized its foreign operations, and reached $1 billion in sales—three notable accomplishments.

When I read the words in his address, I am struck with the enormous sense of continuity in thinking between James Lincoln and Donald Hastings. The culture and practices he describes are the ones that evolved directly from James Lincoln in an almost seamless manner.

To illustrate just how seamless the culture and practices have been at Lincoln Electric from James Lincoln to Donald Hastings, I will cite a few of the passages from the "Chairman's Remarks" made by Donald Hastings at the Annual Meeting of Shareholders of The Lincoln Electric Company held on May 27, 1997.[2] Mr. Hastings retired as chairman of the company after that meeting, having retired as chief executive officer on November 1, 1966.

Mr. Hastings cited three turning points in his career at Lincoln that reflected the direct influence of James Lincoln and the culture and practices he instituted. Hastings was recruited personally by Mr. Lincoln upon graduation from the Harvard Business School in 1953. The tenures of James Lincoln and Donald Hastings at Lincoln Electric overlapped for about 12 years.

Hastings first recounted the influence of Christ, the Sermon on the Mount, and *especially* the golden rule on the way James Lincoln lived, ran the company, and trained the people of Lincoln Electric. Hastings then followed with three concrete examples of how the golden rule of "do unto others as you would have them do unto you" was worked out in practice during his time with the company.

The first example occurred when Hastings was a salesman for Lincoln in Northern California. Hastings asked James Lincoln for permission to increase the number of products sold through distributors. It was the company's practice at that time to sell certain of its products directly to customers bypassing distributors. After saying no, James finally agreed but with the provision that Hastings "treat them right." Hastings followed these instructions with the result that sales volume in the Northern California district, a light manufacturing district, became the second highest in the company!

The second example occurred in Illinois when two prominent customers of Lincoln Electric in Hastings' territories, John Deere and Caterpillar, requested Lincoln to adopt a process called "MIG welding," a welding process that these customers were moving toward but one that Lincoln was planning to avoid. James visited the customers at Hastings request and because these customers requested Lincoln to make this change, James agreed. The company began MIG welding at the highest level of quality. The sales of MIG welding products and related machinery became a critical component of the company's future success—all because James Lincoln was committed to doing what was right for customers.

The third example is one that was recounted in Chapter 1. When Lincoln was in deep financial trouble as a result of the rapid foreign expansion of the late 1980s and early 1990s, the company did not downsize but rather called upon its employees in the Ohio company to work heroically to increase production and sales domestically. The employees responded, helping to restore Lincoln to financial health. Hastings stated that he believed that the current philosophy of downsizing and massive layoffs among U.S. companies is not only contrary to the golden rule but harmful to employees, and in the long run to shareholders. In his words, "when the company cuts the heart and soul out of its organization, it is bound to suffer." Hastings said that these draconian measures represent a massive failure of the management of the companies that take them. Downsizing and massive layoffs are not in Lincoln's "book of values."

After the passage of a century of highly successful operations, doesn't the Lincoln experience have something to teach executives of America? Are we headed on the right path? Is there not a better way? And what are the ingredients of this better way? Not all companies are in the welding business and not all companies are built on the same foundational values as Lincoln Electric.

The key issues that differentiate Lincoln from the majority of public corporations in the United States are:

- The reservoir of *trust* that has been developed between the company's management and workers.
- Trust at Lincoln has been established through the rough and tumble of formal and informal *communications* between labor and management.
- Serving the *customer* has always been the way to economic security for labor and management.
- Continuous *employee development* and *continuous improvements* in quality and productivity have always played a dominant role in the company's management processes.

- *Continuous employment* is earned and not awarded in a paternalistic manner.
- These attributes have led to impressive levels of *creativity* and *flexibility* at the company.
- The company's management systems and processes are in tune with the realities and the needs of *human nature*.
- Employees are *rewarded* based on productivity and quality of output. *Gainsharing* exists along side of *painsharing* at the company.
- Management takes *responsibility* for assuring that the company grows and can continue to provide good jobs for the people who have demonstrated that they are productive and reliable.

Will these principles work elsewhere or is Lincoln Electric an historical accident? The next two chapters are meant to shed light on these issues.

NOTES

1. A transcript of this speech is available from *Vital Speeches of the Day* 62 No. 22 (September 1, 1996): 691–693. The full text is available from UMI Clearinghouse, No. 173, News Publishing Co., 1996. Excerpts are used here by permission of City News Publishing Co., Mount Pleasant, SC 29465.

2. Minutes of the Annual Meeting of Shareholders, The Lincoln Electric Company, May 27, 1997, Cleveland, OH, pp. 4–6.

Chapter
10

Nucor Corporation

Nucor Corporation is the second largest steel producer in the United States. Sales in 1998 were approximately $4.15 billion. Company headquarters are located in Charlotte, North Carolina. The company operates 19 plants in eight states [Alabama, Arkansas (3), Indiana (3), Nebraska, North Carolina, South Carolina (6), Texas (2), and Utah (2)].

As Andrew Carnegie was the architect of integrated steel manufacturing in the United States, Ken Iverson, long-time CEO and chairman, and now chairman emeritus of Nucor, was the father of the minimill. In 1991, Iverson received the National Medal of Technology from President Bush.

Nucor now produces steel products such as hot rolled steel (angles, rounds, flats, channels, sheet, wide-flange beams, blooms, pilings, billiets, and beam blanks), cold finished steel, steel joists and joist girders, steel deck, steel fasteners, and steel grinding balls.

Hot rolled steel is manufactured principally from scrap, utilizing electric furnaces, continuous casting, and automated rolling mills. Cold rolled steel, cold finished steel, steel joists and joists girders, steel fasteners, and steel grinding balls are manufactured by further processing of hot rolled steel. Steel deck is manufactured from cold rolled steel.[1]

Similarities between Lincoln Electric and Nucor's Management Systems

The similarities between the management systems at Lincoln Electric and those at Nucor are numerous. It is almost as if the management systems at Nucor were purposefully and deliberately fashioned after those of Lincoln. The by-products of the formal and informal Mutually Supportive Subsystem Model (MSSM) at Lincoln are the relational qualities of:

- Trust
- Commitment
- Conflict management
- Learning
- Systems thinking
- Agility/speed/adaptability

These relational qualities are not mutually exclusive but often overlap and reinforce one another despite the fact that they have been discussed as discrete qualities.

The qualities are actualized through the management systems at Nucor. Each company has a highly motivated and productive workforce; strong customer loyalty deriving from low prices, high-quality products, and good customer service; a long-standing commitment to technologically superior operations; and a long history of highly profitable operations. Each company is the low-cost producer in its industry.

The Attributes of Nucor's Management Systems Which Have Led to Success

Nucor's success, like Lincoln's, can be attributed to numerous factors but three are especially noteworthy. First and foremost is Nucor's belief in and respect for people which in turn supports an environment of mutual interdependence and cooperation. Nucor maintains a high view of human potentiality, what is commonly referred to as Theory Y management.[2] If you select your personnel carefully and believe that your people are trustworthy, self-starting, self-reliant, hardworking, and motivated, those are the attributes you are likely to find in your workforce. This has certainly been the case at Nucor. Moreover, Nucor's management genuinely cares about its people.

Managers at Nucor serve as mentors who see themselves *working for employees* and helping them to become productive and innovative. Supervisors and managers seek to improve the economic conditions of workers by helping them to become more productive, while at the same time permitting the company to achieve maximum success.

As stated in an article by Nobles and Redpath, "one of management's key responsibilities [at Nucor] is to ensure that the organizational environment sustains and nurtures this potentially 'natural' alignment between employee and company interests."[3] This approach to workers at Nucor propels them to accomplish results beyond what even they believe is possible.

A second attribute of the management systems at Nucor, which reinforces Nucor's belief in people, is a *strong culture*. Nucor's system of values serves as the backbone of the enterprise. Values include but are not limited to fairness, respect, security, humility, honesty, openness, spontaneity, trust, freedom, quality, simplicity, and learning. Every management system at Nucor is rooted in the commitment to these core values, including roles and responsibilities, performance measures, allocation of resources, reward systems, and decision-making processes.

These values guide the decision-making process and help ensure that decisions are made with the best interest of the company and its employees in mind. As noted by Lord Brian Griffiths, "the most critical factor in explaining the superior performance of excellent companies turned out to be the concept of shared values."[4]

The third factor contributing to success at Nucor is executive leadership. Although there are a number of factors that contribute to Nucor's success, all of them are made effective by the actions and support of top management. The management team creates the culture and systems in which employees are empowered and can thrive. Executive management does this by "walking the talk." They are responsible for inspiring members of the organization to be productive, and they create alignment between the organization's mission and individual goals and aspirations. They also develop formal systems and influence the development of informal systems to allow the values of the company to permeate throughout the organization. It is the *vision* of top management that allows for the organization to operate organically and informally—nurturing, growing, and evolving to meet new challenges.

These three attributes—respect for people, strong values, and executive leadership—have provided the driving force for the mutually reinforcing systems that have been designed and developed at Nucor and that have spawned spectacular success. Moreover, it is executive leadership that has been the driving force in the development of the first and second attributes.

Ken Iverson[5] was the former president of Nuclear Corporation. In this position, he became the architect of Nucor Corporation that emerged from the Vulcraft Division of the Nuclear Corporation in 1972. Iverson was the long time CEO and chairman of Nucor until January 1, 1999 when he became chairman emeritus. He attributes the success of Nucor to approximately 70 percent culture and 30 percent technology.[6]

In defining culture, Iverson thinks of it as "all the things that shape interactions among the people in your company, its customers, and suppliers." These interactions are obviously the result of the design of formal management systems and the evolution of informal management systems, which are both determined and influenced by executive leadership. Ken Iverson's leadership at Nucor exemplifies effective executive leadership.

It should be noted that when Vulcraft was part of the Nuclear Corporation, incentives for management and for employees were already in place and working. Nucor simply kept building on that system of management and continuing to improve it.

NUCOR'S MANAGEMENT SYSTEMS

Table 10.1 provides an outline of the style and philosophy of the management of Nucor. One of the most striking things is how determined top executives are to put employees first.

John Correnti, at the time vice chairman, president, and CEO of Nucor, has stated:

> Here's my pecking order: You take care of your employees first. . . . If you have loyal, dedicated, hard-working employees who are happy, they will take care of the customers. If you have disgruntled employees, they

Table 10.1 Management Style and Philosophy at Nucor

The Nucor Story

MISSION AND COMPETITIVE STRATEGY: "to build steel-manufacturing facilities economically and to operate them productively"

VISION OF COOPERATION: "a company is a community of individuals who come together voluntarily to achieve a mission"*

- NUCOR'S ASSUMPTIONS ABOUT ITS PEOPLE
  —Dignity/Self-Worth—treating employees fairly and with respect
  —Rationality/Creativity—promotes entrepreneurship and develops managerial ability in production workers
  —Human Honesty/Morality—culture of freedom
  —Desire to Learn—climate of openness and empowerment
- Egalitarian culture-status symbols distinguishing management and production workers are minimal
- Emphasis on employee development and learning: company growth is pursued in order to provide opportunities for employees to learn, develop, earn, and grow
- Nurturing, coach/team-oriented management style
  —Management actively seeks participation of workers in their areas of expertise
  —"Hands-on" management style
- Servant Leadership Management Style
  —Humility and honesty in management
  —Management sees its role as helping workers to develop and grow
  —Mutual respect and trust between management and production workers
- Order of values regarding stakeholders: employees, customers, and shareholders
- Market-based management versus command and control style
  —21 independently operated businesses
  —Few services centralized at corporate headquarters
  —Belief that spontaneous order will produce superior results
- Emphasis on entrepreneurship and innovation for entire workforce: risk taking and high tolerance for mistakes
- No union or work rules. Four principles governing employee relations:†
  "1. Management is obligated to manage Nucor in such a way that employees will have the opportunity to earn according to their productivity;
  2. Employees should feel confident that if they do their jobs properly, they will have a job tomorrow;
  3. Employees have the right to be treated fairly and must believe that they will be;
  4. Employees must have an avenue of appeal when they believe they are being treated unfairly."
- Management is challenged to maintain culture as the Company continues to grow

---

* Nobles and Redpath, *Market Based Management*™, 106.
† Nucor Corporation, *The Nucor Story* (Charlotte, NC), 6.

are going to run these customers off eventually. The stockholders eventually will benefit from the good customer service.[7]

Both Correnti and Iverson believed that if employees and customers are satisfied, shareholders will be rewarded handsomely, which historically has been true at Nucor. Both Correnti and Iverson were committed to the proposition that long-term survival will benefit the shareholder, employees, and customers. As a result, they were not terribly interested in the short-term goals placed on the company by the investment community.

The company has committed itself to the proposition that it is the employee producing steel who is king. Adam Ritt, executive editor of *New Steel,* summarized the attitude of Nucor's management toward its employees as follows:

> Increasing shareholder value is the phrase du jour in the steel industry. But, how should the worker at the blast furnace of EAF [Electric Arc Furnace] feel when his employer says that the company's primary responsibility is to the stockholders, not to the ones sweating on the shop floor? How hard will that worker push to produce the extra ton?[8]

The company has displayed a high tolerance for trusting its people. There is a commitment to honesty that builds trust. With trust comes a tendency to give managers significant autonomy. This in turn fosters an environment where people are encouraged to take risks in order to improve facilities and processes. Employees at a Nucor plant have to be "Nucorized" by older employees; this means they have to learn to trust one another and to trust management. In addition, they have to be constantly on the lookout for opportunities to improve the functioning and throughput of plant and equipment.

Top management has displayed a servant leadership style of management. They see themselves working for the 6,900 employees to help them do their jobs better, to help them to learn and grow. Making mistakes is often a part of the process of learning and growing. Tolerating mistakes is part of the risk-taking culture of Nucor.

Finally, Nucor's style of management is very "hands on." This is a company that focuses on the production of high-quality, low-cost steel and steel products. The entire management team deals with the operational realities. As a result, the company has not had much success hiring MBAs and has developed a slight hiring bias. Top management believes that most MBAs simply are not interested in working in such a demanding hands-on business, where the emphasis is on throughput and quality of steel production. Moreover, Nucor relies heavily on people skills and generally finds MBAs lacking in these skills.

This philosophy of management and management style is entirely consistent and supportive of the infrastructure of the company. Table 10.1 enumerates all of the elements in the philosophy and management style subsystem.

INFRASTRUCTURE

Nucor has eight autonomous business units; each operates as a profit and investment responsibility center. They are:

- Nucor Steel
- Nucor Cold Finish
- Nucor Grinding Balls
- Nucor Fastener
- Nucor Building Systems
- Vulcraft
- Nucor-Yamato Steel Company
- Nucor Bearing Products, Inc.

In addition, Nucor built an iron carbide plant in Trinidad, West Indies, in 1992.[9] The plant was completed in 1994, but because of mechanical process difficulties, "the first boat load of iron carbide wasn't shipped to the United States until April 1996."[10] The plant began producing iron carbide for use in steel production in Nucor's minimills in 1996. Iron carbide may be converted to metal and then substituted for a portion of the scrap metal that is used as an input in producing steel. The advantage of iron carbide is that it can be produced at a lower cost than the scrap metal it replaces in the production process. Trinidad was chosen for the site of the new plant for numerous reasons, most particularly its abundant supply of iron carbide. The company also negotiated "permanent tax-free status" in the Republic of Trinidad.[11]

The experiment in Trinidad, however, was later deemed uneconomical. Nucor suspended operations in Trinidad in 1998. This experiment, however, illustrates Nucor's high-risk, high-reward culture. The use of iron carbide, along with scrap steel, had never been used before in minimills. Nucor tried and failed! Failure is also a part of Nucor's culture, but so is the success they previously have achieved in the implementation of new technologies!

Nucor Steel

Nucor Steel operates eight ministeel mills, using scrap steel to manufacture various steel products. Nucor produces commodity steel products such as "bars, angles, light structural, sheet, and special steel products."[12]

Nucor Cold Finish

The three plants produce steel for shafts and precision parts. The advantages of the cold finish process are that steel can be produced with smoother surfaces and more accurate dimensions than hot steel. Cold steel is used in buildings, equipment, and household appliances. The diverse uses of cold finish steel somewhat buffer the impact of the business cycle on Nucor.

Nucor Grinding Balls

This single steel plant produces steel grinding balls of one- to five-inch circumference. These balls are used in the mining industry for processing copper, iron, zinc, lead, gold, silver, and other ores.[13]

Nucor Fastener

Nucor maintains two facilities that are devoted to making steel fasteners such as screws and bolts. The first fastener facility was built in St. Joe, Indiana, in 1986 and "produced hex-head cap screws, hex bolts, and socket head cap screws."[14]

Nucor Building Systems

This division designs and builds preengineered steel buildings and frames in two plants. Commercial and industrial buildings are the primary markets for its steel frame products, which are sold directly to building contractors.

Vulcraft

Vulcraft is the largest producer of joists and horizontal steel beams to support industrial, commercial, and institutional buildings in the United States. These beams are used in high-rise office buildings, apartments, and homes. Vulcraft operates six plants in six states, all within the United States. Its steel is purchased from Nucor Steel.

Nucor-Yamato Steel Company

In 1988, Nucor formed an alliance with one of Japan's leading producers of wide-flange steel beams to construct a minimill in Arkansas. This is the first minimill to make "40-inch I beams." This plant uses continuous casting technology that forms beams to much closer specifications than traditional methods. Construction of the mill was completed and operations began in 1993. In 1997, Nucor shipped over 2.2 million tons of steel products from this plant in Blytheville, Arkansas, making Nucor-Yamato Nucor's largest division.

Nucor Bearing Products, Inc.

This single plant produces steel bearings that are used in motors, automobiles, and other devices that contain moving parts. It also produces machined steel parts.

ADDITIONAL ASPECTS OF THE INFRASTRUCTURE

Each of these autonomous units at Nucor is composed of one or more plants. Each plant manager is a general manager. Each general manager is held responsible for earning a return on assets (ROA) of 25 percent and has substantial autonomy in the operations of its plant so long as the target ROA is achieved. Input may be purchased either from another division of Nucor or an outside source. This freedom in sourcing decisions follows from and is consistent with the high degree of autonomy given to each plant manager.

Only three restrictions exist. Each general manager may not sell assets without approval from corporate headquarters, may not engage in significant financing activity, and must obtain approval from corporate headquarters for major capital expenditures. Otherwise, the autonomy of each general manager is complete.

One might ask where the synergy is among plants in such a decentralized organization that concentrates in a single industry? After all, shouldn't a firm striving to be the world's low-cost producer of steel seek economies of scale among its various plants? Nucor's answer to the preceding questions is profound. Nucor believes there is synergy in comparing the performance of very similar plants. It simplifies the control system at Nucor and thus saves time and money!

> Another way to simplify controls—this time at the evaluation stage—is to rely on "deadly parallels." Two or preferably more operating units are deliberately organized along comparable lines; then the results of one unit are compared with achievements by parallel units. The assumption is that external opportunities and problems are about the same for all units, so "if the Dallas unit can do it why can't you? . . . A competitive pride leads each manager to try to look good relative to his peers."[15]

This is exactly the strategy used at Nucor. By meeting three times a year and by comparing performance of plants on a monthly basis, *informal peer pressure* is created to increase productivity, lower cost, and raise quality. High throughput is the key to keeping costs down, and peer pressure is used to raise throughput. In addition, best practices are shared so that all plants can benefit from innovations at other plants. For this simplified control system to work in creating peer pressure, multiple plants of a similar nature are needed.

The informal organization at Nucor is unique in that it not only is not bureaucratic but it emphasizes employee freedom, thus creating the ability to get things done quickly. The cost of this "chaos" is mistakes that are made by employees and managers who operate without extensive supervision. Also, the lack of strong staffs at corporate headquarters minimizes Nucor's ability to achieve scale economies in those areas where scale economies are possible, such as in purchasing and transportation. Top executives at Nucor firmly believe that the informal systems are more important and more responsible for the company's success than its formal systems.

The company is in effect trading off the benefits of autonomy, empowerment, speed, agility, and adaptability for potential economies of scale. Management has concluded that the trade-off is favorable in terms of the motivational effects it creates. In a sense, this runs counter to the common practice of companies seeking to be low-cost producers. In this regard, Nucor is unconventional and even radical in the autonomy it grants plant managers.

The small staff at corporate headquarters follows from the desire of top management to empower divisions, plants, and employees. In fact, the staff at corporate headquarters in Charlotte, North Carolina, is so small (under 25) that it would have real difficulty meddling too deeply into the affairs of the divisions. Micromanagement thus becomes impossible at Nucor. Again, the existence of a small corporate staff is consistent with the intention of management to give general managers significant levels of autonomy.

The recruiting practices at Nucor are very selective and emphasize self-reliance and a strong work ethic. The company seeks workers who desire to work hard, demonstrate a strong commitment to the company, enjoy the "thrill of the game," and desire to make a lot of money. No specific level of educational requirements for its production workers has been set. The company does, however, encourage all employees without high school diplomas to obtain their General Education Diploma (GED). The working environment at Nucor is very demanding. As a result, turnover is very high at new plants. However, the rewards at Nucor are such that this permits the company to maintain a nonunion shop and eliminates work rules that may prohibit the agility and adaptability that is widespread among the teams at Nucor.

Employees tend to be very loyal and demonstrate a strong tendency to encourage relatives and friends to come to work for Nucor. In fact, for existing employees, Nucor often means *Nephews*, *Uncles*,

Cousins, and Other Relatives. Therefore, it is not uncommon for a Nucor plant to take on a small-town America, family-and-friends atmosphere. The company has always sought to build upon "small-town American values."

The company has done very few acquisitions. The reasons are related both to technology and the workforce. Potential acquisitions tend to have older technology that would have to be updated substantially by Nucor. In addition, acquisitions tend to be problematic because they often involve workers who are unionized. Nucor's desire to run a nonunion shop with highly motivated and hardworking people creates a bias toward building new plants. The strong tendency is to build these plants in rural locations and hire local people with a strong work ethic. Costs for land and construction for these facilities are less than in major metropolitan areas. In addition, the cost of living for employees is less. This further magnifies the "real income" of employees.

To ensure that these new plants are "Nucorized," the company transfers approximately 30 employees at various levels of the new plant. Production workers are hired locally. Although the company is very committed to promoting people from within, they also hire middle managers from other steel companies. It then becomes the job of the newly promoted managers and transferred employees to demonstrate the "Nucor Way" to new employees and to managers recruited from the outside. The task is to convince these new employees and managers that the culture and management systems at Nucor really work although they are often very different from those these new recruits have ever experienced.

Although there is an attempt to adopt the same culture in every plant, each facility has its own peculiarities. There is no attempt by top management to force the Nucor culture on a facility, but there is every attempt to convince personnel that the Nucor culture is good and effective. The emphasis of management is on "what is right" not "who is right."

Teams are formal structures at Nucor plants. A weekly bonus system results in strong incentives for the teams to achieve high levels of productivity and quality. Teams solve problems. The productivity statistics to be reviewed later bear out the effectiveness of the team and

Table 10.2   Infrastructure at Nucor

Organization Structure

- Flat Organization Structure-Four Layers of Management-Streamlined Chain of Command
  —Chairman/Vice chairman/President
  —Vice president/General manager
  —Department manager
  —Supervisory/professional
  —Hourly employee
- Nine Business Units Operate as Highly Autonomous Units
  —Each General Manager is responsible for business planning, marketing, sales, product pricing, R&D, and human resources
  —Good ROA leads to increased autonomy for plant managers
- High worker autonomy within business units
  —Empowered employees
  —Spontaneous order, not controlled order
  —Nonbureaucratic behavior, high level of informal interaction
  —No "sandbagging" and "gamesmanship," no work rules—workers do what is necessary
- Little Direct Staff Support of Business Units
  —Small corporate headquarter staff
  —Technology, project management, R&D, finance, and technology assessment staffs at headquarters
  —Strong plant independence
- Selective Recruiting Process
  —Locate plants in rural locations across America
  —Screen people to fit with Nucor's culture
- Emphasis on Creating Teamwork, Mutual Interdependence, and Immediate Problem Solving
  —Project teams with 20 to 40 production workers and 1 supervisor/facilitator
  —Team members function in a flexible manner
  —No job descriptions
- Project Managers of New Plants Become Plant Managers
  —Much parallel processing
  —Project management process is *organized chaos* but projects are managed at substantial cost savings over competitors
  —Key to Nucor's project management system is the culture of employee freedom
  —Project Manager spending authority is $1 million
  —Project Manager may offer bonuses to suppliers

Table 10.2 *(Continued)*

Responsibility-Measurement Methods

• 25 percent ROA for plant managers
• Transfer pricing for transfers of steel products between plants
• Strong emphasis on teamwork in productivity and quality measurements

Informal Organizational Relationships

• Nonbureaucratic behavior
• Workers encouraged to assume new roles as needed to solve problems—no work rules restricting tasks
• High level of informal interactions
• Not status oriented—few traditional executive perquisites
• Competition among plants for improvements in productivity and cost control

incentive structure at Nucor. When receiving the National Medal of Technology, Iverson paid tribute to the adaptability contributed by the people at Nucor when he said: "Our most valuable asset is a workforce that can rapidly solve the processing problems and make technology work."[16]

Finally, the infrastructure allows Nucor to manage projects in a manner that is far more effective and efficient than that of its competitors. Each project manager has more stake in the results of the project than if he or she were passing off responsibility to another manager to operate the plant. Managers are held accountable for a 25 percent ROA. As a result, managers are very concerned about the cost, schedule, quality, and completion time of the plant.

The result of the project management methods at Nucor is that the company is able to construct minimills "at between $200 to $500 per ton of annual manufacturing capacity, as compared to $1,400 to $1,700 per ton to build mills favored by integrated steel producers."[17]

Table 10.2 presents a complete representation of the infrastructure at Nucor.

Consistent with the company's view of human nature and the servant leadership style of management is a coordination and integration subsystem that emphasizes trust, extensive formal and informal communications, an open-door policy, and elaborate grievance procedures. The impression one gets in examining this subsystem is that the company is "walking the talk" with its employees. The result is very low employee turnover and very high employee productivity. Table 10.3 lists the formal and informal coordination and integration mechanisms at Nucor.

Most noteworthy in Nucor's rewards and recognition system is the weekly team-based bonuses that can be large in relation to the base

Table 10.3   Coordination and Integration at Nucor

- High level of trust and openness
- Emphasis on spontaneous order
- Council of general managers plus top management
- No games and sandbagging in planning and resource allocation process
- Regular meetings between plant management and employees to discuss performance and problems
- Quarterly general manager meetings at headquarters to review performance and to plan for the future. Meetings often *generate strong conflict* and conflict is encouraged so long as the motives are for what is best for the company as a whole
  —Meet to decide which capital projects get funded in case of a need for capital rationing
  —Meet to decide budget and capital budget
  —Meet to decide on any changes to the management system
- Employee grievance procedures provides for employee appeal process
  —Employee appeal process can move from supervisor to department to corporate headquarters until grievance is resolved
- Open-door policy of top officers to production employees and to middle managers
- Extensive formal and informal communications network
- Generation and use of the knowledge system facilitates coordination among plants
- Fair amount of job rotation and cross-training so people can perform many different tasks
- Numerous training programs
- Cross-functional teams of 20–40 members is the basic mode of operation in plants
- Employee opinion survey every three years
  —Has led to significant policy changes such as random drug testing and mandatory firings for drug violations
- Goal-oriented and self-reliant workers—workers who are skilled at solving problems themselves on the spot
- The appeal to dignity, rationality, creativity, fair division, and honesty unleashes tendencies among employees toward natural alignment with interests of managers, customers, and shareholders

wage. Although the structure of incentives at Lincoln is much more individualistic, the upside rewards at Nucor are more substantial than at Lincoln. The base pay at Nucor, however, is somewhat below average for the steel industry. On the other hand, the bonus at Nucor can average between 100 to 200 percent of base pay per week depending on the quantity of "on-spec production" by a team. Average wages plus bonus of production workers at each steel mill in 1996 was approximately $60,000. This is approximately the same total compensation earned by Lincoln workers in 1996.

Consistent throughout the rewards and recognition subsystem at Nucor is the notion of *fair division* of output. As a result, Nucor is the most productive manufacturing company in the world! Clearly, fair division and productivity are not at odds with each other. Nucor is the lowest cost producer of steel per ton, in the nation, if not in the world.

The team-based bonus system at Nucor is especially important given the cost structure of Nucor's plants. It is true that variable costs, as a percentage of total costs, are lower in minimills such as Nucor than at integrated mills. Nevertheless, fixed costs are still substantial. For example, the fixed cost of electricity to operate an electric arc furnace per year is approximately $1.4 million. As a result, throughput is crucial for reducing average total unit cost per ton.

In setting standards for production bonuses, Nucor uses meticulous, detailed records on production levels of mills in the past. In addition, Nucor uses estimates of practical annual capacity provided by equipment suppliers. Benchmark estimates from suppliers are given heavy weight, especially with new technology. Nucor pays its crews bonus pay for every additional ton of "on spec" production beyond practical capacity.

This incentive system in turn motivates crews to work toward improving the output capacity of each machine, which leads to attempts by workers to reengineer the equipment so as to increase capacity. The equipment is essentially "Nucorized" by employees. Again, peer pressure is used between teams at a given plant just as it is used between plants.

There is a substantial commitment to *continuous employment at Nucor as long as the employee is performing his or her job.* Employee termination decisions for those with 10 or more years of service are treated as "conscience" decisions and are made at corporate headquarters, illustrating the importance the company places on the security of income for employees even in a cyclical business.

The Nucor team-based production system is very taxing on employees. Although the record age for an employee working on a production team is 82 years, many employees move off production teams and take less demanding jobs elsewhere in Nucor's plants as they age. These jobs are also lower paying. Surveys indicate that these aging employees have met their most significant financial obligations and are more interested in free time than money at this point in their lives.

Informal rewards are also prominent at Nucor. Exemplary employees, for example, receive new leather jackets. Nucor surveys all of its employees every three years to assess employee satisfaction. In past surveys only 15 percent to 17 percent of employees expressed unhappiness with any aspect of their jobs. Management uses the results of these surveys to address genuine employee concerns.

Incentive compensation decisions for plant managers and other officers of the company are made based on ROA and ROE as specified in Table 10.4. Bonuses for plant managers are as high as 90 percent of their base salary. All nonproduction employees at each plant are covered by a bonus plan that is tied to the same ROA target as the plant manager's bonus system. Bonuses for this group of employees may be as high as 32 percent of their wages and salaries.

Bonuses to senior officers begin after the company earns 8 percent ROE and "is capped at 24 percent of [or return on] shareholder's equity, at which point officers receive a bonus of about 200 percent of their base pay in cash plus a bonus of 100 percent of base pay in stock."[18]

PLANNING, RESOURCE ALLOCATION, AND REPORTING

Nucor is in a very cyclical business, yet over the past 11 years, only in 1991 did sales fall from the preceding year and then only by 1 percent. Rates of growth in sales have ranged from a low of −1 percent to a high of 39 percent with the average year-to-year rate of growth in sales over the 11-year period being 16 percent. "Between 1966 and 1996, Nucor Corporation grew at an annual compound rate [of sales] of approximately 17 percent."[19]

Table 10.4   Rewards and Recognition at Nucor

- Emphasis on fair division of the output of the firm
- Incentive pay for all production employees
  - —Pay according to productivity
  - —Weekly bonuses for production workers averaging 100 to 200 of base pay
  - —Determination of bonuses is based on team efforts
  - —Bonuses are paid based on quantity and quality of production
  - —Product complexity taken into account in bonus formula
- Peer pressure within teams motivates improvements in productivity, quality, and innovation
- Job security—continuous employment after a probation period if performance remains satisfactory
- Plant manager incentive compensation based primarily on ROA of their facility
- Nonproduction employee incentive compensation based on plant ROA
- Senior officer incentives based on pretax ROE performance above a minimum level ROE and are 60 percent stock and 40 percent cash
- Rare special cash semiannual bonuses for all employees during very profitable years
- Profit-sharing program minimum of 10 percent of pretax earnings with seven-year vesting period
- Matching stock purchase plan up to 10 percent of pay
- 401K plan for all employees with Nucor matching contributions with percentage match depending on company ROE
- College scholarships for college-age children of employees—$2,200 per year per child
- Tendency toward equality of benefits among all employees of Nucor reinforcing egalitarian culture
- Pride of workmanship, dignity, and self-esteem
- Sense of personal ownership and belonging to a team
- Job satisfaction
- Monthly management evaluation report publicizes all plant ROAs creating informal rewards and penalties for good and poor performers

---

Earnings per share adjusted for stock splits have ranged from a low 60 cents to a high in 1997 of $3.35. The average year-to-year rate of growth in earnings per share from operations, excluding gains from the sale of assets, during the past seven years has been 33 percent.

Given the importance of productivity and cost reduction and control to the overall strategy of Nucor in this commodity business, it is important to note that average growth in sales per employee increased by

13.2 percent over the past 11 years. Although this is not a perfect measure of productivity, spurious growth fluctuations may be assumed to be minimized given the length of time involved. These numbers give credence to Nucor's claim to be the most productive manufacturing company in the world. Furthermore, Nucor estimates that its unit labor cost per ton of steel is approximately $25. The company believes this is approximately half of the cost per ton incurred by other large integrated steel companies in the United States. At $25 per ton, unit labor costs are below the cost of shipping steel from abroad to the United States thus insulating Nucor from the competitive effects of low-wage foreign labor. These productivity and unit labor cost numbers have led to high rates of year-to-year growth in sales and in earnings per share.

Finally, percentage return on average equity ranged from a low of 9.5 percent in 1991 to a high of 22.4 percent in 1994. The average return on equity from 1987 to 1997 was approximately 15 percent. Financial performance information on Nucor from 1966 to 1997 is presented in Appendix 10.1 thru Appendix 10.5 at the end of this chapter.

Table 10.5 enumerates the characteristics of the planning, resource allocation, and reporting process at Nucor. Note Nucor's tremendous commitment to technological superiority. Three evidences of this are the huge investment in thin-slab continuous casting in the Crawfordsville, Indiana, plant; the Nucor-Yamato joint venture emphasizing continuous casting methods of wide-flange steel production; and the amount Nucor has invested in building and upgrading its plants and equipment over the past 11 years. Capital expenditures have totaled approximately $3 billion from 1987 to 1997. As a final note regarding capital expenditures, Nucor follows rather conservative accounting policies. For example, "pre-operating and start-up costs of new facilities reduced net earnings by 46 cents per share in 1998. These costs were $72,400,000 in 1998, compared with $59,700,000 in 1997 ($88,900,000 in 1996)."[20]

One of Nucor's key values is its commitment to remain at state-of-the-art technology. This has been demonstrated by its high-risk culture and its capital expenditures. Nucor's reputation for technological excellence has encouraged vendors from all over the world to visit and present their technological innovations to management. Top management is continuously evaluating the technological ideas of

Table 10.5 Formal Planning, Resource Allocation, and Reporting Process at Nucor

Operations
- Strong product and technology innovation and market planning
- Plants and minimills located in farming areas
- Core competence
- Theory of the Business—all products are commodities so key success factors are low cost and high quality coupled with highly motivated workforce and technological leadership
  —May operate at 140 percent of capacity if tap employee knowledge of bottlenecks
- Keep business simple and straight forward
- Internal market system (transfer pricing at market) encourages smart purchases

Planning and Resource Allocation
- Strong focus on customer satisfaction
  —Integrity in pricing
  —High-quality products and customer service
- Strong emphasis on growth in new plants: high capital expenditure budgets and sales revenues
- Corporate headquarters responsibility for overall strategic planning:
  —Establishing new plants and products
  —Introducing new technologies
  —Financing strategy and implementation
  —Identification of cash flow and capital needs
  —Helps and encourages managers who are having difficulty achieving their ROA
  —Management development and succession
  —Termination decisions of employees with more than 10 years of experience
  —Collection and sharing information among the management team
- Annual planning process with each plant doing its own planning for its operations
  —Each plant takes advantage of local market information and does its own strategic planning
  —High degree of decentralization in capital investment decisions
  —Cost controls at local level

Reporting and Evaluation Process
- Council of managers consider and evaluate funding for new products
- Strong emphasis on cost control and productivity at all plants
- Well-defined reporting system linked to responsibility success measures
- Commodity products assessed in terms of cost and quality
- Monthly management report shared with all plants
  —Common plants share and compare information and improvements
  —Plants not in competition with each other
- Frequent employee evaluations
  —Weekly for production teams
  —Heavy emphasis on self-control within teams

others. They are looking for ideas to perfect through engineering and manufacturing, and they are constantly looking for technological breakthroughs, not merely small derivative improvements but those ideas leading to breakthrough improvements.

Appendix 10.1 presents financial data for the Nucor Corporation from 1966 through 1997. This is the period in which Nucor emerged from the previous Nuclear Corporation under the leadership of Ken Iverson. Appendix 10.2 is a graph depicting the annual return on equity of the Nucor Corporation and is derived from Appendix 10.1. Appendix 10.3 presents the annual earnings per share data in a graphical format. Appendix 10.4 provides annual growth rates in earnings per share for this period. Finally, Appendix 10.5 provides the rate of growth in the price of Nucor's common stock during this period of time.

We have completed a detailed review of each subsystem of the formal and informal management systems at Nucor Corporation (Figures 10.1 and 10.2). Each subsystem follows the values and management style of the organization and boosts each other in a mutually supportive way. Furthermore, the formal management systems support the informal systems and make each other more effective, thus further boosting potential performance.

In general, whether the formal and informal management systems result in boosting performance depends on how well both sets of systems are aligned with the realities of the specific and general environments faced by the company. This is a subject to which we now turn.

Figure 7.1 contained both the *macro* and the *industry specific environments* faced by Lincoln. Refer back to that figure as we discuss the environmental forces facing Nucor.

THE MACROENVIRONMENT IN THE STEEL INDUSTRY

Steel is a worldwide industry, and as such Nucor is affected by both supply and demand factors across the world. In fact, many of the innovations perfected by Nucor and reviewed previously had their origin in other parts of the world.

Figure 10.1 Formal Management Systems.

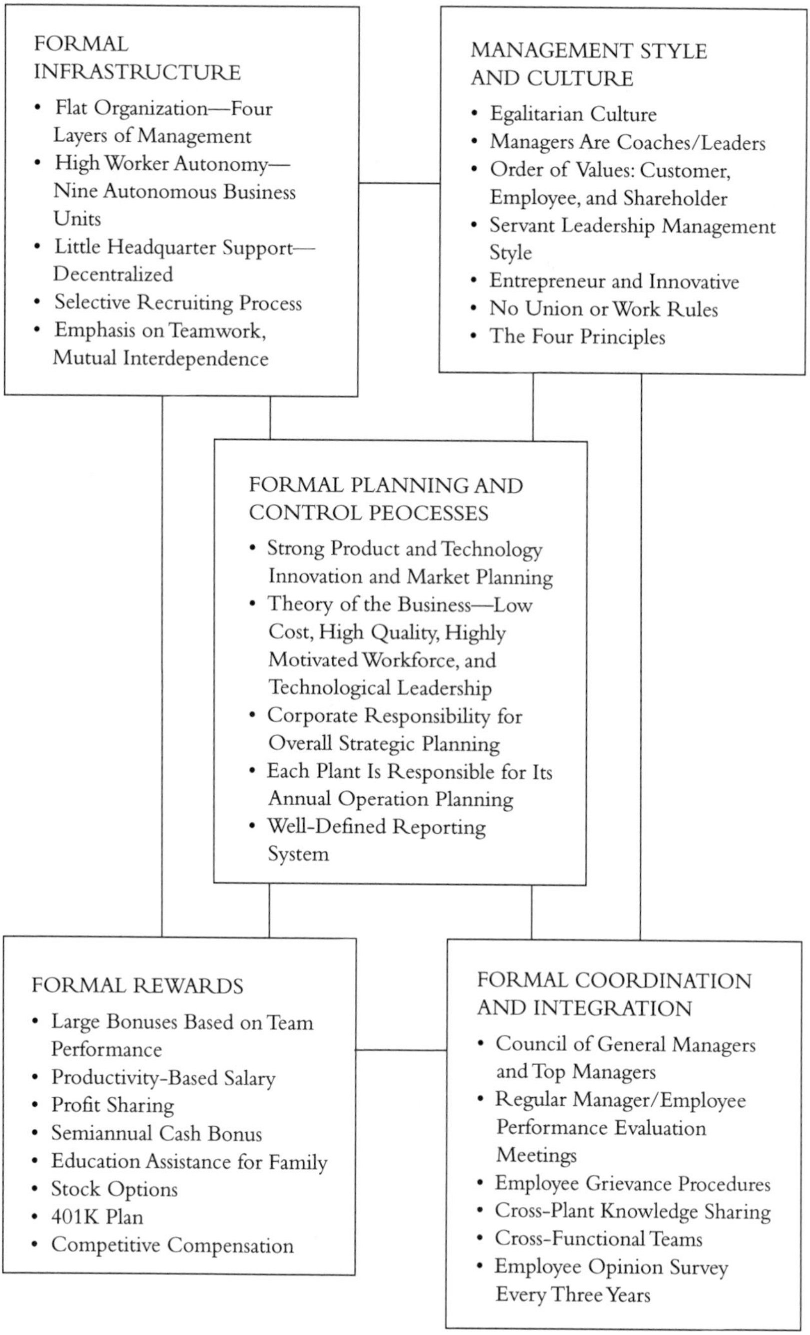

FORMAL
INFRASTRUCTURE

- Flat Organization—Four
  Layers of Management
- High Worker Autonomy—
  Nine Autonomous Business
  Units
- Little Headquarter Support—
  Decentralized
- Selective Recruiting Process
- Emphasis on Teamwork,
  Mutual Interdependence

MANAGEMENT STYLE
AND CULTURE

- Egalitarian Culture
- Managers Are Coaches/Leaders
- Order of Values: Customer,
  Employee, and Shareholder
- Servant Leadership Management
  Style
- Entrepreneur and Innovative
- No Union or Work Rules
- The Four Principles

FORMAL PLANNING AND
CONTROL PEOCESSES

- Strong Product and Technology
  Innovation and Market Planning
- Theory of the Business—Low
  Cost, High Quality, Highly
  Motivated Workforce, and
  Technological Leadership
- Corporate Responsibility for
  Overall Strategic Planning
- Each Plant Is Responsible for Its
  Annual Operation Planning
- Well-Defined Reporting
  System

FORMAL REWARDS

- Large Bonuses Based on Team
  Performance
- Productivity-Based Salary
- Profit Sharing
- Semiannual Cash Bonus
- Education Assistance for Family
- Stock Options
- 401K Plan
- Competitive Compensation

FORMAL COORDINATION
AND INTEGRATION

- Council of General Managers
  and Top Managers
- Regular Manager/Employee
  Performance Evaluation
  Meetings
- Employee Grievance Procedures
- Cross-Plant Knowledge Sharing
- Cross-Functional Teams
- Employee Opinion Survey
  Every Three Years

Figure 10.2   Informal Management Systems.

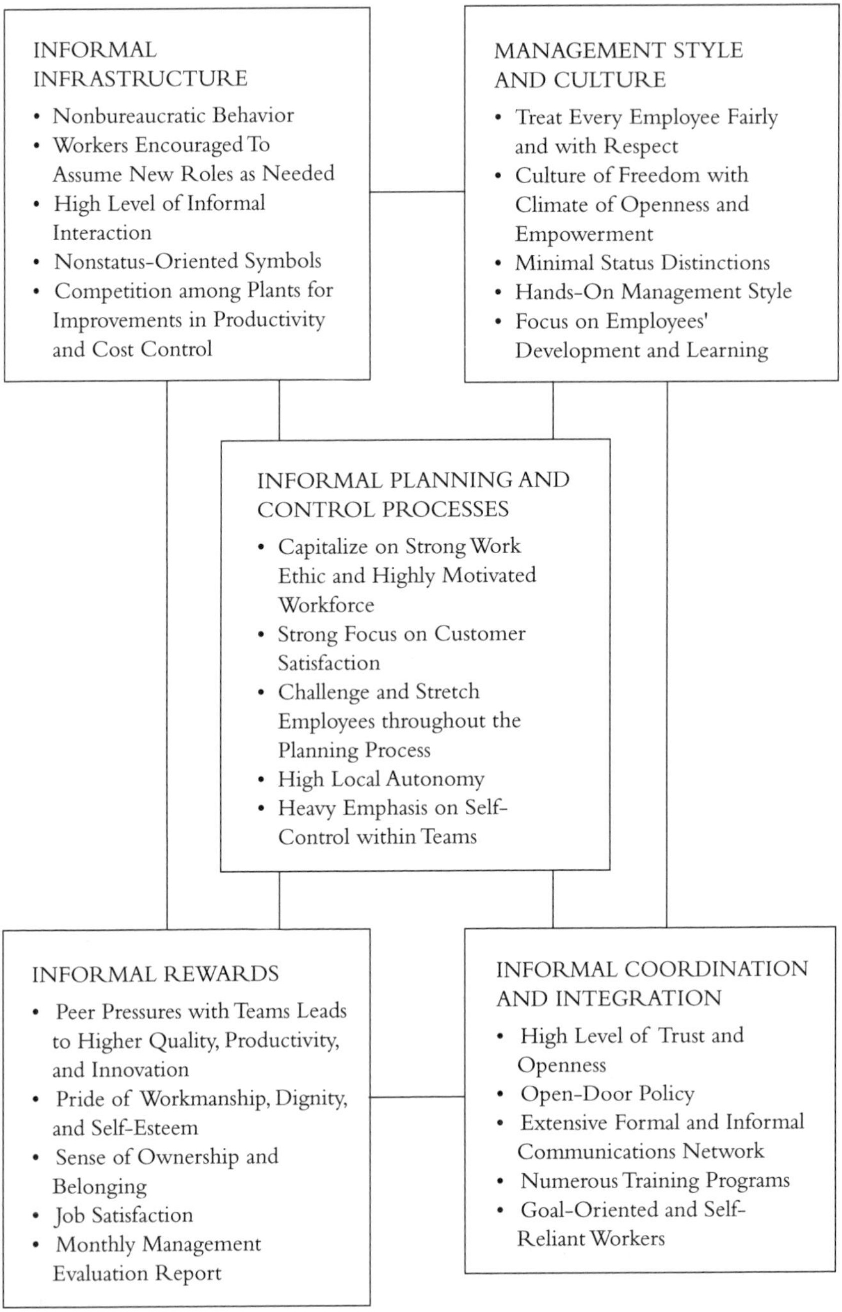

INFORMAL INFRASTRUCTURE

- Nonbureaucratic Behavior
- Workers Encouraged To Assume New Roles as Needed
- High Level of Informal Interaction
- Nonstatus-Oriented Symbols
- Competition among Plants for Improvements in Productivity and Cost Control

MANAGEMENT STYLE AND CULTURE

- Treat Every Employee Fairly and with Respect
- Culture of Freedom with Climate of Openness and Empowerment
- Minimal Status Distinctions
- Hands-On Management Style
- Focus on Employees' Development and Learning

INFORMAL PLANNING AND CONTROL PROCESSES

- Capitalize on Strong Work Ethic and Highly Motivated Workforce
- Strong Focus on Customer Satisfaction
- Challenge and Stretch Employees throughout the Planning Process
- High Local Autonomy
- Heavy Emphasis on Self-Control within Teams

INFORMAL REWARDS

- Peer Pressures with Teams Leads to Higher Quality, Productivity, and Innovation
- Pride of Workmanship, Dignity, and Self-Esteem
- Sense of Ownership and Belonging
- Job Satisfaction
- Monthly Management Evaluation Report

INFORMAL COORDINATION AND INTEGRATION

- High Level of Trust and Openness
- Open-Door Policy
- Extensive Formal and Informal Communications Network
- Numerous Training Programs
- Goal-Oriented and Self-Reliant Workers

In mid-1998, the domestic demand for steel was 125 million tons. This represents a 1.5 percent increase over 1997. This level of demand in the United States is the highest in 30 years. Steel is used in automobiles; construction projects such as buildings, bridges, and roads; capital expenditures by industry; and other consumer expenditures such as washers and home appliances.

Each of these sectors expanded in 1998, thus providing an increased demand for steel. According to recent estimates,[21] approximately

- 35 percent of all steel is used in construction of buildings, bridges, and roads
- 25 percent is used in the manufacture of industrial machinery
- 22 percent is used for consumer durable goods such as automobiles and home appliances

Although demand was expected to increase by 1.5 percent in 1998 to 125 million tons in the United States, domestic supply was expected to increase by 2.5 percent to 109 million tons.[22] Moreover, with a strong dollar, imports are increasing from Asia, Russia, Korea, and Brazil as these steel-producing nations try to export their way out of deep recessions. Worldwide steel production capacity significantly exceeds worldwide demand for steel at the present time. Therefore, predictions are for a continued decline in steel prices around the world, which should put pressure on all domestic producers in spite of rising domestic demand for steel.

After almost 20 years of reductions in U.S. steel capacity, from 160 million tons (mt) to approximately 95 mt, domestic capacity has begun to expand again as a result of the cost-efficient minimills pioneered by Nucor. As a result, Nucor has become the second leading supplier of steel in the United States with the highest market capitalization in the industry.[23]

On the plus side, improvements in technology at the minimills have resulted in lowering the cost of production, thus making it possible for companies like Nucor to meet the declining prices while stabilizing profits. It is difficult in the current environment to continue the growth pattern that Nucor has experienced in the past.

To realize the macrodifficulties, with a forecasted demand of 125 mt and a domestic supply of 109 mt and imports of 31 mt, there is excess supply in the domestic market. The problem is further complicated in that Japan's largest export market, China, is beset by numerous economic problems which has reduced demand for Japanese exports dramatically. This further intensifies Japan's drive to export to the United States. During the first half of 1998, Japan's exports to China decreased by approximately 13 percent, whereas Japan's exports to the United States have increased by more than 170 percent.[24]

ANTIDUMPING LAWS AND POTENTIAL U.S. GOVERNMENT INTERVENTION

As the economies of Russia, Japan, Korea, and Brazil weaken, there are charges from steel industry executives that international laws against dumping are being violated by the exporting nations. Dumping occurs when steel is sold below its production cost or when different prices are charged in home and foreign markets.

As the domestic steel industry is threatened, Congress and the president could invoke antidumping laws and punish violators. In 1974, the U.S. Congress passed the 1974 Trade Act. In 1988, Congress passed the Omnibus Trade and Competitiveness Act. Under Section 301 of the 1974 act, the president was given authority to rectify trade injustices against U.S. companies. In combination, these two acts of Congress give the president and his cabinet the ability to place restrictions on imports, raise tariffs, and restrict imports from nations engaged in unfair trade practices.[25]

Officials from the U.S. steel industry are now lobbying to impose import tariffs on "cheap imports" or to establish import quotas for each exporting nation. To substantiate their claims, industry officials point out that "the United States imported 1,029 mt. of hot-rolled sheet in October 1998, up 103 percent from a year earlier."[26]

The most likely scenario, given the desire to spare the economies of Asia, Russia, and Latin America further harm, is for the U.S. Department of Commerce to negotiate voluntary quotas with these exporting nations.

THE SUBENVIRONMENT AT NUCOR: PRODUCTS, MARKETS, AND TECHNOLOGY

Macrofactors in the environment are important to Nucor and must be monitored closely, and appropriate adaptations must be made. In addition, there are a number of very specific factors related to Nucor's plants, products, competition, technology, and personnel that are of at least equal importance.

Nucor's response to domestic and international competition has been to raise production to 100 percent capacity to achieve scale economies and improved productivity. Next, the company has proceeded to cut prices. From June to December 1998, Nucor dropped prices by 25 percent in three discrete moves.[27] Nucor believes that it is one of the world's low-cost producers, and although it must deal with poor exchange rates, the company believes it can be successful pursuing this pricing and productivity strategy. If it succeeds, it may force less efficient producers to exit from the market.

As a part of this strategy, Nucor is now building a 1.2 mt plant to make plate steel in Hertford County, North Carolina. Technological improvements that will improve productivity and reduce costs are being made. If the company can continue to operate as the low-cost steel producer in the world, it can survive this depression in steel prices.

Nucor currently has less than 10 percent of the U.S. market for steel. In the specific environment it faces, in order to grow substantially—say, to double its size—it would have to do so by taking business away from other domestic steel producers.

Current steel imports, however, are in products that compete with only 40 percent of Nucor's products. The remaining 60 percent of Nucor's products are for use in the construction and consumer product markets. They have not yet been affected by imports.[28]

Another specific company factor is the price of inputs. Nucor's minimills make steel from scrap steel. Scrap steel prices are at their lowest level in decades due to the recession in Asia.

The combination of reductions in scrap prices, increased productivity derived from operating plants at 100 percent of capacity, and firming steel prices is expected to offset the reduction in profits that will come about by the price reductions announced during 1998.

COMPOSITE CYBERNETIC MANAGEMENT

Figure 10.3 represents a diagram of the *composite cybernetic management process* used by Nucor to meet customer needs through employee performance. Figure 10.3 may be specified for each of the stakeholders separately, as well as for the internal business processes that are

Figure 10.3   A Composite Cybernetic Management Process.

Employee and Customer Goals and Strategies

- On Spec Production
- Continuous Cost/ Price Reductions
- New Technology Development
- High-Quality Customer Service
- Highly Motivated Workforce
- Highly Productive Workforce

Improvements/ Adaptations

- Heavy Capital Investment in New P&E
- Cut Prices to Meet International Competition
- Invest for the Long-Term Regardless of Short-Term Pressures
- Maintain Continuous Employment during Recessions

Status

- Growth in Sales and Net Income
- Employee Team Performance ROA
- Sales per Employee
- Cost per Ton

Compare

Critical Success Factors

- Cost/Price
- Employee Satisfaction
- Product Quality and Service
- Selective Workforce
- State-of-Art Technology
- High Rates of Productivity Growth

Performance Measures

- Team Productivity and Quality
- Cost Relative to Industry
- Market Share in Specific Market Segments
- Team Productivity and Quality Performance
- Plant ROA
- Plant Capacity Use
- Company ROE

Ideal

Benchmarks from Past Performance and Competition

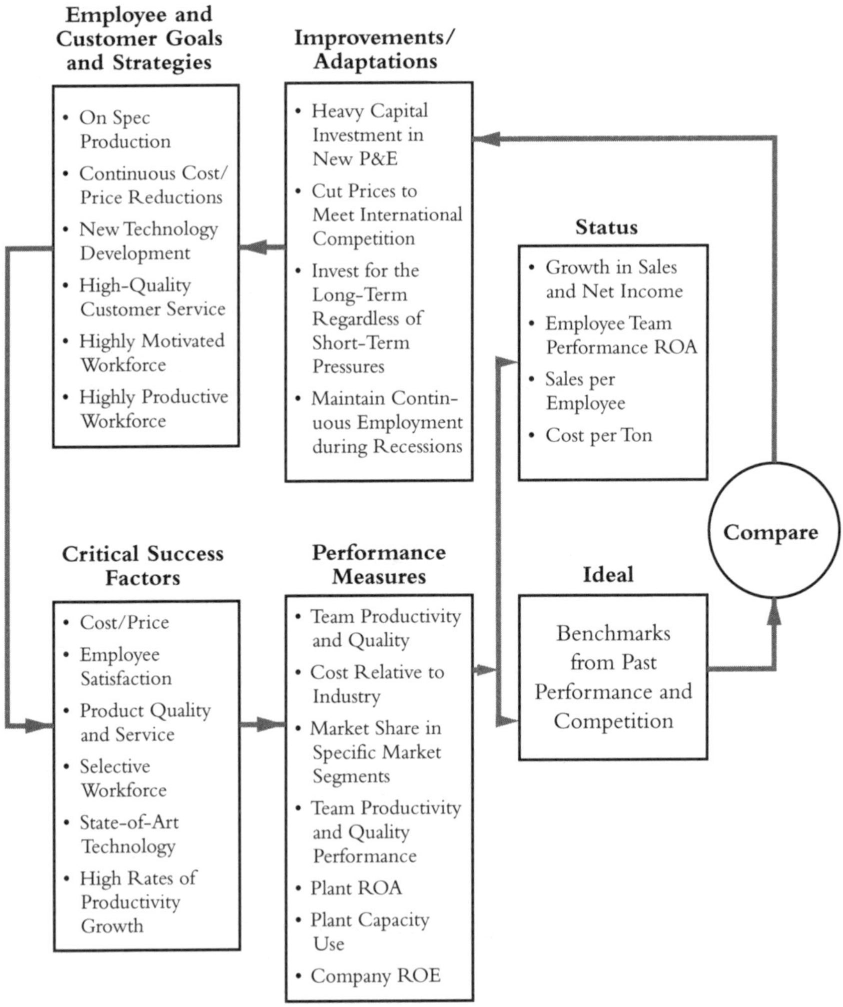

necessary for meeting all stakeholder needs, following the pattern suggested by Kaplan and Norton.[29]

RELATIONAL QUALITIES YIELDING AGILITY AND ADAPTABILITY

As we have seen in the Lincoln case, the six relational qualities are highly interdependent, but trust is the key to successful dynamics in the agile model of management. Once high levels of trust are produced in an organization, it is relatively easy to gain employee commitment which in turn enhances the ability of an organization to manage conflict in a way that is constructive in making tough decisions without destroying the fabric of human relations. Learning is a by-product of employee interaction in problem-solving situations within the context of informal relationships and cross-functional teams. Systems thinking is encouraged by cross-functional teams as well as by job rotation and by extensive communication and education of employees by management. These five relational qualities have much to do with producing the attribute of agility.

The next question in terms of dynamics is: How do these two sources of agility—executive leadership and formal and informal management systems—produce the six relational variables that so significantly contribute to organizational success?

Relational Variable: Trust

"Trust is the expectation that arises within a community of regular, honest and cooperative behavior, based on commonly shared norms with other members of that community."[30] This definition of trust is echoed in Nucor's belief that a "company is a community of individuals who come together voluntarily to achieve a mission." Trust is demonstrated in this proposition first by the choice of words and then through action.

- "Community" implies a mutually, beneficial coexistence.
- "Voluntarily" acknowledges that people are free thinkers who have a choice.

- "Mission" implies cohesive action that has drawn the group to act in concert.

Nucor honors its commitments starting with its commitment to provide job security for people who are performing their jobs properly. This is not a trivial matter, and Iverson takes job security very seriously as the major factor contributing to the creation of trust.

> Look at what employees typically get in corporate America.
>
> Most don't get job security. Workers' short-term interests tend to run a distant third behind those of shareholders and executives. When those short-term interests conflict, people lose their jobs, no matter how hard they have worked (and no matter how much the company may need them down the line). That is why, through the longest economic expansion in history, many people remain haunted by the specter of recession and by memories of massive, dispassionate "reductions in force." And that is why so many workers remain deeply distrustful of management, even when managers try to rebuild the bridges of trust. After all, it was managers who tore down those bridges in the first place.[31]

Earning trust at Nucor is also done by establishing a system of open communications among team members and between management and workers. Management does not penalize people for making mistakes or for speaking out about problems and opportunities. This high degree of trust and openness is demonstrated by the employees' willingness to candidly discuss past mistakes without fear of repercussions.

Open communications are facilitated by Nucor's flat organization structure and by its open-door policy. Decisions occur at the lowest possible level in the organization. Decentralization provides evidence that a significant amount of trust exists in the judgment of employees on the part of top management.

Regular staff meetings are held to keep the lines of communication open, thus reducing suspicion and building trust. Workers can approach management with their problems, criticisms, and suggestions. In addition, the employee appeal process sets forth a course of action in case employees believe that the company has in some way breached the value system. The grievance procedure is one of the core values of the company.

encourages team members to work out the conflict because it will affect productivity and compensation of the entire team. Thus, incentives are in the right direction for resolving conflict.

In addition, the employee appeal process provides an orderly way to resolve individual employee grievances. Moreover, termination decisions for long-term employees are handled at corporate headquarters, thus permitting resolution of some of the most potentially serious conflicts at the very highest levels of the company.

At the top level, all general managers at Nucor are officers of the company. They meet three times a year. During these meetings, they remove their "operating hats" and put on a Nucor perspective. The meetings are designed to discuss plans and performance, to share good ideas, to drop poor practices, and to knit the company together.

Plenty of expected conflict surfaces at these meetings. They are designed for this purpose. All the general managers, by seeking to do what is best for Nucor, resolve these conflicts.

Relational Variable: Learning

All learning requires feedback—the quicker and more accurate the feedback, the greater the learning. Team environment and cooperation facilitate learning. Mistakes at Nucor are viewed as *learning opportunities.*

Learning is clearly a cornerstone of Nucor's success. The company challenges people to generate new ideas. One example occurred during a recessionary period in which a prefabricated steel roof was invented by Nucor's employees.

Nucor's management also provides opportunities for employees to learn by urging them to go beyond their zone of comfort and accept greater responsibilities. In one case, a factory worker was assigned to a team with the responsibility for the construction of a $250 million plant; then that factory worker was put in charge of the melt shop. Not only are employees challenged, but managers also enlist feedback.

The idea that sometimes you can learn more from your mistakes than your success is a key belief at Nucor. The ability of employees and managers to take responsibility for their mistakes as long as there is a lesson to be learned from them clearly provides opportunities for growth. Nucor's commitment to continuous improvement permits organization members to take risks and to learn from their mistakes.

Employees at Nucor are cross-trained; in the process, they learn new functions and assist each other. This ties directly into the ongoing process at Nucor to continuously improve production techniques and methods.

Formal and informal information sharing is prevalent. Information sharing (or knowledge) systems are in place so that employees can learn from each other's successes and failures. The monthly evaluation report also facilitates this process.

Relational Variable: Systems Thinking

Although individual incentives are used to motivate employees to higher levels of productivity, team incentives help keep employees focused on overarching company goals. Nucor's value systems also appeals to what Maslow has described as the need for self-actualization: higher level needs beyond narrow self-interest that have a far-reaching effect on motivation.[33] By focusing on qualities such as teamwork and community, trust and honesty, respect and dignity, employees are encouraged to think beyond their own self-interest to satisfy the needs of the organization as a whole. If they feel like partners, they will act like partners!

Moreover, the fact that plant managers and nonproduction employees receive bonuses based on Nucor's overall return on assets rather than on individual performance further brings employee and company goals in sync and contributes to a systems perspective. Finally, the management systems reinforce one another.

Nucor believes that "spontaneous order" will bring superior results to "controlled order." In that spirit, each of the subsystems of the management systems at Nucor supports one another.

The annual planning process at Nucor is an attempt to knit Nucor together and to create a systems view of the corporation. The annual planning process seeks to collect and share information throughout the company, to identify cash flow and capital needs, and to provide opportunities for corporate managers to coach plant managers.

Relational Variable: Agility/Speed/Adaptability

The qualities of agility/speed/adaptability serve as a source of Nucor's competitive advantage and are reflected in a number of ways. Project management experts accelerate the learning process by transferring knowledge about plant construction to the managers responsible for each new plant. A central research and development organization allows managers to leverage specific expertise without having to dedicate their own time and effort to this research.

The use of internal markets creates an environment wherein innovation and adaptability is facilitated. Because Nucor's plants operate as autonomous business units, they have the ability to react and adapt quickly to changes in the marketplace and to changes in technology. In addition, the high degree of autonomy that managers enjoy allows them to be creative and to take independent action.

For instance, project managers have the authority to offer bonuses to contractors if they deem these bonuses to be appropriate. Nucor's rapid construction of plants is further evidence of the company's agility. Plants are built using many parallel activities and without excessive reliance on blueprints. Managers direct contractors where to place conduits, drains, and so forth. These building methods of "organized chaos" result in construction costs that are 8 percent lower than the industry norm.

A flat organization, teamwork, and spontaneous order create an environment in which quick reaction and change is facilitated. Employees are encouraged in this environment to change direction as needed. Cross-trained employees can change functions as the need arises to permit rapid responses to unforeseen situations. The attitude that "management thinks, employees do" is nonexistent at Nucor.

Finally, continuous improvement processes have resulted in changes to technology and new product introductions in order to adapt to local needs.

In summary, commitment, the ability to manage conflict, learning, and systems thinking require high levels of trust in an organization and these create agility. Nucor is and has been one of the most agile companies in the United States.

RECENT DEVELOPMENTS AT NUCOR

In early June 1999, John Correnti, CEO, president, and vice chairman of Nucor resigned over a dispute with the board of directors concerning the future directions for the growth of the company.

Nucor currently finds itself at a strategic turning point. Nucor's historic growth rates have been so great that one research analyst, Richard Aldrich of Lehman Brothers, is predicting that Nucor will produce and sell 11.4 mt of steel by the year 2000 making Nucor the single largest steel producer in the United States, surpassing US Steel.[34] With U.S. demand for steel growing at 1.5 percent per year, it will be very difficult for Nucor to continue to achieve past growth rates if it simply continues its current strategy. The minimill concept has been widely duplicated in the United States and inexpensive foreign imports are flooding the country. Nucor has fared particularly well during these turbulent times although in the first quarter of 1999, sales fell by 22 percent and net income dropped 27 percent from the first quarter of 1998.

Now that Nucor has succeeded in becoming the nation's largest steel producer, how should it proceed? Should Nucor simply try to take more business away from the integrated steel producers in a sort of a zero-sum game? Should Nucor expand internationally as Lincoln has done? Should Nucor diversify and if so into what markets? If Nucor diversifies should it do so by acquisitions or by constructing greenfield operations?

Differences also exist as to management practices. By any measure, Nucor's management systems are heavily informal, with very little formal strategic planning done at corporate headquarters. Should the companies management system become more formalized? Should the company expand its very small staff at corporate headquarters?

Lincoln Electric faced a similar turning point in the late 1980s and early 1990s. It chose to expand internationally. The change was very bumpy to say the least. Yet the culture and management systems at Lincoln proved agile and the company made the transition to a global company. Nucor faces similar questions. The culture and management systems will permit the company to adapt, but there may be some turbulence ahead.

NUCOR'S MANAGEMENT SYSTEM CONTRASTED WITH LINCOLN'S

Nucor's management system can be compared and contrasted with Lincoln. Similar to Lincoln Electric, Nucor, places a high value on employees. This is demonstrated through management's open-door policy, an emphasis on trust and openness, a performance-based compensation system, job security, and personal responsibility and accountability. Other similarities include Lincoln's guaranteed cost reduction program, as contrasted to that of Nucor's integrity in pricing strategy, selective recruiting processes, and the absence of excessive perks for executives.

Although both Nucor and Lincoln place a high priority on the transfer of knowledge through open communication channels, Lincoln has developed an employee elected advisory board to further facilitate access to management. Superior performance is also similarly rewarded at Lincoln and Nucor. At both companies, employees have the ability to earn according to their productivity and innovation based on a bonus system. Both companies include team performance in bonus calculations but Nucor's bonus is exclusively team-based whereas Lincoln's is predominately based on individual performance.

INTERNAL MARKET CONCEPTS

Both Nucor and Lincoln have adopted the internal market concepts to some extent. The internal market concept, as applied to organizations, seeks to capitalize on those instincts in human nature that seek to pursue self-interests while operating to further organizational goals. To ensure that the overall interests of the organization are met while members pursue their own self-interests, management systems should be designed to create the incentives for individuals that allow them to attain the goals of the company. As a result, the internal market concept stresses *entrepreneurial action, powerful incentives,* and *accountability.*

The belief is that by facilitating the pursuit of one's self-interest, more innovation and higher rates of productivity can be achieved in organizations. As a result, business units and employees become more efficient, adaptable, and profitable.

Both Lincoln and Nucor operate on the premise of self-management and view themselves as a confederation of entrepreneurs. This is observed at the operating level at Lincoln and at most levels at Nucor.

James Lincoln believed that there were two different ways to manage a company—entrepreneurially or administratively. He chose the entrepreneurial system. It manifested itself in incentives placed on virtually every position in the company according to the four criteria of merit. He placed no upper limit on the wages that could be earned by production workers, and he also required workers to share the pain when profits were poor and when quality was defective. At Nucor, each worker is part of a team whose weekly income is determined based on "on-spec" production. Each plant manager's bonus is based on the plant's ROA; each officer's bonus is based on ROE.

Innovation at Nucor has come from everywhere in the company. Production employees are expected to solve the problems they confront even if the problems are novel. General managers at Nucor have come from the factory floor. A very high view of human potential exists at Nucor as it does at Lincoln.

Both companies are highly selective in their hiring, and both companies have successfully resisted unionization. Iverson states:

> When a company's managers treat employees as equals, they earn trust. And the bond of trust enables managers to do things that would never fly in a company based on "*We* vs. *They.*"[35]

Both Lincoln and Nucor pay the highest wages in their industry to production workers yet each is the low-cost producer in their industry.

CHALLENGES TO THE VIABILITY OF THE INTERNAL MARKET CONCEPT

Challenges exist in applying the internal market concept because roles and responsibilities become blurred as employees are encouraged to act as entrepreneurs, creating messy working relationships. The role of top managers is that of advisors and mentors rather than directors.

Senge also challenges the internal market concept as the solution to today's organizational dilemmas.[36] He notes that "[c]hanges in the 'outer world' do not necessarily produce changes in the 'inner world'" (p. 88). For instance, he raises the issue of the complexity of information. If managers have difficulty understanding the wealth of information generated in organizations, how can those at lower levels be expected to do so effectively? In addition, he argues that by encouraging open communication and honesty and internal markets, firms may actually threaten the team spirit that they are attempting to create. "If candor prevails, it often leads to different patterns of defensive behavior" (p. 92).

At both Lincoln and Nucor, we have demonstrated that the internal market concept does not exist in a vacuum. Rather it exists with mutually reinforcing sets of management systems that do alleviate the potential problems associated with merely internal markets and competition within organizations and among workers.

NOTES

1. *Form 10-K,* Nucor Corporation, for fiscal year ending December 31, 1997, filed with the Securities and Exchange Commission, March 23, 1998, p. 2.

2. First named and described by Douglas McGregor in *The Human Side of Enterprise* (New York: Harper Publishers, 1954).

3. William Nobles and Judy Redpath, "Market Based Management™—A Key to Nucor's Success," *Journal of Applied Corporate Finance,* 10, No. 3 (fall 1997): 105.

4. Lord Griffiths of Fforestfach, *The Business of Values,* The HANSEN-WESSNER Memorial Lecture, The ServiceMaster Company, Downer's Grove, IL, 1996, pp. 8–9.

5. Ken Iverson with Tom Varian, *Plain Talk: Lessons from a Business Maverick* (New York: John Wiley & Sons, 1998), 8–9.

6. Ibid., 75.

7. Adam Ritt, "Nucor's Investment in Loyalty," *New Steel,* Charners Business Information (August 1998): 12.

8. Ibid., 1.

9. Iverson with Varian, p. 159.

10. Jeffrey L. Rodengen, *The Legend of Nucor Corporation* (Fort Lauderdale, FL: Write Stuff Enterprises, 1997), 126.

11. Ibid.

12. Nucor Corporation, *1997 Annual Report,* Charlotte, NC, 5.

13. Form 10-K, page 11.

14. Jeffrey L. Rodengen, p. 113.

15. William H. Newman, *Constructive Control: Design and Use of Control Systems* (Englewood Cliffs, NJ: Prentice-Hall, 1975), 133.

16. Press release from Nucor Corporation. "Nucor's Iverson Receives National Medal of Technology," September 16, 1991. Quoted on page 124 of Rodengen, *The Legend of Nucor Corporation.*

17. Iverson with Varian, p. 178.

18. Ibid., p. 112.

19. Ibid., p. 183.

20. Nucor News Release, February 3, 1999, Charlotte, NC, http://www.nucor.com/pressrel.htm.

21. Equity-Basic Industries, *Back to Basics,* April 24, 1998, BT Alex Brown Research, New York, NY, pages 101–105.

22. Ibid., p. 101.

23. Ibid.

24. *Notes from the Front: The Imports Are Coming, The Imports Are Coming!* Vol. 13, No. 7, August 5, 1998, BT, Alex Brown Research, New York, NY, pp. 1–2.

25. Edwin Mansfield, "International Trade Disputes," in *Managerial Economics: Theory, Applications and Cases,* 3d ed. (New York: W.W. Norton, 1996), 637–638.

26. Emily Schwartz, Merrill Lynch Research Bulletin, "Steel Imports Surge," Washington, DC, p. 1.

27. There are signs that world steel prices are firming, and Nucor has recently (April 1999) raised prices on some of its commodity steel products.

28. Interview with Neil Cavuto, *The Cavuto Business Report,* Transcript of interview with John Correnti, Nucor, CEO, *Fox News Report,* December 2, 1998.

29. Robert S. Kaplan and David P. Norton, *The Balanced Scorecard: Translating Strategy into Action* (Boston, MA: Harvard Business School Press, 1996).

30. Lord Griffiths of Fforestfach, *Business of Values,* 13.

31. Iverson with Varian, p. 22.

32. Ibid., p. 76.

33. A. H. Maslow, "A Theory of Human Motivation," *Psychological Review,* 50 (January, 1943): 370–396.

34. "Nucor CEO Steps Down Unexpectedly," *The Wall Street Journal* (June 4, 1999): A3 and A6.

35. Iverson with Varian, p. 70.

36. Peter M. Senge, "Internal Markets and Learning Organizations," in *Internal Markets: Bringing the Power of Free Enterprise Inside Your Organization,* edited by William E. Halal, Ali Geranmayeh, and John Pourdehnand (New York: John Wiley & Sons, 1993), Chap. 5.

Appendix 10.1 Historical Financial Data for Nucor Corporation from 1966–1997

	Net Earning	Total Equity	ROE	EPS	EPS Growth	Stock Price per Share	Stock Growth
1966	$ 1,333,900.00	$ 2,239,882.00	59.6%	$0.02		$ 0.23	
1967	1,703,256.00	6,581,876.00	25.9	0.03	50.0%	0.64	178.3%
1968	2,238,936.00	9,288,771.00	24.1	0.03	0.0	0.78	21.9
1969	2,335,083.00	11,938,178.00	19.6	0.03	0.0	0.45	−42.3
1970	1,140,757.00	13,101,313.00	8.7	0.02	−33.3	0.27	−40.0
1971	2,740,694.00	15,892,357.00	17.2	0.04	100.0	0.41	51.9
1972	4,668,190.00	20,929,525.00	22.3	0.07	75.0	0.54	31.7
1973	6,009,042.00	26,620,195.00	22.6	0.09	28.6	0.41	−24.1
1974	9,680,083.00	37,103,939.00	26.1	0.14	55.6	0.30	−26.8
1975	7,581,788.00	44,549,735.00	17.0	0.10	−28.6	0.41	36.7
1976	8,696,891.00	54,084,970.00	16.1	0.11	10.0	0.74	80.5
1977	12,452,592.00	66,295,405.00	18.8	0.16	45.5	1.02	37.8
1978	25,848,849.00	92,129,119.00	28.1	0.33	106.3	1.74	70.6
1979	42,264,537.00	133,257,816.00	31.7	0.52	57.6	3.32	90.8
1980	45,060,198.00	177,603,690.00	25.4	0.55	5.8	5.82	75.3
1981	34,728,966.00	212,376,020.00	16.4	0.42	−23.6	4.98	−14.4
1982	22,192,064.00	232,281,057.00	9.6	0.27	−35.7	5.21	4.6
1983	27,864,308.00	258,129,694.00	10.8	0.33	22.2	7.13	36.9
1984	44,548,451.00	299,602,834.00	14.9	0.53	60.6	5.38	−24.5
1985	58,478,352.00	357,502,028.00	16.4	0.68	28.3	8.98	66.9
1986	46,438,888.00	383,699,454.00	12.1	0.54	−20.6	7.72	−14.0
1987	50,534,450.00	428,009,367.00	11.8	0.60	11.1	9.91	28.4
1988	109,439,842.00	532,281,449.00	20.6	1.29	115.0	11.94	20.5
1989	57,835,844.00	584,445,479.00	9.9	0.68	−47.3	15.06	26.1

(Continued)

Appendix 10.1 *(Continued)*

	Net Earning	Total Equity	ROE	EPS	EPS Growth	Stock Price per Share	Stock Growth
1990	$ 75,065,261.00	$ 652,757,216.00	11.5%	$0.88	29.4%	$15.50	2.9%
1991	64,716,499.00	711,608,991.00	9.1	0.75	-14.8	22.34	44.1
1992	79,225,709.00	784,230,713.00	10.1	0.92	22.7	39.19	75.4
1993	123,509,607.00	902,166,939.00	13.7	1.42	54.3	53.00	35.2
1994	226,632,844.00	1,122,610,257.00	20.2	2.60	83.1	55.50	4.7
1995	274,534,505.00	1,382,112,159.00	19.9	3.14	20.8	57.13	2.9
1996	248,168,948.00	1,609,290,193.00	15.4	2.83	-9.9	51.00	-10.7
1997	194,482,440.00	$1,876,425,866.00	10.4	3.35	18.4	48.31	-5.3

Appendix 10.2   Annual Return on Equity of Nucor Corporation.

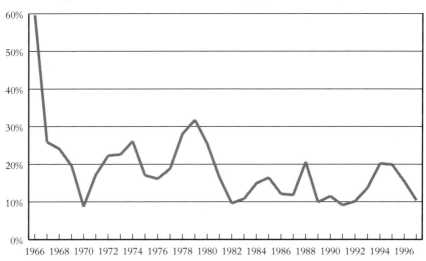

Appendix 10.3   Annual Earnings per Share.

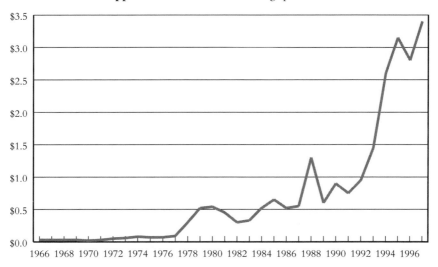

Appendix 10.4   Annual Growth Rates in Earnings per Share.

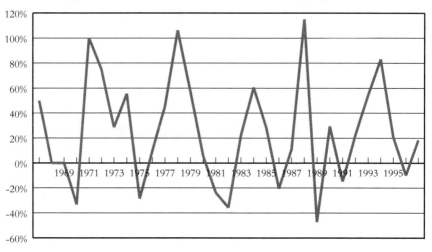

Appendix 10.5   The Rate of Growth in the Price of Nucor's Common Stock.

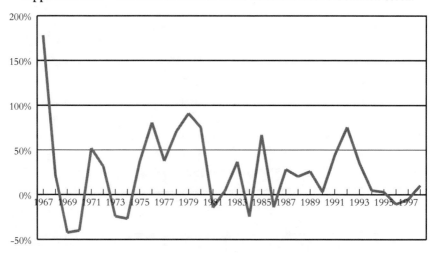

Chapter
11

Worthington Industries

W orthington Industries was founded in 1955 by John H. Mc-
Connell when he borrowed $600 on his 1952 Oldsmobile,
and together with $1,200 that he had in his checking ac-
count, he bought a supply of steel and processed it for sale. McConnell
made $600 profit on that initial transaction. And that was the start of
Worthington Industries. The company, headquartered in Columbus,
Ohio, is a leading manufacturer of processed steel products.[1]

Then and now the company is guided by a philosophy based on the
golden rule. Worthington is now a global company with annual sales
of $1.6 billion and 53 facilities in 20 states, and 11 countries. The
company currently employs approximately 7,500 people.

Worthington has made a very successful, critical corporate transition
from father to son. John P. McConnell, the son of the founder, was
named chairman and CEO of the company in 1996. John P. McConnell
worked his way up through the company, beginning with positions on
the plant floor in the company's Louisville plant, as head of human resources at the cylinder plant in Columbus, and as vice president of operations for the company as a whole. John P., like his father, is very
committed to the corporate philosophy of Worthington Industries.

After divesting itself of its noncore businesses, the company's operations consist of only processed steel products and the equity in joint
ventures related to these products. The processed steel segment is made
up of four lines of businesses. For 1998, 1997, and 1996, the percentage of sales from continuing operations was as follows:

	1998	1997	1996
Steel processing	56%	56%	68%
Pressure cylinders	14	14	15
Metal framing	21	21	8
Automotive body panels	9	9	9

STEEL PROCESSING

Worthington Industries is an intermediate processor of flat rolled steel. This is the company's largest business segment. Worthington's customers require specialized steel services and processing. The company currently has approximately 1,700 customers, principally in the automotive, automotive supply, appliance, electrical, communications, construction, office furniture, office equipment, agricultural, machinery, and leisure-time industries.

The company's steel "processing capabilities include pickling, slitting, rolling, annealing, edging, tension leveling, cutting-to-length, configured blanking, laser blank welding, painting, nickel plating, and hot dipped galvanizing."[2]

Worthington has a strong commitment to quality. Orders meeting all customer requirements exceed 99 percent in an industry that historically has had a much higher defect rate.

In 1998, Worthington began operations at its new and largest steel processing plant located in Decatur, Alabama. This new 750,000-square-foot facility has greatly expanded Worthington's steel processing capacity. Its location adjacent to a steel minimill owned and operated by TRICO provides Worthington with a low-cost steel supplier for its processing operations.

PRESSURE CYLINDERS

The company is a leading supplier of low- and high-pressure cylinders on a global basis and is the major supplier in North America. The company operates seven wholly owned facilities and participates in one joint venture devoted to cylinders. Three major types of pressurized cylinders are manufactured and distributed:

1. Refrigerant gas cylinders used to charge air-conditioning and refrigeration systems.

2. Liquid propane gas cylinders sold to manufacturers and distributors of barbecue grills as well as to users of material handling, heating, cooking, and camping equipment.

3. High-pressure cylinders sold primarily to gas fillers and suppliers as containers for various gases used in industry and by health care facilities. Included in this business is the growing market for tanks containing helium that are used to inflate balloons for social events.

METAL FRAMING

Worthington acquired Dietrich Industries in 1996. "Dietrich is the nation's leading producer of metal framing products for the commercial and residential building industries."[3] Dietrich currently operates 18 facilities throughout the United States and its products include steel studs, floor joists, and other metal accessory products used by commercial and residential contractors. It is the only metal framing company with a national distribution network in the United States.

AUTOMOTIVE BODY PANELS

As a part of Worthington's strategic plan to focus on its core businesses related to steel processing, the company acquired Gerstenlager in 1997. Gerstenlager is located in Wooster, Ohio. John H. McConnell originally bought Gerstenlager through JMAC, a holding company of the McConnell family; the company became part of Worthington in 1997.

Gerstenlager is the country's leading independent producer of after-market body panels for the automotive industry. It stamps galvanized steel into automotive components, such as doors, fenders, and hoods. Its principal customers are domestic and transplant auto manufacturers in the United States, as well as medium- and heavy-duty truck manufacturers.

Gerstenlager competes with captive, in-house auto body stamping plants and with other suppliers. Its main competitive advantage is the diversity of its die sets and its ability to supply replacement body frames for older automobiles. Worthington's main customer is General Motors Corporation, which purchases frames through its divisions and subsidiaries. Worthington's dependence on GM makes them sensitive to changes in managerial decisions and to cyclical economic factors.

JOINT VENTURES

The joint ventures have been structured in a number of different ways: sometimes Worthington is the principal owner and sometimes they are the minority partner. Worthington generally takes the position that they would like to run the operations-side of the business. The company believes that managing operations is one of their comparative advantages.

As a part of its strategy to focus on its core businesses and to grow globally, the company participates in six joint ventures. The six joint ventures are:

1. *WAVE (Worthington/Armstrong Venture).* WAVE is a leading global supplier of metal suspended ceilings. These ceilings are made of thin-galvanized steel, which is formed into ceiling sections and used in commercial and residential buildings. Worthington is an equal partner with Armstrong World Industries in this joint venture. This venture has operating facilities in four states in the United States and in England, France, Spain, and China.

2. *Spartan Steel Coating.* Spartan is a joint venture with Rouge Industries of Dearborn, Michigan, which is located in Monroe, Michigan, and is engaged in producing "light gauge, hot galvanized and galvanneal sheet steel."[4] Spartan was spun-off from the Ford Motor Company several years ago and is an integrated steel producer.

   This joint venture commenced operations in the May 1998. The hot-dipped galvanized steel produced by Spartan is used primarily for value-added automotive applications. Worthington is a majority owner in this venture with Rouge Industries.

3. *TWB (Worthington and Thyssen Stahl).* This joint venture, which operates in Monroe, Michigan, was formed in 1992 between Worthington and Thyssen Stahl of Germany. The venture added three minority partners in 1997—LTV Steel, Bethlehem Steel, and Rouge Steel—bringing Worthington's equity interests down to 33 percent. TWB is the leading supplier of laser-welded blanks. Lasers permit welding of much thinner steel blanks for use in the automotive industry. These laser-welded blanks use advanced technology and result in lighter and less expensive metal frames. Laser welding is, in many respects, an extension of Worthington's metal framing business.

4. *Worthington S.A.* This is a joint venture of Worthington Cylinders with three propane producers in Brazil. Worthington S.A. operates a cylinder manufacturing facility in São Paulo. This is a 52 percent owned joint venture and is a facility positioned to serve the growing market for cylinders in South America. Worthington entered into this joint venture because the company wanted to compete in the South American cylinder market and thought they needed local partners to be successful.

5. *Worthington Specialty Products (WSP).* WSP is a joint venture equally owned by Worthington and USX Corporation, located in Jackson, Michigan. This joint venture is devoted to supplying processed steel to USX Corporation.

6. *Acerex S.A.* Acerex is an equally owned joint venture between Worthington and Hylsamex, Mexico's leading steel-processing company. This venture was established in Monterey, Mexico, and serves the markets for steel slitting and "cut-to-length" requirements of customers in Mexico and the United States.

MACROENVIRONMENT IN THE PROCESSED STEEL INDUSTRY[5]

As one of the largest steel processors in the United States, Worthington Industries is in a position whereby general macroeconomic and specific conditions in the steel industry influence its overall operating and financial performance. In many ways, the macroenvironment of the processed steel industry is similar to the general industry environment of raw steel producers such as Nucor.

As a manufacturing leader in the world market for processed steel, Worthington is affected by changes in worldwide prices, supply and demand for steel, and steel processed products. Domestically, the demand for processed steel products has been largely driven by a strong consumer demand for finished automotive parts, appliances, and machinery.

In 1998, domestic demand for steel–processed products increased steadily, although international economic slowdowns continued in South America and Asia. Because of this situation, these nations have concentrated on exporting steel to the United States, creating a supply glut of raw steel that has caused the prices of steel to fall in the United States.

Worthington, like Nucor, has reduced prices during 1998, but because the majority of Worthington's business is in the value-added, steel-processing market, it has been somewhat buffeted from the full effects of the excess supply conditions in hot- and cold-rolled steel products.

Worthington believes that the best defense against foreign competition is a strong offense. As the world's steelmakers look to markets in the United States, Worthington continues to focus on expanding internationally. They have pursued an aggressive strategy of expansion through joint ventures and acquisitions. These strategic alliances have been focused on Worthington's core businesses of processed steel products. One such merger was with Heiser of Gaming, Austria. Heiser is Europe's leading producer of high-pressure cylinders.

As Worthington has increased its presence overseas, it has increased its vulnerabilities to international economic and political conditions, including increased exposure to currency risk. For example, Worthington, through its joint venture in Brazil, is presently exposed to a volatile currency situation.

ENVIRONMENTAL REGULATION

Worthington is subject to federal, state, and local laws regulating the environmental impact of steel manufacturing. These regulations and laws do differ from state to state and from city to city, subsequently influencing the company's choice of facility locations. Nevertheless, Worthington continues to explore ways to reduce its emissions and waste.

Specific Environmental Factors

During the fourth quarter of fiscal year 1998, Worthington performed a strategic review of two aspects of its operations to evaluate the level of economic value of the company. The focus of this review was centered on the Custom Products Segment, comprised of Worthington Custom Plastics, Inc., Worthington Precision Metals, Inc., and the Cast Products segment, consisting principally of the Buckeye Steel Castings Company.

At the end of this strategic review, Worthington concluded that it would divest itself of the above businesses and concentrate on its core strengths: processed-steel products. Worthington's core businesses within this segment are steel processing, pressure cylinders, metal framing, and automotive body parts. As the company focused the scope of its operations during 1998, Worthington continued to pursue a strategy of expansion and growth within its marketplace niche. This is evident in its strategic alliances, both domestic and international, and in the opening of new, wholly owned plants in the United States.

Worthington products compete on the basis of quality, the company's ability to meet delivery requirements of customers, and price. The physical proximity of its plants to its customers has a significant positive effect on the company's ability to meet customer delivery requirements.

Demand for Worthington's product lines from continuing operations was up from 1997. This increase is attributed to new automotive business, gains in traditional markets, and the overall strength of the U.S. economy.

MARKET SEGMENTS

Market segments include automotive body panels (fully described on p. 175), steel processing, pressure cylinders, and metal framing.

Steel Processing

This segment consists of 11 processing facilities. In fiscal year 1998, steel processing accounted for 56 percent of the company's sales. Worthington Steel's 1,700 industrial customers are concentrated in the automotive, automotive supply, appliance, electrical, communications, construction, office furniture, office equipment, agriculture, machinery, and leisure-time industries. Worthington competes within a highly competitive intermediate steel-processing segment that purchases its steel from steel mills, including Nucor. Worthington has been able to differentiate itself by offering a variety of value-added technical services, including toll processing. Toll processing is an activity usually carried out by steel producers.

Pressure Cylinders

This segment of Worthington's operations accounted for 14 percent of its total sales in fiscal year 1998. Sales concentration is with major accounts, although Worthington has a total of over 2,000 customers for its pressurized cylinders.

Eight plants are located in Ohio, Oklahoma, Alabama, Ontario, Austria, and a joint venture in São Paulo, Brazil. Worthington has the majority share of the market in the low-pressure cylinder segment. In the high-pressure cylinder segment, the company competes with two rivals, each of which has a larger market share than Worthington.

Through its Heiser acquisition in Austria, Worthington has been able to achieve the largest market share in Europe's industrial gas cylinder market.

Metal Framing

Worthington has grown its metal framing business through the acquisition of Dietrich Industries. Dietrich is the largest supplier of metal framing products in the United States. The metal framing segment of Worthington accounted for 21 percent of total sales for fiscal year 1998. Dietrich is the single national supplier of metal framing products and as such competes with five regional competitors, and many small, localized firms.

MANAGEMENT SYSTEMS AT
WORTHINGTON INDUSTRIES

Worthington has been guided in its operations by its well-developed philosophy statement. The values of the company are those developed by John H. McConnell; they are based on the golden rule and they have not changed materially over the history of the company. These values are the company's core foundation.

The company executives try to live these values day-by-day, week-by-week, and month-by-month. Through words and actions, they also try to influence the behavior of all their employees. Worthington's philosophy, which is visible in all of their operations and in all of their literature, is reproduced in the box that follows.

Worthington's ranking of its stakeholders is different than either Lincoln's or Nucor's. When Lincoln ranks its stakeholders, it places the customer first, the employees second, and the shareholder third. When Nucor ranks its stakeholders, it places the employees first, the customer second, and the shareholder third. Worthington, on the other hand, places its shareholders first.

Further investigation reveals that the shareholder first premise may, in fact, work itself out in very much the way it works out at Lincoln and Nucor. First, Worthington encourages everyone in the company to own stock.

The company also is very customer focused—and emphasizes cost, quality, and service. Worthington takes great pride in quality and service levels and is striving for zero defects. This care extends to an elaborate Internet site that customers may use to purchase products and services. The company seeks to improve quality and service for its customers on a continuous basis.

Moreover, the company is very focused on the growth and development of its employees. It believes that people are their greatest asset. They believe their employees will be honest and give the company a good day's work for a good day's pay. The company believes that encouragement and praise will promote employee development. They take a very high view of what people are capable of accomplishing, and they have historical evidence to support their views. For example, Donald Malenick who retired as president of Worthington on May 26, 1999, began his career at the company on the

WORTHINGTON INDUSTRIES' PHILOSOPHY

Earnings: The first corporate goal for Worthington Industries is to earn money for its shareholders and increase the value of their investment. We believe that the best measurement of the accomplishment of our goal is consistent growth in earnings per share.

Our Golden Rule: We treat our customers, employees, investors, and suppliers, as we would like to be treated.

People: We are dedicated to the belief that people are our most important asset. We believe people respond to recognition, opportunity to grow, and fair compensation. We believe that compensation should be directly related to job performance and therefore use incentives, profit sharing or otherwise, in every possible situation. From employees we expect an honest day's work for an honest day's pay. We believe in the philosophy of continued employment for all Worthington people. In filling job openings, every effort is expended to find candidates within Worthington, its divisions or subsidiaries. When employees are requested to relocate from one operation to another, it is accomplished without financial loss to the individual.

Customer: Without the customer and his need for our products and services we have nothing. We will exert every effort to see that the customer's quality and service requirements are met. Once a commitment is made to a customer, every effort is made to fulfill that obligation.

Suppliers: We cannot operate profitably without those who supply the quality raw materials we need for our products. From a pricing standpoint, we ask only that suppliers be competitive in the marketplace and treat us as they do their other customers. We are loyal to suppliers who meet our quality and service requirements through all market situations.

Organization: We believe in a divisionalized organizational structure with responsibility for performance resting with the head of each operation. All managers are given the operating latitude and authority to accomplish their responsibilities within our corporate goals and objectives. In keeping with this philosophy, we do not create corporate procedures. If procedures are necessary within a particular company operation, that manager creates them. We believe in a small corporate staff and support group to service the needs of our shareholders and operating units as requested.

Communication: We communicate through every possible channel with our customers, employees, shareholders, and the financial community.

Citizenship: Worthington Industries practices good citizenship at all levels. We conduct our business in a professional and ethical manner when dealing with customers, neighbors, and the general public worldwide. We encourage all our people to actively participate in community affairs. We support worthwhile community causes.

production floor. John Christie succeeded Malenick as president on June 1, 1999.

Worthington's attitude toward their suppliers and community is just as it reads on the philosophy card. In a real sense, the philosophy and culture at Worthington is very well developed; it influences every aspect of their management systems and processes. My approach in describing the management systems at the company will directly follow the statements on its philosophy card.

Shareholders/Earnings

Worthington's performance with regard to their shareholders has been consistent and strong. Most strikingly, perhaps, is the fact that the company has been profitable in each of the 44 years of its existence.[6]

Table 11.1 presents data regarding the financial performance of Worthington during the past 18 years. Figure 11.1 presents a chart of

Table 11.1 Financial Performance of Worthington: 1981–1998

	ROE	ROC	EPS	EPS Growth	Dividends per Share	Dividends Growth
1981	24.6%	14.2%	$0.54		$0.18	
1982	17.9	10.3	0.31	−42.6	0.13	−25.9
1983	16.6	9.6	0.33	6.5	0.14	7.8
1984	18.7	12.4	0.43	30.3	0.11	−24.8
1985	20.3	15.0	0.40	−7.0	0.12	9.7
1986	19.2	14.9	0.45	12.5	0.13	11.7
1987	17.0	13.9	0.45	0.0	0.16	17.4
1988	20.5	17.3	0.58	28.9	0.18	16.8
1989	21.2	18.3	0.69	19.0	0.20	12.2
1990	16.0	14.1	0.62	−10.1	0.25	24.5
1991	12.7	11.1	0.54	−12.9	0.27	6.7
1992	15.4	13.4	0.65	20.4	0.30	12.6
1993	16.4	14.4	0.76	16.9	0.33	7.3
1994	18.1	15.9	0.73	−3.9	0.37	12.2
1995	21.7	18.7	0.94	28.8	0.41	11.8
1996	15.8	11.9	0.76	−19.1	0.45	9.8
1997	13.5	8.8	0.69	−9.2	0.49	8.9
1998	13.3	8.2	0.85	23.2	0.53	8.1
Avg.	0.1772	0.1347				
Avg.	ROC	0.1409	w/o 97,98			

Figure 11.1   Average Return on Equity from 1981–1998.

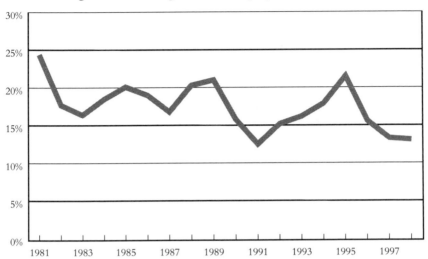

the average ROE for this period. The average is 17.7 percent for the 18-year period *without one losing year*. This performance is considerably above average for the metals industry of which they are a part.

Figure 11.2 is a graphical representation of the company's earnings per share of common stock, and Figure 11.3 represents the company's growth in earnings per share. If we exclude the boom year of 1981, earnings have grown at a compound rate of slightly better than 6 percent over a 17-year period. From 1982 to 1995, earnings grew at the compound rate of slightly greater than 8 percent. As far as dividends are concerned, if we exclude 1981, dividends have been increased in all but one of the past 17 years. The compounded rate of growth in dividends per share for the past 17 years has been approximately 9 percent.

Based on an analysis of these data, Worthington has performed well financially, especially in light of industry performance during this same period. They have recorded profits in every year of their existence and record profits in 36 of the company's 43 years. They have increased dividends in all but one year since their shares were offered to the public in 1968.

Therefore, Worthington has performed according to the goals stated in the philosophy card. Specifically, they have shown consistent growth in earnings per share.

Figure 11.2 Worthington's Earnings per Share 1981–1998.

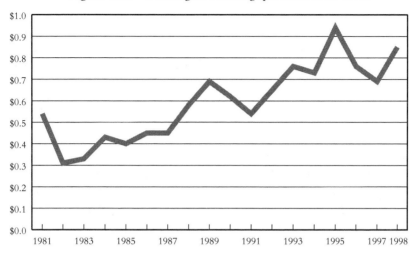

Figure 11.3 Worthington's Rate of Growth in Earnings per Share.

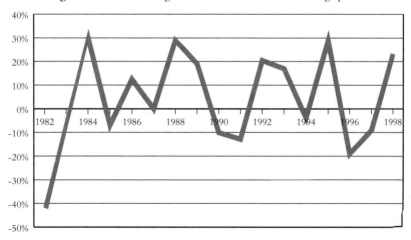

Additional Steps to Increase the Value of Shareholder Investment

Worthington conducted a strategic review of all of its subsidiaries during the fiscal year ending on May 31, 1998. This review was motivated by the company's desire to continue to focus on value-added activities that will generate superior long-term growth and financial performance. As a result, the company decided to continue to pursue its core competency in metal processing and to divest itself of three other operations.

The decision to sell three of its subsidiaries was announced in June 1998. Sale of the subsidiaries was completed during fiscal year 1999. The three subsidiaries are Worthington Custom Plastics, Worthington Precious Metals, and Buckeye Steel Castings. These three subsidiaries make up two of Worthington's three business segments: processed steel products, custom products, and cast products. As a result of the divestiture, Worthington intends to focus on its core competence: value-added products that are expected to generate high long-term returns and bring the return of total capital (ROCE) back up above the cost of capital, thus furthering shareholder goals.

The company plans to use cash inflows from the sale of these three subsidiaries to enhance the competitive strength of its metal processing business and to strengthen its capital structure by paying down its debt and by repurchasing its own common shares.

This strategy follows directly the company's number 1 goal to increase the value of shareholder investments. One investment research firm, Goldman Sachs, estimates that Worthington "will grow earnings by 35 percent over the next two years."[7]

To summarize this section, Worthington Industries is striving to improve its recent financial performance. Nevertheless, in the five-year period from 1993 to 1997 its return on average invested capital was approximately 14 percent whereas the median returns in steel was 10.4 percent; for metals it was 9.7 percent; and for all industries it was 10.5 percent. So, even with one sub-par year (1997) in that five-year period, Worthington has been an "outperformer" on a relative basis.[8]

People

As outside verification that Worthington does indeed view their employees as their most important asset, the two issues of *The 100 Best*

Companies to Work for in America[9] place the company on the list of the top 100. These two issues were separated in time by approximately a decade.[10] The company was ranked 48th in 1988 and 89th in 1999. Robert Levering and Milton Moskowitz conducted all of these studies.

To back up their rankings, these studies point to the company's employee councils that are appointed in most of Worthington's plants and assist management with a number of decisions. One of the most important decisions made by these councils is the decision to move an employee from probationary to regular status. When an employee begins at Worthington, that individual is placed on probation. At the end of a 90-day period, the employee becomes eligible to be considered for regular status. Once the employee is accepted by majority vote of the plant council, the employee moves from hourly pay to salary. Moreover, the employee then becomes eligible to participate in the company's profit-sharing program.

Management does play a role in the decision to make an employee permanent, and often makes recommendations to the council. If management has some doubts, the tendency is to discharge the worker. Worthington is a demanding place to work and some people don't last a week. They are expected to hustle.

Because management is not down on the floor working with employees all the time, employees are in a better position to judge whether a person should become a regular employee, and therefore a participant in the profit-sharing pool.

If a probationary employee is being considered for regular status, the employee council members will speak to that employee's coworkers and ask how the employee appears to be performing. If the opinions are favorable, then the council votes the employee regular status.

The employee councils at each plant meet frequently, at least once a month. The councils also plan activities together and discuss safety issues. At least every quarter, the councils are used to share business results with the employees of their plant.

Management enjoys great *teamwork* and comraderie in working with the employee councils. The councils often surprise management with the insights they bring to problems and opportunities faced by the company.

Employees display a great deal of trust and openness toward the management of the company. Top management places a heavy emphasis on the company's open-door policy. Company management works a lot on communications. Open-door, face-to-face communication leads to resolving conflicts when they are small and prevents them from festering and becoming big.

Managers are appointed who truly care about employees, and they try to keep politics out of company discussions. Because the profit-sharing program at Worthington is group-centered, it helps break down some of the walls between workers and between production workers and management. It helps to unify each division.

As another example of how Worthington works out its philosophy toward people, consider the recent transportation initiative undertaken by the company.

The Recent Transportation Initiative at Worthington

Worthington has recently (1998) chosen Ruan Transportation Management Systems as their partner to bring dispatching, trucking, and tracking system under one umbrella. Ruan is a leader in the transportation field.

The objective of this partnership is to experiment with the outsourcing of the company's transportation activities to a specialist in this field and in the process to add value to the company. The program is currently being run on a pilot basis in four plants—the Delta, Monroe, Porter, and Columbus plants of Worthington Steel. The pilot project began in March 1999. Worthington will make a decision by the end of 1999 on extending the relationship with Ruan to other company locations. Ruan is to assemble people, processes, technology, and partner carriers to carry out all the transportation activities for these four plants. Worthington has established a program with Ruan in which Ruan will share in a portion of the any savings realized by Worthington. Gain sharing will of course occur only when Worthington realizes actual savings in its cost of transportation.

Measurements are made at each plant. Feedback is provided for continuous improvement through the company's reporting systems. The company believes that significant opportunities exist by viewing shipments from all parts of the organization and by routing trucks across the entire organization. Moreover, they anticipate further benefit by centralizing the dispatching operations. Worthington anticipates annual savings to the company will reach $8 million per year by

2002, at which time the pilot program will be extended to all of the company's operations. The transportation initiative is viewed as a win-win gain-sharing agreement with Ruan.

Nevertheless, the program has and will create dislocations among Worthington's truck drivers. In essence, they will lose their current positions. In keeping with its philosophy, Worthington has offered numerous options to its displaced employees.

Any employee dislocated as a result of the transportation initiative has several options. First, they may choose to join the Ruan team. If they wish to stay at Worthington, other jobs within the company will be offered and the company will apply its moving policy to this group. Or, the employee may make an offer to buy one of the company trucks and become independent. Early retirement options are to be offered to eligible employees. Finally, for those employees who choose to leave Worthington, generous severance packages will be offered.

This demonstration of Worthington's commitment is especially important for younger employees because as a group they are more cynical. They have seen their parents upsized, downsized, right-sized, and so on, in other companies, and this has created cynicism toward business in general.

Emphasis on Internal Promotion

Levering and Moskowitz report that 95 percent of jobs are filled by internal candidates.[11] And many of the top executives start at the bottom. Donald Malenick started as a general laborer and became president of the company. Five of the nine vice presidents [at the time] started in entry-level positions. According to cylinder plant supervisor Jim Knox: "The opportunity exists unlike any other company as far as moving up through the ranks. If you set a goal, you can reach any level of management you want."

Merit is the key to promotion at Worthington. Education helps, and the company does have a have tuition reimbursement program for all employees. Employees are encouraged to help themselves develop through education and through seeking other jobs within the company to broaden their knowledge and to become more "promotable."

In looking for plant managers, for example, the key ingredients the company looks for in candidates are leadership and people skills as opposed to immediately germane product knowledge. They look for a hands-on management style and for common sense. Because Worthington is very team focused, they also look at the ability of potential supervisors and managers to work in teams.

Emphasis on Employee Rewards

How does Worthington implement compensation? Worthington sets its salary scale at the *top quartile of salaries*[12] for comparable work in the localities in which they operate. *Profit sharing distributions are made each quarter* and average between "35 to 55 percent of an employee's base salary."[13]

The overall profit-sharing plan is subdivided into four different group plans. One group consists of production workers; the second is an administrative group; the third is a professional group; and the fourth is an executive group.

The ratio of base salary to total compensation varies among these four groups. The higher up in the organization the more total compensation is at risk. The higher up in the organization, the smaller the base salary is as a percentage of total compensation. For production workers, 75 percent to 80 percent of total compensation is made up of base salary; the other portion consists of profit sharing. At the executive level, however, base salary is more like 40 percent of total compensation. Nevertheless, Worthington wants all their people to be well paid, significantly above the market average. To accomplish this, a great deal of total compensation must be at risk each year.

Although the percentages have changed from year to year, the size of the profit-sharing pool for production, professional, and administrative employees depends on both the performance of each local plant and corporate performance. At the executive level, however, there is a set formula for profit sharing, and this formula doesn't change very often.

Customers

We turn now to Worthington's implementation of the golden rule as far as its customers are concerned. The attitude toward customers at Worthington is just as it reads on the philosophy card. The company is very customer focused. They emphasize cost, quality, and service in their performance measurement systems and take great pride in the quality of their products and the service levels they provide customers. The company continuously seeks to improve customer service.

One of the major factors contributing toward customer satisfaction among the customers of Worthington is a sales training program remarkably similar to the one at Lincoln Electric. At Worthington, salespersonnel are required to work in a plant that produces the products which the salesperson will sell. This training period lasts six months.

Salespersons learn to work with production personnel as a team in filling the needs and orders of customers, and in understanding plant capability and order profitability. With further training in areas of technical skill, the salesforce is able to offer customers the highest quality products and services that meet or exceed their needs. Orders that are not profitable for Worthington are simply not taken.

By providing effective and continuous service to customers, the salesforce is better able to develop and nurture good relationships with customers. This in turn leads to repeat business.

The outcome of this philosophy is that each employee believes that he or she is doing important work that will beneficially affect the customers.

Because the company pays for performance and provides a substantial opportunity for employees to share in the profits of the company, quality and service to customers must be high—otherwise there will be no profits. Treating the customers well is part of the entire system of stakeholder relationships and management. The results speak for themselves: high earnings for shareholders, good pay for employees, and good quality and service for customers.

Suppliers

Here the company asks to be treated as suppliers would want to be treated themselves. In turn, the company expresses a commitment to be loyal customers for these suppliers in return for fair prices, good-quality products, and services. Nucor is both a supplier and competitor of Worthington. Although the competitive markets these two companies serve don't overlap too much, the company considers

Nucor to be a supplier that it values because Nucor meets the supplier test.

Citizenship

One of Worthington's employees summed up the company's attitude toward the social impacts of the company beautifully when she said:

> At Worthington Industries, we don't have to practice the golden rule,
> it is in our hearts. We are a team. We take the Worthington philosophy
> into all areas of our lives—including into the community.

Company management encourages employees to participate in community affairs. Pride in the community enhances employee motivation at work.

The company also conducts a legislative affairs program for employees and encourages employees to contact local officials, members of Congress, and U.S. senators to inquire about pending legislation and to make their views known.

The two remaining issues of management philosophy are closely tied to the *infrastructure* and to the *coordination and integration* subsystems of the mutually supportive systems model and can be beneficially described in this section. We turn first to the issue of organization and autonomy.

Organization

Worthington Industries maintains a very decentralized organization, that is, individual locations have a great deal of autonomy. Nevertheless, unlike Nucor, functions such as purchasing are centralized. The company tries to centralize those functions in which significant scale economies exist. The decision to begin outsourcing the transportation and dispatch functions has already been discussed.

In the human resource area, the individual units of the company use more shared services. This allows the company to offer human resource services to all locations so that everybody can have access to the same services. This is especially important for newly acquired acquisitions.

Nevertheless, the bias in the company is toward small plants of under 150 employees to enhance communications and the sense of identification and commitment on the part of all employees. Plant managers are generally granted substantial autonomy. The company prides itself on maintaining a flat organization structure with few procedures, and managers at all levels are encouraged to be accessible to their employees.

The company is also forming strategic business units (SBUs) by grouping certain similar operations. One SBU is Towlling. Towlling involves processing hot- and cold-rolled steel. Nucor and other major mills are customers of this SBU. Another SBU consists of a few plants involved in cold-rolled strip products. These latter products are processed to very close tolerances.

The cold-rolled strip SBU has somewhat the same structure as does the cylinder product line which has been organized as an SBU for many years. For example, propane gas cylinders for gas grills are made in many locations, and these locations are grouped into an SBU. Propane cylinder tanks that are made for heating products are in different locations, and they too are grouped into an SBU.

Communication

The requirement for people skills on the part of managers and supervisors at Worthington and the organization and role of the employee councils at each plant are very strong mechanisms for communicating with employees.

The sales training program and the emphasis the company places on understanding and communicating effectively with their customers speaks eloquently. The company also communicates with current and prospective shareholders through a well-developed Internet site.

COMPOSITE CYBERNETIC MANAGEMENT PROCESS

We have now completed a detailed review of each subsystem of the management systems at Worthington Industries. Figures 11.4 and

Figure 11.4   Formal Management Systems.

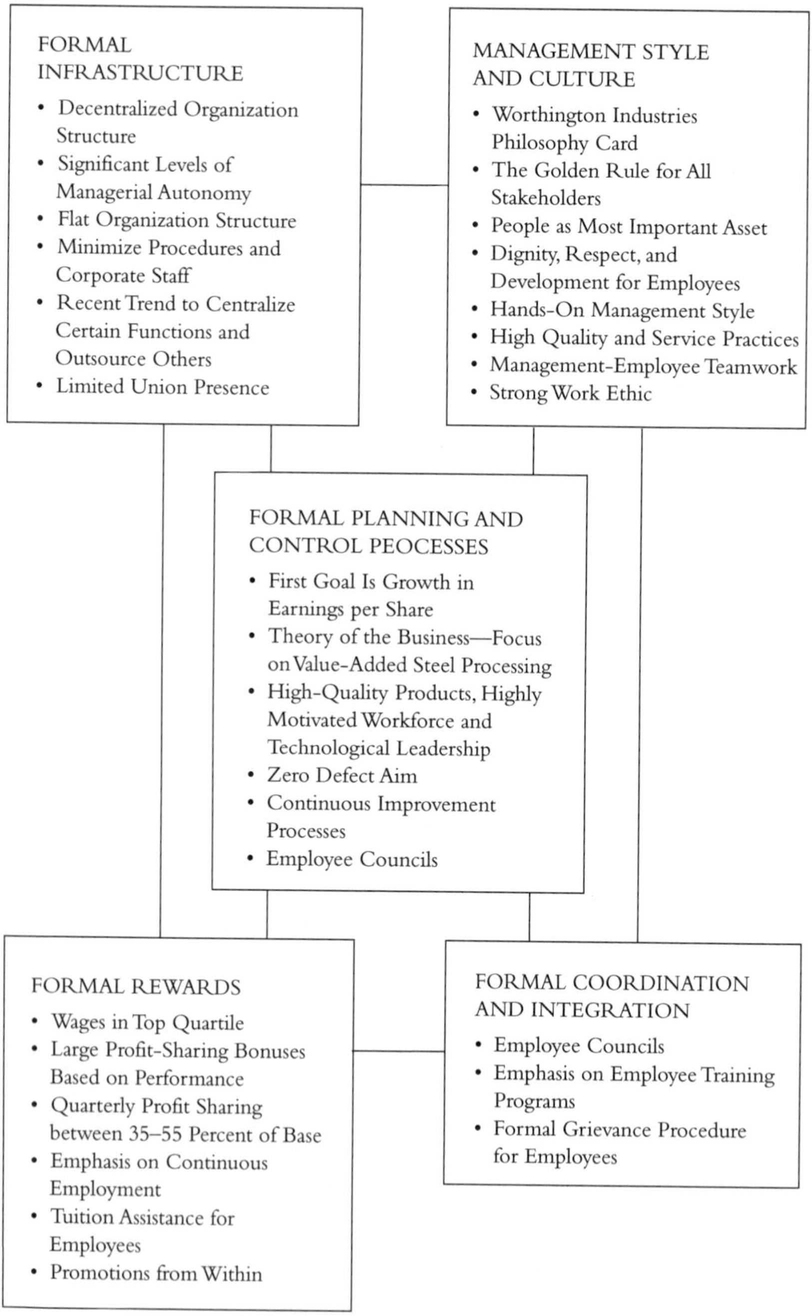

FORMAL
INFRASTRUCTURE

- Decentralized Organization
  Structure
- Significant Levels of
  Managerial Autonomy
- Flat Organization Structure
- Minimize Procedures and
  Corporate Staff
- Recent Trend to Centralize
  Certain Functions and
  Outsource Others
- Limited Union Presence

MANAGEMENT STYLE
AND CULTURE

- Worthington Industries
  Philosophy Card
- The Golden Rule for All
  Stakeholders
- People as Most Important Asset
- Dignity, Respect, and
  Development for Employees
- Hands-On Management Style
- High Quality and Service Practices
- Management-Employee Teamwork
- Strong Work Ethic

FORMAL PLANNING AND
CONTROL PEOCESSES

- First Goal Is Growth in
  Earnings per Share
- Theory of the Business—Focus
  on Value-Added Steel Processing
- High-Quality Products, Highly
  Motivated Workforce and
  Technological Leadership
- Zero Defect Aim
- Continuous Improvement
  Processes
- Employee Councils

FORMAL REWARDS

- Wages in Top Quartile
- Large Profit-Sharing Bonuses
  Based on Performance
- Quarterly Profit Sharing
  between 35–55 Percent of Base
- Emphasis on Continuous
  Employment
- Tuition Assistance for
  Employees
- Promotions from Within

FORMAL COORDINATION
AND INTEGRATION

- Employee Councils
- Emphasis on Employee Training
  Programs
- Formal Grievance Procedure
  for Employees

11.5 summarize the formal and informal management systems at the company.

Each subsystem results from the philosophy statement of the company and as such boost each other in a mutually beneficial manner. In addition, the formal management systems support the informal systems and make each other effective, thus further boosting potential performance.

Figure 11.6 represents a composite cybernetic management process for Worthington to meet shareholder goals by meeting customer needs through a well-paid and highly motivated workforce.

RELATIONAL QUALITIES YIELDING AGILITY AND ADAPTABILITY

As we have seen previously in the Lincoln and Nucor cases, the six relational variables are highly interdependent, but trust is the key to successful dynamics in the agile model of management. Systems thinking occurs when there is reinforcement among the components of the management systems of the firm and when the informal management systems reinforce the formal management systems. Systems thinking is further stimulated when the management systems are synchronized with a management process that meets the goals of the organization. Finally, these factors promote the ability of the organization to be proactive and reactive with respect to its environment, a condition that I refer to as agility. Table 11.2 lists the aspects of the management systems that contribute to the presence of each relational variable at the company.

CONCLUSION

In concluding this chapter on Worthington Industries, I would like to emphasize two points. First, although Worthington's first goal is to meet shareholder expectations, the company is balanced. It believes that the first goal is met by doing an extraordinary job for its

Figure 11.5   Informal Management Systems.

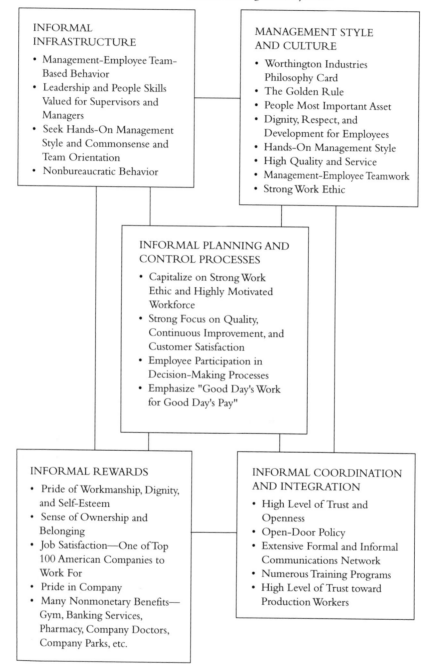

INFORMAL
INFRASTRUCTURE

- Management-Employee Team-Based Behavior
- Leadership and People Skills Valued for Supervisors and Managers
- Seek Hands-On Management Style and Commonsense and Team Orientation
- Nonbureaucratic Behavior

MANAGEMENT STYLE
AND CULTURE

- Worthington Industries Philosophy Card
- The Golden Rule
- People Most Important Asset
- Dignity, Respect, and Development for Employees
- Hands-On Management Style
- High Quality and Service
- Management-Employee Teamwork
- Strong Work Ethic

INFORMAL PLANNING AND
CONTROL PROCESSES

- Capitalize on Strong Work Ethic and Highly Motivated Workforce
- Strong Focus on Quality, Continuous Improvement, and Customer Satisfaction
- Employee Participation in Decision-Making Processes
- Emphasize "Good Day's Work for Good Day's Pay"

INFORMAL REWARDS

- Pride of Workmanship, Dignity, and Self-Esteem
- Sense of Ownership and Belonging
- Job Satisfaction—One of Top 100 American Companies to Work For
- Pride in Company
- Many Nonmonetary Benefits—Gym, Banking Services, Pharmacy, Company Doctors, Company Parks, etc.

INFORMAL COORDINATION
AND INTEGRATION

- High Level of Trust and Openness
- Open-Door Policy
- Extensive Formal and Informal Communications Network
- Numerous Training Programs
- High Level of Trust toward Production Workers

Figure 11.6 A Composite Cybernetic Management Process for Worthington Industries.

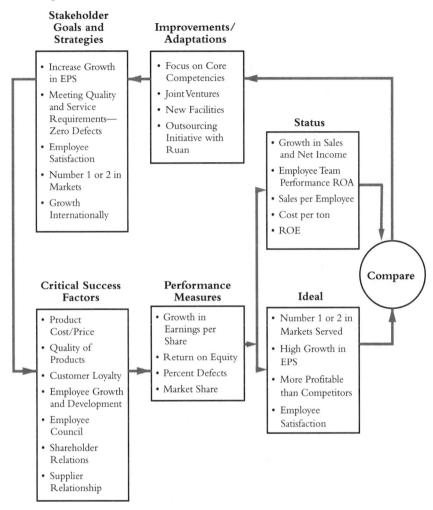

customers and by treating its employees as its most important asset. It is truly a golden rule company in words and deeds.

From the founding of the company in 1955, John H. McConnell always emphasized the unlimited opportunities that exist at Worthington. His often-repeated words are, "we have only scratched the surface." This spirit is very much alive today.

Table 11.2   Sources of the Relational Qualities at Worthington Industries

---

1. Trust
- High levels of employee Autonomy and Empowerment
- Employee councils
- Golden rule philosophy applied in genuine manner to all stakeholders
- People treated as though they are the No. 1 asset of the company
- Open-door policy
- Opportunities for people to develop and grow
- Egalitarian environment

2. Commitment
- Salaries in top quartile
- Considered one of the best 100 companies in America
- Continuous employment for responsible and productive workers
- Profit-sharing plan
- Emphasis on internal promotions
- Employees encouraged to own stock
- Pride within local communities

3. Conflict Management
- Equitable procedure to process grievances
- Employee councils conduct peer reviews
- Little tolerance for politics
- Limited unionization of workforce
- Application of golden rule to stakeholders
- Managers with good leadership and people skills
- Open-door policy and management by walking around

4. Learning
- Heavy emphasis on individual and organizational learning
- Strong sales training program
- Employees encouraged to grow and develop by tuition assistance program

5. Systems Thinking
- Worthington structures profit sharing on corporate basis
- Management systems mutually reinforcing
- Strong focus on customers, employees, shareholders, suppliers, community

6. Agility/Speed/Adaptability
- Small corporate staff and relatively flat organization
- Nonbureaucratic behavior
- Focus on core competencies
- High levels of autonomy and empowerment
- Joint-venture strategies
- Profit-sharing program

NOTES

1. In addition to interviews conducted at corporate headquarters, this chapter reflects information processed from three company videos, eight years of *Annual Reports,* 10-K annual filings with the Securities and Exchange Commission, and the company's Internet page, http://www.stockprofiles.com/wthg/logo.htm.

2. Form 10-K, Worthington Industries, Inc., for the fiscal year ending May 13, 1998, filed with Securities and Exchange Commission, August 28, 1998, pages 1–2.

3. http://www.stockprofiles.com/wthg/logo.htm.

4. Ibid.

5. This section of the chapter is derived from information contained in the company's 10K-R405 form filed with the Securities and Exchange Commission on August 28, 1998, for the fiscal year 1998 ending on May 31, 1998.

6. 1998 Summary *Annual Report,* Worthington Industries, 1205 Dearborn Drive, Columbus, OH, 2.

7. "Increase Your Yield," *Money Magazine* (November 1998).

8. http://www.forbes.com/tool/toolbox/jan1/1998/8149.htm.

9. Robert Levering and Milton Moskowitz, *The 100 Best Companies to Work for in America,* rev ed. (New York: Penguin Group, 1994), 489–493.

10. *Fortune,* Time, Inc., New York, January 12, 1998, and January 11, 1999.

11. Levering and Moskowitz, *The 100 Best Companies to Work for in America,* 492.

12. Ibid., p.490.

13. Ibid.

Chapter
12

Lessons from Lincoln Electric and Nucor Corporation

EXAMPLES OF LEARNING ORGANIZATION

As we have seen, Nucor and Lincoln use teams extensively. At Nucor, teams are central to the production process; most production work takes place in teams of between 20 and 40 members. The teams are designed as small as necessary for a complete, recurring task to be accomplished.

The management system of each company is highly supportive of the requirements for developing learning organizations both within teams and within each company.

AN EXAMPLE OF A HIGH-PERFORMING TEAM AT NUCOR[1]

The following is an example of a high-performing team at Nucor's Vulcraft plant in Florence, South Carolina:

> "If your shift starts at two o'clock, you should be there by one or one-fifteen. The latest anybody on our team shows up is one-thirty," says Tony Myers, a production worker from our Vulcraft plant in Florence. "We all get our equipment ready. We talk about what we have to do to make things go right. It's like a football team before a game. You

don't show up for the kickoff. You get there early and you get yourself ready. When that horn blows, we have to be primed. We've got eight hours to make us some money. The more we get done, the more money we make."

Steel joists are a key component of the metal skeleton that supports most industrial, commercial, and institutional buildings. We fabricate joists to the specs provided by construction engineers for a specific project. Joist manufacture is something of a specialty, so the automation options are limited. You need people, working in teams, to do it right.

Ham Lott calls the rigging table and welding pit—successive stations on the Vulcraft line where Tony Myers works—"the best show of labor in the United States." A partially assembled open web joist comes rattling down the line. Six riggers quickly heft the 30'–50' frame onto the rigging table and start clamping the metal angles into place, custom-forming the complex structure called for in a schematic, which each team member has studied. In less than a minute, the joist is ready to move down the line to the welding pit, where the crew of eight converges on it like the tentacles of a highly synchronized machine. Safety masks flip down and torches flare brilliant white as workers apply a series of precise welds. Speed is everything. Yet speed without accuracy is nothing. A quality inspection waits at the next station. Miss a weld, and the joist may be rejected and yield no bonus to the group.

What about the supervisor? "You wouldn't know who the supervisor is by watching us work," Tony says. "He's part of the team. He shares in the same bonus. He's not worried about being the big man in charge. He's worried about making things so we can all earn more money. We're all looking at this the same."

The pressure to perform is intense, but virtually all of it comes from peers—the other members of the group—rather than from anyone in management.

"If you're the last man welding, or if you are screwing up your welds, everybody knows. And you better believe they get on you, too," Tony says. "The company gives the new guy on the crew ninety days to prove himself. But we know in about a month if he is going to make it. At first, we just tell him things. Explain what he needs to know. We work hard at training him because, if we do, he's going to make us some money. If a guy won't work, though, the team will run him off. It's not about liking him or not liking him. It's about making a living. That man's gotta make it or break it."[2]

An Example of a High-Performing Team at Lincoln

Lincoln's first acquisition was in the United States. They were acquiring a company on a Friday; the previous Monday a top executive of Lincoln was asked to participate, but no employees were available because of the normal plant shutdown during the August vacation period. He was given the responsibility of moving the entire acquired company, all raw materials and finished goods from two plants in downtown Cleveland to the main plant on the outskirts of the city. Next he was required to tear down the two factories and remove all key equipment so that operations could not continue in the old location the next Monday morning. He was told that it had to be a highly secretive operation because there were going to be negotiations with the union representing employees at the acquired company the following Monday.

The executive had to visualize the job without examining the site and estimate what resources were going to be required. He estimated a need for 170 forklift drivers and 34 semi-trucks that he would have to obtain on contract. He then brought in supervisors so that they could pick the team members who were needed to do the job and notify them of the need for their help during their vacation period. They then had to train forklift drivers since they did not have 170 of them available in the Cleveland plant. And they had to act at 6:30 on Friday night—with the precision of a military operation.

He took over the plant and called in 220 employees for 4:30 P.M. on Friday. At 4:10 P.M., the vice chairman of Lincoln told him that the papers for the acquisition had not yet been signed. The vice chairman then told this executive, "If I don't get these papers signed I am not coming back; you figure out what to do with the employees." The papers were signed at 4:20!

The Lincoln employees who were called in went out and with minimum supervision moved 24 million pounds of product. By Sunday morning at 11 A.M. they were up and running at the main plant ready to manufacture product and by Monday morning at 8 A.M. they started to manufacture competitive product. They had no injuries; two minor accidents—the only complaint was from local police who asked that the semi-truck drivers slow down (Lincoln was paying them on piece rate, by the load!).

The management team of the acquired company could not believe that the Lincoln people were moving *9 trucks of material per hour* whereas the acquired company output for moving product was *4 truck loads of material per day.* Forklift drivers would drop their load and go back after another while other people came along and reloaded the pallets.

That's the kind of workers they have at Lincoln Electric. Their workers have been so good at responding to unusual challenges that top management has tremendous faith in them.[3]

THE INGREDIENTS OF THE AGILE/LEARNING ORGANIZATION: A SYSTEM DYNAMICS MODEL

We now examine the aspects of teams that create agility and learning by examining a systems dynamics model of the requirements for a learning organization.[4]

THE NEED FOR COMPANIES TO BECOME LEARNING ORGANIZATIONS

The rate of change in the world of business has intensified. The causes of the increased pace of change include an explosion in new knowledge and technology, in industrialization, in world population, and in the interdependency of the world business system. This rate of change places a premium on the ability of organizations to learn and to become agile so as to adapt proactively to competitive threats and to seize on new opportunities.

Increasingly, an organization's ability to develop and sustain competitive advantage is dependent on its ability to learn on a continuous basis and to create knowledge. And increasingly, this competitive advantage resides in its people, more specifically in its highly trained knowledge workers.

The challenges facing an organization can be met by redesigning its management systems so as to facilitate learning—that is, by creating the learning or agile organization. Drawing from studies by Senge[5, 6] a learning organization requires the development of five personal and organizational disciplines. These five disciplines are found at Lincoln Electric, Nucor, and Worthington but discussions of these disciplines is limited to the specific examples from Lincoln and Nucor.

These five disciplines include:

- *Systemic thinking* about business processes and problems
- *Personal mastery* through encouraging conditions in organizations for the establishment of personal vision, learning, and growth
- *Shared visions* growing out of the visions of individuals, of what a group, a multidisciplinary team, a policy committee, a concurrent engineering group, a planning group, executive staff, or an organization as a whole would like to create
- Development of new and improved *mental models* of the cause-and-affect relationships that influence business problems
- Development of processes for *team learning.*

It is especially important to note that when team learning occurs, individual members of a unit learn to work together in harmony, using their peculiar skills to reinforce the talents of others on the team. The objective of team learning is to create solutions to problems that generate greater value than the sum of the value that could have been generated by team members working independently on the solution to business problems.

We turn now to examine the conditions under which each of these disciplines is created through the design of an organization's management systems.

Systemic Thinking

The design of management systems has a significant influence on the ability of an organization and the teams within it to learn and to develop competitive advantages in learning. As an organization progresses in time, the various aspects of the subsystems of these management systems interact with each other. These interactions can be described as various patterns of cause-and-effect relationships. When the subsystems are appropriately aligned, they produce mutually supportive interactions that contribute to the development of the learning organization. In contrast, when the subsystems are out of alignment, they frustrate attempts to create a learning environment.

Systems thinking views patterns of causality as circles, not as straight lines. At the heart of systems thinking is the concept of feedback.

Patterns of feedback are at the heart of an understanding of dynamic processes; these patterns can explain how variables involved in dynamic processes can balance or reinforce each other.

Circles of causality often cause problems. These circular patterns of cause-and-effect in systems link one variable back to the first variable. We call these circles of causality causal loops.

Figure 12.1 is an example of a causal loop. Activity A influences B which in turn influences C which then influences A. Let's review another example of how such a causal loop works but this time in the context of the dynamics of the management process.

Let's assume that a member of the organization expresses trust in another member (Action A). The second member, influenced by this action, might take on expanded responsibilities to ensure that an expected outcome is achieved (Action B). The improved outcome might lead a third member to comment to the first member that the second member can be counted on to perform, thus increasing the first member's trust in this person (Action C). This then becomes an example of a *reinforcing* causal loop in a positive direction. The opposite can also occur. Reducing trust might cause a member to reduce effort, thus leading to further reductions in trust. This too is a reinforcing spiral but in a downward direction.

A reinforcing loop does not occur forever. Limiting forces materialize. Systems thinking recognizes that a change in one variable

Figure 12.1   A Causal Loop.

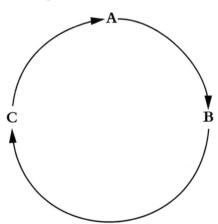

can cause changes in secondary variables. These secondary changes, not so obvious at first, can begin to create influences over time, which limit the reinforcement process. For example, if a third party overheard the lack of trust member one has in member two, that third party might begin expressing trust in member two, thus *balancing* the downward spiral in trust in member two. The second causal loop thus balances the first.

Many reinforcing processes take time to work out; in other words, *delays* are present. Delays are the time it takes for a change in one variable to affect another. The second causal loop which balanced the first, took some time to take effect. The concept of delay is therefore the third building block of systems thinking along with *reinforcing* and *balancing* (feedback) loops. Many of the dynamics we observe in management practice are due to unrecognized or unforeseen delays. The longer and the more variable the time associated with a delay, the greater will be the tendency to overshoot the goal of a system. From a management systems perspective, the designer can use this understanding of dynamic system thinking to enhance the mutually supportive and adaptive dimensions of the management system.

A general principle to note based on the preceding discussion is, when a reinforcing process is set into motion to achieve a desired result, it also sets into motion secondary, balancing, effects which usually slow down the primary effect.

When a subsystem or element is changed in the mutually supportive subsystems model (MSSM), each other subsystem and element should be examined to understand the secondary effects. For example, to reduce costs, management could reduce the number of phones in the entire organization. If informal communications were carried out in the organization by phone messages, the loss of efficiency due to reduced coordination might increase costs more than the reduction due to lower phone costs. This is the result of viewing the change systemically.

Another problem, this one caused by delays, occurs frequently in the management process when management tends to *overreact* to a problem—to bring too strong or repetitive corrections to a problem. Still another dynamic problem involves *lowering expectations*. This situation occurs when a problem is complex and management lacks resolve. Lowering expectations or *eroding goals* reduces tension to resolve the gap between performance and expectations. This relaxation, however, typically results in reduced accomplishments.

For an organization to operate as a learning organization, it must be viewed and analyzed in terms of its being an open system. A learning organization is one that is open to changes in its environment. It is continuously seeking to adapt to these changes; it has developed a shared vision of what the organization wants to accomplish among its members. The shared vision is one that encourages individual learning and team problem solving, and it is one that is continuously seeking new knowledge as a source of motivation and competitive advantage. We certainly see these attributes at both Lincoln and Nucor.

The management style most supportive of the learning organization is a *coaching and participative* one. Because the rate of change is so great, authoritarian, command, and control management systems, where corporate executives develop the strategy that is then implemented by the rest of the organization, are not agile enough for the environment. Moreover, they never tap the full potential of people at all levels of the organization.

The learning organization requires management systems that encourage the development of the talent of all of the people in the organization. Moreover, the talent of each member should be applied in a manner that it is consistent with the vision of the organization as a whole. People become an organization's most valuable asset in a learning organization, and the development of people becomes the most important task of management if a company is to cope successfully with a rapidly changing environment.

MANAGEMENT SYSTEM DYNAMICS OF THE LEARNING ORGANIZATION

A Culture of Openness and Trust

The first step a leader must take in a newly formed team is to create a culture of openness and trust—without such a culture (or without such values), the team will have its potential as a successful learning organization crippled. Openness is a disposition that one has toward another, and it "emerges when two or more individuals become willing to suspend their certitude in each other's presence. . . . If openness is a quality of relationships, then building relationships characterized by openness may be one of the most high-leverage actions for building organizations characterized by openness."[7] There is little question that both James Lincoln and Ken Iverson thought this to be true.

How is the quality of openness created on a team or in an organization? William O'Brien, former president of Hanover Insurance Companies, believes, "The impulse towards openness is the spirit of love." O'Brien believes that "the best definition of love that underlies openness is the full and unconditional commitment to another's completion, to another being all that she or he can and wants to be."[8] *The strong emphasis on developing people and placing no upper limits on their development is the hallmark of the human resource practices at Lincoln Electric and Nucor Corporation as well as at Worthington.*

Openness and trust are very closely related. Trust is manifested when one person chooses to reveal something of themselves that they would otherwise conceal. It requires a level of experience and affection among members of a group. *Affective trust* is based on limited but successful experience in sharing sensitive information with another, whereas *resilient trust* is developed over longer periods of successful interaction with the same person or group of people.

By cultivating a culture of openness and trust, the leader establishes a climate in which all members of the team are encouraged to participate fully in the activities of the team. Participation occurs without the undue influence of authority (note the presence of this in both the Lincoln and Nucor team examples). The idea is that free and open communications prevail among team members. The benefit of openness and trust is the potential that team members will not proceed with team activities under strong preconceived notions imposed on them by dominant team members, thus unleashing ideas from all members of the team. For example, the top management at Nucor told me that they often have strong disagreements among themselves. But they agree on objectives and vision, and this permits them to move on in the solution of problems. Hastings spoke of the rugged give and take at Lincoln, yet management and workers agree on the goal of the company.

The highly expedited schedule of one particular Lincoln project could only have been achieved with a high degree of trust by top management in the executive in charge of the project and in the supervisors and workers called in from their vacations. The coordination that took place among team leaders and members demonstrated a wide-open communication process and an extraordinary level of trust among all members of the team.

Developing Shared Vision

With a culture of trust and openness in place, team members are able to come to team activities with few preconceived assumptions or beliefs about the "best way" to perform a given action. A free interchange of ideas (dialogue) may then be used in problem-solving sessions to weigh the benefits of suggested actions. This free interchange of ideas is very conducive to the development of a shared vision for a project or for a team activity, and is also helpful in a search for the alternatives that allow a team to optimize its effort in order to achieve a goal. It should be noted, however, that causation may work in reverse: the strength of a new and inspirational vision could itself stimulate openness and trust on a team!

A shared vision is a positive picture of the future, a future that is important to each of the team members. It answers the question: What do we as a team want to bring into being? In the Lincoln example, it was to tear down and move the equipment of one company to Lincoln's main plant and have the equipment functioning in 72 hours in its new location. At Nucor, the team's vision is to continuously increase on-spec production so as to earn higher and higher bonuses. It is the vision that creates the energy to learn and to seek solutions to the problems that will inevitably arise and have to be solved for us to create the "desired future state." It forces us to stretch and the stretching activity forces us to learn. Without a positive vision of the future, the natural enthropic forces will begin to pull a team in separate and opposite directions. Moreover, a strong shared vision for a team assists team members in developing trust in one another because in sharing the vision, they hold in common a major issue on which they agree.

A culture of openness and trust allows individuals to share their personal dreams and aspirations. In sharing personal visions and aspirations over a period of time a *listening environment* among team members allows an overall shared vision for the team to emerge. The overall shared vision is one that allows the fulfillment of the personal visions of each of the team members.

Those committed to the shared vision have an enormous amount of energy to apply to its fulfillment. They feel responsible for the success of the vision, and they will be able to recruit others who are committed to the vision. The vision and talk of the vision creates energy, excitement, and action.

This shared vision is not to be expected from every member of a team. Various degrees of commitment are more the norm. Those who are committed to the vision must sell those who are not sold on its importance and merit. The level of commitment from the latter will be much less than from the former. For those who are merely compliant, the vision is instrumental to something else that the person wants—money, security, status, associations, lifestyle, and so on. Yet all team members must at minimum be compliant to the vision for the organization or team to be effective. Skepticism may be expressed, but cynicism cannot be tolerated if a team is to be successful.

All these aforementioned activities represent *informal* planning activities. Once the process of making improvements is underway, team members may assume roles that better support the process of further improvement. This leads to an environment that fosters team or staff learning—one team member contributes to the insights of another and the whole becomes greater than the sum of the parts. After some time operating in this environment, during which time teams develop and refine these skills, the process begins to provide reinforcing feedback for increasing the level of trust and openness. This further reinforces the other activities and accelerates their efficiency.

Figure 12.2 shows this reinforcing system of informal activities that assists teams in achieving their goals and becoming learning organizations. One should not be surprised to find so much informality in the management systems of Lincoln and Nucor. They are high-powered learning organizations.

Search and Improvement Processes for Problem Solving

Search and improvement processes are informal planning and problem-solving processes that involve team members searching for an understanding of current problems in order to determine future actions. These processes involve data gathering, contacting experts on the team and elsewhere inside or outside the organization, recalling past experiences, and in general seeking to increase an understanding of the

Figure 12.2 Reinforcing System of Informal Activities Leading to Team Learning.

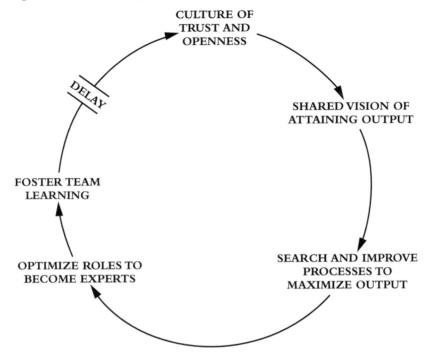

problems faced by the team. These processes are critically dependent on free and open communications, both vertically and laterally. With little cross-functional communications and problem solving, search and improvement processes will be hindered. That's why work rules are so damaging to the learning process and why Nucor and Lincoln have been so resistant to the unionization of their workforce. Empowerment of the workforce has been in place at Lincoln for almost a century and at Nucor for decades. Empowerment is not a new management idea: It is standard operating procedure.

With a climate of openness and trust and a shared vision, team members are prepared to engage in dialogue and discussion to determine the best course of action to take in solving problems. Solving problems requires accurate identification and analysis of the cause-and-effect relations surrounding problem areas. A number of tools are available for understanding the meaning of data and for facilitating specific actions. Problem situations can require a complex array of data. Structured techniques of analysis may be used beneficially to solve problems. These techniques include many of the tools associated with total quality management (TQM).

One of the reasons why our visions for our teams do not get translated into reality is because our models of cause-and-effect are often faulty (we do indeed perceive the world dimly!). In other words, our models of reality are often incorrect which means that when we act on them we do not necessarily achieve what we intend to achieve. Many problems involve circles of causality in which elements in a problem are both the cause and the effects of other elements. To uncover appropriate mental models for solving problems requires contributions from the entire team. This in turn requires dialogue, open discussion, and conflict among team members.

To solve problems, we must attempt to make our understanding of the problem and its solution explicit and expose our reasoning to the rest of the team. Others should be encouraged to speak and expose their views. We ought to have freedom to question the assumptions underlying each other's assumptions of cause-and-effect. We should run experiments or surveys if advisable. Problem-solving techniques new to the team can be made available.

Competition can force us to change our mental models. Drastic reductions in cost or cycle time by competitors, for example, can cause us to question the way we produce our products and services.

Firms that have emphasized certain dimensions of functionality may come under severe pressure from competitors that begin to emphasize cost of service (e.g., low cost, low amenity airlines). The firm thus is forced to reconsider its model (or theory of the business) of how its markets respond to cost, quality, and functionality issues. In the Nucor team example, one cannot determine by observation alone the identities of the supervisor and steel workers. Since members of a team including the team supervisor have the same objective, each member does what is necessary to achieve team objectives. This is possible under conditions of very flexible work rules.

Emerging into Roles as Experts on Teams

Once the process of making improvements is underway, team members should be encouraged to assume roles that effectively support the process of further improvement.

Emergent roles are the informal relationships and responsibilities that emerge on a team, based on the needs of the team and on the expertise of team members. Cooperative norms on a team permit individual team members to assume leadership responsibilities for which their expertise makes them most qualified as specific problems develop. This is very clear on both the Nucor and Lincoln teams.

The results achieved by Nucor and other minimills have certainly caused integrated steel producers to question their methods and mental models. Production workers at Nucor are always trying to improve processes and equipment to boost on-spec production.

Informal relationships, based on openness and trust and shared vision, allow these informal relationships to emerge and the commitment to the vision of the project enhances the "willingness to serve" of each member in a way most helpful to the team and its vision. This dimension of the learning organization has each member conscious of each other and of the talents of others. It has them adjusting her or his own talent to the talents of other members—like a good basketball team. Individual members of the team are not absorbed in either role ambiguity or in restrictive work rules as who can do what. They fit their talents to the needs of the specific task.

Team Learning

The entire reinforcing system in Figure 12.2 creates the potential for fostering team learning and knowledge creation. It presumes a number of ingredients that are not common to the realities of the way organizations typically function. Let's review some of the key ingredients that are required to foster team learning.

The reinforcing cycle reflects a deemphasis on command and control hierarchical organization and an emphasis on work-based horizontal organizations. These organizations are based heavily on teams—management teams, product development teams, project management teams, cross-functional teams, reengineering teams, and project improvement teams—teams that are chartered to solve significant business problems. The horizontal cut allows for more effective use of the higher qualities of human nature—morality, dignity, creativity, rationality, management capacity, and relatedness.

Learning is a fundamental instinct in human nature, and it is one of our stronger instincts. It takes place at a very rapid rate when people are allowed to develop a vision—personal and shared—as to what they would like to create.

We become open to new approaches for solving problems, and we are ready to let those with special expertise needed on a project assume leadership for that task. The more progress that is made on a project, the more we are encouraged to continue to cooperate with and enjoy team membership. Being a part of a high-performing team is exhilarating, motivating, and intrinsically very rewarding.

After some time operating in this environment, during which time teams develop and refine these skills, the process begins to provide reinforcing feedback for increasing the level of trust and openness among team members. This further reinforces other activities, thus accelerating their effectiveness.

The bonus system at Nucor and the piece-rate and bonus system at Lincoln create a vested interest in team members training new team members so as to improve quality and quantity of production. The two team examples are micro examples of the learning processes that are in place within each company.

After looking at the competitive power and human motivational potential of the learning organization, including the examples of Nucor and Lincoln, we are left with the nagging question: Why do we not see more of them in practice?

Balancing Factors Limiting the Growth and Development of the Learning Organization

Figure 12.3 introduces a number of potential limiting or balancing factors to the development of the learning organization represented in Figure 12.2. These are factors that either limit the effectiveness of the learning organization or actually shut it down. Given the scarcity of these learning organizations in practice, we must assume that many or most of these limiting factors are alive and well in most organizations. There seems to be at least five categories of limiting factors. They should be expected to one degree or another on all teams and in all organizations. The organizations that minimize them should be expected to excel in performance and to achieve sustainable competitive advantage.

Figure 12.3   Limitations to the Development of the Learning Organization.

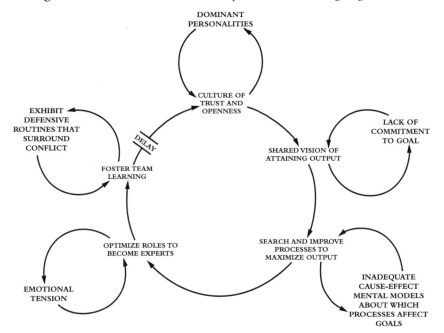

Teams that begin to fail or actually fail may have a leader or *dominant member* who holds strong preconceived beliefs about how the management team should proceed and act. The dominant member or leader manipulates team behavior for self-serving purposes, not for the best interests of the team. Line managers may engage in bureaucratic infighting rather than behave in a way that promotes the cross-functional integration necessary for team behavior to succeed in solving problems. This type of bureaucratic behavior prevents the development of openness and trust and must be reversed by a culture of cross-functional cooperation if the effort of a team is to succeed. Our case examples from Lincoln and Nucor illustrate these points.

The presence of a dominant member, who may emerge out of a position of organizational rank, balances the culture of openness and trust. Because it threatens the key team processes of dialogue and discussion, it may be fatal to the success of the team. One engineering organization the author is familiar with had a manager of product engineering who acted as a manager of projects in a product-development group. He in turn reported to the director of engineering of the overall organization. By flattening the organization and by eliminating the position of manager of product engineering, the project development work functioned with less direct day-to-day supervision and with an atmosphere of openness and trust.

This manager had been a dominant force in the day-to-day management of product development work and attempted to tightly control the communication flows within the organization of projects. The result of his removal was to decrease political infighting and to increase openness and trust in the organization. This had positive effects on other aspects of the reinforcing systems of informal project activities.

Proceeding clockwise along the reinforcing loop, another limiting factor is a gradual *erosion of the commitment* to the goals of the team which erodes the common vision. There are various degrees of commitment, the minimum being apathy and the maximum being total commitment. A team member who is totally committed to the vision will do whatever is necessary to make it succeed. As levels of commitment fall, the amount of energy and motivation directed toward accomplishing the goal falls.

Genuine commitment to a vision is rare in an organization. Often, the plurality of people are in general acquiescence with what an organization wants to achieve, but organizational members are not ordinarily in high states of commitment. That is what makes the Lincoln and Nucor examples so unusual.

The worst position a team member may take is active resistance or apathy toward the vision. The team leader should not tolerate these positions in order to succeed. A person who is truly committed to a vision brings a level of passion and energy to the task that one cannot bring about through seeking merely a low-level of compliance.

A lack of commitment to a goal may be altered abruptly as a result of a significant threat from a competitor. Fear does produce strong motivation to actively share the vision of the team and to grow and develop, but it doesn't endure as a continuing source of learning and human development. Therefore, the emotion of fear can produce change and commitment, but the drive to fulfill dreams and aspirations is a much stronger and sustainable source of growth and development for the individual and organization.

Here we see the importance of the desire to achieve personal mastery on the part of the individual to the development and implementation of the shared vision on a team.

There is an important feedback relationship from development of shared vision to the development of openness and trust. A new vision that captures the imagination of the team can create a fervent willingness to participate in problem-solving activities. This, in turn, can lead to a new degree of openness and trust—in other words, the new vision acts as a vehicle for developing a new level of openness and trust.

Even if a staff remains committed to a goal and subscribes to a culture of openness and trust, the team can still be unsuccessful if it lacks an adequate model of cause-and-effect. Search and improvement efforts suffer from the inability to see the effects of many of our actions because of the presence of delays and because of the influence of intervening events. System models help improve our mental models, but in the final analysis many problems faced by teams are at least partially intractable. By encouraging lateral communications, members emerging as experts, total participation in problem solving by team members, and high levels of activity that recognize the success of team members in problem solving, a team leader goes a long way toward improving the chances of the team arriving at solutions that solve problems and improve processes.

Although team members come to team projects with their well-developed areas of expertise, they must also adjust both to project work requirements and to the skills of other members of the team. As team members begin to perform tasks on team projects, they often experience role ambiguity and conflict in cross-functional work relations. Role conflict may lead to emotional tension and to a deterioration of team performance. The focus may shift from productive creative tension to destructive emotional tension (or back-biting). Emotional tension limits the ability of team members to build personal mastery.

A significant source of emotional tension is also what we feel as we seek to solve creative problems in our new or emergent areas of expertise on a project. Emotional tension, stemming from interpersonal conflicts, is different and may lead teams to a lower vision; in that sense, it may work against the learning process. On the other hand, emotional tension of the creative variety may be a very positive force in motivating team members to adjust to roles and to go the extra mile to solve problems on the project.

In other words, emotional tension may be a positive force emanating from the tension between the vision and current reality—what Senge refers to as creative tension—or emotional tension may distract members from pursuit of their goal by forcing them to spend increasingly larger amounts of time in ambiguous roles.

To summarize this discussion on emotional tension, the wrong kind of emotional tension may tend to balance the positive forces that encourage mutually supportive emergent roles, but the right kind may energize the individual and the team.

For learning to occur, there must be open dialogue and discussion of the issues surrounding the vision and of the problems involved in achieving the vision. Defensive routines are "habitual ways of interacting that protect us or others from threat or embarrassment, but which also prevent us from learning."[9] Because defensive routines move us away from the truth, they also move us away from learning and from the achievement of our vision.

As teams begin to experience the exhilaration of learning and of making progress toward a vision, defensive routines begin to subside and commitment to the truth and to helping each other grow further enhances knowledge creation. The diminution of defensive routines makes room for increased learning activity. The reinforcing cycle is thus strengthened further.

In summary, our analysis indicates that team learning is facilitated or hindered by informal systems of management. But, the formal elements of the control system also interact with the informal elements to reinforce or to hinder learning. Figure 12.4 shows the interaction of the informal with the formal elements of the control process.

The two activities shown on the left of Figure 12.4 come from the informal management systems and involve searching for data, seeking new directions, and formulating plans. These activities are most prevalent during times when organizations are facing periods of great change. The balancing feedback on the right illustrates the relationships of formal and informal processes. Formal planning and control processes are seen as the formal aspects of attaining intermediate goals leading to the shared vision. These formal activities on project work involve assessing

Figure 12.4   Interaction between Formal and Informal Control Processes.

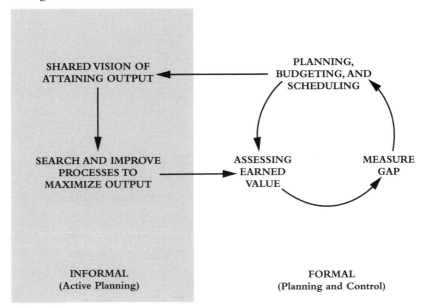

SHARED VISION OF
ATTAINING OUTPUT

PLANNING,
BUDGETING, AND
SCHEDULING

SEARCH AND IMPROVE
PROCESSES TO
MAXIMIZE OUTPUT

ASSESSING
EARNED
VALUE

MEASURE
GAP

INFORMAL
(Active Planning)

FORMAL
(Planning and Control)

the gap between performance and the vision (or milestones toward the vision) and taking steps in the planning and budgeting, resource allocation, and reporting processes to close the gap.

The formal processes interact with the informal processes to allow the team to achieve its goals. The informal activities provide the vision and energy to fulfill the vision and the formal gap—determined by formal measurement—allowing the team to guide its efforts toward goals. Both formal and informal activities are associated with the learning organization. But as the examples at the beginning of this chapter illustrate, the informal activities are often more important.

Showing the formal and informal activities within the context of the entire dynamic management system produces a mutually supportive reinforcing learning system. Figure 12.5 displays a reinforcing loop that we might call the adaptive management or learning engine. The reinforcing loop shows the additional influence of formal and informal rewards (as a result of measurement) on team learning, thus linking the structural aspects of the management system to the process aspects.

No one examining the Lincoln or Nucor rewards and recognition systems can doubt the power of incentives, rewards, and recognition

Figure 12.5   The Learning Engine.

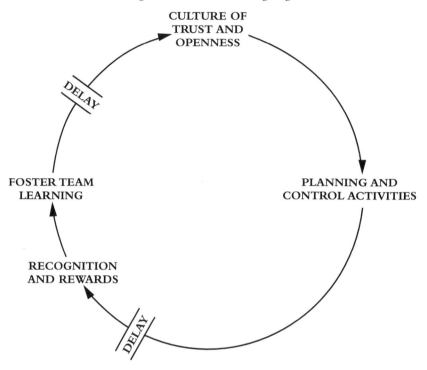

to produce outstanding results for a company. Yet in each company, strong rewards work because of other elements within the mutually reinforcing set of management systems. Rewards do not work in isolation from other *trust-producing elements* of the management systems of an organization. This is a firm belief of the top managements of both of these organizations and of their founders.

Finally, we are in a position to view the entire dynamic of the management system as it affects team performance. Figure 12.6 is such a view. Two elements of the management structure not previously discussed are included at the top left. Both set the initial conditions for teams. *Prior training or indoctrination* for the team is one element, and *infrastructure or formal chartering of the team* is the other. We see both elements in operation at Nucor and Lincoln.

The familiar reinforcing loop of culture, vision, search, and so on, is the upper reinforcing loop along with the five potentially balancing

Figure 12.6   Dynamics of the Entire Management System.

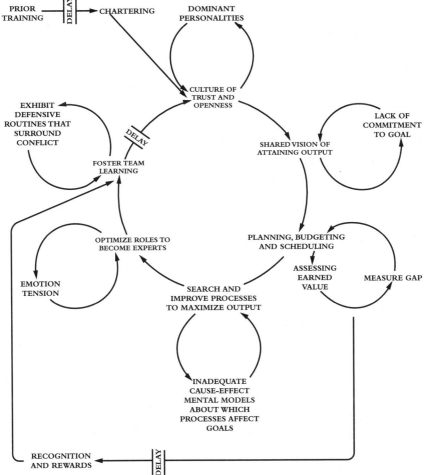

items shown along the outside. The formal planning and control balancing activities support the informal planning processes. The outer loop of measurement and rewards reinforces team learning at the bottom of the structure.

The progress of the team is influenced significantly by how closely the leadership of the team can come to creating the mutually supporting reinforcing loops by using appropriate elements of the informal and formal management systems in a dynamic manner while minimizing the inhibitors.

SUMMARY

Many of the characteristics of the learning organization described in this chapter may be found in well-run organizations. One of the major purposes of this book is to present systematic examples of public companies that have developed learning organizations, not by design but by applying fundamental principles and values derived from good management practice. As described by Robert N. Bellah et al.:

> We can see among us examples of institutions that are functioning well, that give the individuals within them a purpose and an identity not through molding them into conformity but through challenging them to become active, innovative, responsible and thus happy persons because they understand what they are doing and why it is important.[10]

Moreover, we can see the difficulties posed by the institution of capitalism on the organizations of America as they try to meet the demands placed on them by the financial markets. Meeting these demands may have devastating effects on the culture of trust and openness needed to develop learning organizations; Robert N. Bellah et al., state:

> The prospect of takeovers create an atmosphere in which everyone is suspicious, ready to bail out, looking out for number 1, trying to make the next quarterly statement look good at whatever long term cost so as to advance the prospects of getting another job. By strip-mining our most valuable economic asset—namely, the creative interaction of people who have grown to understand and to trust each other—we sink our long term viability, while we appoint another commission on competitiveness.[11]

Organizations, especially in this new era of knowledge work, should expand their notions of just what its assets are. In essence, we need a new and radically different method of accounting. We not only should be concerned with financial and physical aspects of capital, but we should also be vitally concerned with human capital and its development. The effectiveness of human capital, in turn, is increasingly dependent on the communities we are able to build and evolve at the workplace. These communities create another form of capital—social capital. Robert Putnam develops the analogy between physical and human capital and social capital as follows:

[S]ocial capital refers to features of social organization, such as networks, norms, and trust, that facilitate coordination and cooperation for mutual benefit. Social capital enhances the benefits of investment in physical and human capital. Stocks of social capital, such as trust, norms, and networks, tend to be self reinforcing and cumulative. Successful collaboration in one endeavor builds connections and trust—social assets that facilitate future collaboration in other unrelated tasks. As with conventional capital, those who have social capital tend to accumulate more— them that has gets. Social capital is what social philosopher Albert O. Hirschman calls a "moral resource," that is, a resource whose supply increases rather than decreases through use and which (unlike physical capital) becomes depleted if not used.[12]

Building social capital is fundamental and at the heart of the learning organization. The three organizations described in this book have built high levels of social capital.

NOTES

1. Reprinted from Ken Iverson with Tom Varian, *Plain Talk: Lessons from a Business Maverick* (New York: John Wiley & Sons, 1998), 108–110. Reprinted by permission of John Wiley & Sons, Inc.

2. Ken Iverson with Tom Varian, *Plain Talk: Lessons from a Business Maverick* (New York: John Wiley & Sons, 1998), 108–110.

3. This case example was described to the author by Richard Sabo, longtime assistant to the CEO of Lincoln Electric, October 1996.

4. The systems dynamics model applied in this chapter to analyze these two teams was developed by Robert Severino using a framework designed by Joseph Maciariello and Calvin Kirby.

5. Peter Senge, *The Fifth Discipline* (New York: Doubleday/Currency, 1990).

6. Peter Senge, Richard Ross, Bryan Smith, Charlotte Roberts, and Art Kleiner, *The Fifth Discipline Fieldbook* (New York: Doubleday/Currency, 1994).

7. Definition attributed to David Bohm in Peter M. Senge, *The Fifth Discipline,* 284.

8. Ibid., p. 285.

9. Ibid., p. 237.

10. Robert N. Bellah, Richard Madsen, William Sullivan, Ann Swindler, and Steven M. Tipton, *The Good Society* (New York: Vintage Books, 1991), 50.

11. Ibid., p. 95.

12. Robert D. Putnam, "The Prosperous Community: Social Capital and Public Life," *American Prospect* (spring 1993): 35–38.

Epilogue

Lasting Value: Incentive Management as Cradled by the Culture and Management Systems at Lincoln Electric

T his concluding chapter places the findings from our analysis of Lincoln Electric's incentive system, culture and management systems into historical perspective. You will see a company that has been managed for a century under some of the best management practices known to man.

We begin our reflections with the work of Frederick Winslow Taylor (1856–1915). If we look at his work closely, we see that it was during his most productive period (the late 1890s and the early 1900s) that John C. Lincoln founded the Lincoln Electric Company. Moreover, in 1911, when James F. Lincoln assumed operating control of Lincoln Electric, Taylor published an extensive paper on "Shop Management," which was first presented at a meeting of the American Society of Mechanical Engineers in Saratoga Springs, New York, in 1903.[1] The paper outlines the details of piece work and piece-rate systems for managing work. Some of his comments were mirrored in the views of James F. Lincoln. For example, Taylor states:

> It is safe to say that no system or scheme of management should be considered which does not in the long run give satisfaction to both employer and employe[e], which does not make it apparent that their best

224

interests are mutual, and which does not bring about such thorough and hearty cooperation that they can pull together instead of apart. . . . This book is written with the object of advocating *high wages* and *low labor cost* as the foundation of the best management.[2]

Taylor then goes on to detail how piece rates should be set in order to motivate production workers to increase productivity, their wages, and to reduce unit labor costs. Taylor recognized how few employers seemed to be operating in this manner but had worked with some that were.

In commenting on the influence of Taylor, Drucker notes that "Morgensen's, one of Taylor's disciples showed that unschooled people who, however, knew what working was, could obtain results as good as those of the most highly trained engineers."[3] Drucker goes on to note that [c]reativity, if by this is meant undirected, unstructured, untutored, and uncontrolled guessing is not likely to produce results. But a system that does not tap and put to use the knowledge, experience, resources and imagination of people who have to live with the system and make it work is as unlikely to be effective.

Although it is clear that James Lincoln based his philosophy of management on the golden rule, he did see piece rates and the bonus system as fundamentally consistent with the implementation of his philosophy.

Lincoln's views and practices concerning the potential of individuals when provided with the best materials and equipment and when properly motivated by management extended management practice considerably beyond the practices pioneered by Frederick Taylor. Like Taylor, however, he was interested in piecework as a vehicle to raise labor productivity and wages while lowering costs to customers.

Another influential innovator and practitioner in the years preceding World War I was Henry Ford. Not only did Henry Ford introduce the assembly line, standardization of parts, and mass production in the United States, he also saw the wisdom of paying each production worker $5 per day, "three times what was then standard." This resulted in a dramatic increase in productivity and a dramatic reduction in turnover. Moreover, Ford's initiative consequently *reduced the actual cost of labor* in an automobile.[4]

Taylor and Ford were beginning to innovate in the areas of industrial engineering, time and motion studies, mass production, and productivity increasing compensation schemes for production workers. All this was occurring in America as James Lincoln began his career at Lincoln Electric.

Lincoln went much further in the design of his management systems than either of these two contemporaries ever dreamed. In that sense, he was a pioneer. He did so by placing much more emphasis on the development of people and on organizational systems and processes that could create an enduring organization. Although Henry Ford ultimately mismanaged the Ford Motor Company and needed the help of his grandson Henry Ford II to revive it, James Lincoln built an organization that has survived and prospered for over a century.

Lincoln clearly built upon the works of these two giants but his contribution has been less recognized.

LINCOLN ELECTRIC AND TENANTS OF GOOD MANAGEMENT PRACTICE[5]

The Spirit of the Performance

Drucker states, "the purpose of an organization is to enable common men to do uncommon things."[6] Drucker believes that to empower common men to do uncommon things is only possible in the "moral sphere."[7] This is not a matter of preaching morality by management: It is a matter of carrying out *practices*. Drucker enumerates as follows:

- "The focus of the organization must be on performance." High-performance standards characterize the achieving organization.
- "The focus of the organization must be upon *opportunities* rather than on problems."
- "The decisions that affect people: their placement and their pay, promotion, demotion, and severance must express the values and beliefs of the organization. They are the true controls of an organization."

- "Finally, in its people decisions, management must demonstrate that it realizes that *integrity* is one absolute requirement of a manager, the one quality that he has to bring with him and cannot be expected to acquire later on. And management must demonstrate that it requires the same integrity of itself."[8]

After reviewing the culture and management systems of Lincoln Electric along with those of Nucor and Worthington, do we not see this spirit of performance? Do we not see a deep respect for the dignity and talent of human beings on the part of the founders of the management systems of these organizations—James Lincoln, Ken Iverson, and John H. McConnell? And do we not see organizations that are performance and people driven? And although each organization perceives their people to be their "greatest assets," they are not organizations that we would characterize as "warm and fuzzy" in their operations.

Motivation

Douglas McGregor developed two theories of motivation.[9] The *Theory X* person is undeveloped and finds work distasteful. This type of worker needs strong monitoring and supervision to motivate performance. The *Theory Y* person, on the other hand, comes to work with internal motivation to perform and to develop his or her talents. This type of worker is motivated by challenging conditions and can be brought to high levels of development, performance, and creativity if properly managed. Both types of people are present in the workforce at all times.

In commenting on McGregor's models of human nature, Drucker believes that

> [T]here are different human natures which behave differently under different conditions. Individuals can acquire the habit of achievement but also can acquire the habit of defeat.[10]

To achieve Type Y motivation at work, very high demands must be placed on managers and workers. Moreover, as to the power of material incentives to motivate productivity and profitability, Drucker believes that "[t]here is not one shred of evidence for the alleged turning away from material rewards. Yet there is more to human motivation besides material rewards. . . . The work relationship has to be based upon human respect."[11]

A manager cannot assume all of the workers are wrong. This attitude is all a part of respecting the worker.

The evidence at Lincoln, Nucor, and Worthington is that there are a number of employees and potential employees who either fit the Type Y description or with wise management can be transformed into a Type Y person. Lincoln's advisory board, Worthington's employee councils, and Nucor's active hands-on management and open-door policy all demonstrate a sincere respect for the dignity and creativity of production employees. In addition, each of these companies is egalitarian in their wage and salary structure.

Job Security and Income Stability

Drucker explains why the Japanese employment system is of interest to us in the United States: "[I]t satisfies two apparently mutually contradictory needs: (1) job and income security; and (2) flexible, adaptable labor forces and labor costs."[12]

Although the Japanese have evolved a system of job and income security and adaptability, James Lincoln had pioneered these concepts in the United States in 1934, much earlier than the Japanese. Moreover, both Nucor and Worthington also provide the opportunity for continuous employment.

James Lincoln believed that the need for continuous employment and income was one of the greatest needs that the worker faced. This led to the guaranteed employment policy in the Ohio Company. During hard times, there is at Lincoln "painsharing" and flexibility. Each of the other two companies discussed have employed similar practices. Notably, Lincoln and Nucor are not unionized, whereas Worthington has shed the majority of its operations that were unionized. This gives each of these companies the flexibility to offer continuous employment and to achieve flexibility and adaptability during changing times.

The Nature of Work and Achievement

Often management is defined as *getting work done through people*. In the discipline of economics, the worker is considered a *factor of production*, a means to an end comparable to capital and technology. But if the worker is treated merely as an instrument of production, damage will be done to his or her nature and the result will diminish achievements.

Drucker is concerned with the task of "making work suitable for human beings." This "implies consideration of the human resource as human beings and not as things, and as having—unlike any other resource—personality, citizenship, control over whether they work, how much and how well, and thus requiring responsibility, motivation, participation, satisfaction, incentives and rewards, leadership, status, and function."[13]

Lincoln Electric has embraced an approach toward its people based on the golden rule. Although it ranks consumers as its dominant stakeholder, the focus of the company's management system is to accomplish its objectives and to maintain employee relations. Historically, this has produced a high-trust culture between management and production workers.

Nucor unabashedly asserts that its business is all about its people. Treating them well, paying them well, granting them autonomy, allowing them to fail as they try to innovate and welcoming their ideas is the "Nucor Way." As we have seen earlier, Iverson sees it as simply a matter of applying the golden rule to all of Nucor's constituents.

Worthington, on the other hand, ranks investors as the key stakeholder. However, this primary ranking for the stockholder is strongly couched within their golden rule philosophy. In this philosophy, the people of Worthington are considered the company's most important asset.

The Responsible Worker

Drucker believes that the goal of business is to make workers managers; by that he means that workers should take responsibility for achieving the results expected on his or her job and for the output of the work group.[14] For each job, standards are established, timely feedback on performance is provided to the worker, and continuous training is provided to improve knowledge and upgrade worker skills.

Clearly, the production worker at Lincoln is motivated to perform by the piece-rate system and by the semiannual evaluations according to the four merit criteria. Similarly, Nucor's teams have established standards for productivity and for quality. Once productivity standards are met for a team, the bonus system kicks in. The bonus calculations are group related so that each person is accountable to the group for his or her bonus payment. Worthington's employee councils monitor admission of employees to those who will contribute to the profitability of the plant and therefore to employee quarterly bonuses.

Although the feedback and training processes differ among these three companies, they all have responsible workers.

Workers at Lincoln often refer to themselves as entrepreneurs, with a span of control of 100:1 there is little direct supervision. Nucor uses the internal market concept extensively. In each of the three companies, the opportunity for promotion is virtually unlimited. This encourages employees to take responsibility and expand their knowledge of company operations.

Finally, Drucker believes that

> Living in fear of loss of job and income is incompatible with taking responsibility for job and work group, for output and performance. . . . To accept the burden or responsibility, the worker, the unskilled as well as the skilled worker, and the manual as well as the knowledge worker, needs a fair measure of security of job and income.[15]

The Need for Economic Growth

James Lincoln established the primary business objective of producing "more and more at less and less" while simultaneously increasing quality and service to customers. Nucor has followed essentially the same objective.

With the guarantee of continuous employment, and very rapid rates of productivity improvement, the only alternative open to Lincoln is economic growth in a basic, cyclical industry. This is no small feat!

How is this accomplished? First, the market expands as prices fall. Second, the company has been able to achieve a dominant position in welding consumables and equipment in the United States. Third, James Lincoln initiated expansion into international markets, building plants first in Canada, then in Australia and in France. Moreover, a great deal of international trade has always been conducted from Cleveland.

Nucor has not expanded internationally but has been successful in gaining larger shares of the domestic market and has introduced a steady stream of new products and innovative technologies. Worthington has sloughed off its least productive product lines and has pursued an aggressive program of domestic and international expansion.

These three companies have still an additional reason to pursue growth. The metals industry is not considered glamorous. In fact, motivating the best and the brightest young people to join these organizations is difficult. It is only possible if there is some distinction, such as innovation, or a reputation for the growth and development of its people.

Drucker states the problem as follows:

> A company that is not able to attract, motivate, and hold men of talent and competence will not survive. Increasingly, this will mean attracting, motivating, and holding the knowledge worker. Unlike the manual worker of yesterday, the knowledge worker does not, however, look just for a job. He looks for a career. He looks for an opportunity. . . . The advent of the knowledge worker creates pressure for at least some, and in many cases, for considerable growth.[16]

Reinforcing Drucker's point about the potential problems of recruiting knowledge workers, a recent report by Bloomberg News[17] directed attention to the problems certain steel companies are having recruiting engineers. Lincoln, Nucor, and Worthington have marketed themselves successfully to knowledge workers through growth and through other aspects of their culture and management systems. As a result, they have not encountered the recruiting problems of other companies in the metals industry.

Drucker goes on to talk about the need for continuous learning if a company is to grow:

> . . . a company, to be able to grow, must, within itself, create an atmosphere of continuous learning. It must be managed in such manner that all its members—down to the lowest ranking employees—are willing and ready to take on new, different, and bigger responsibilities as a

matter of course, and without trepidation. A company can grow only to
the extent to which its people can grow.[18]

Continuous learning is deeply ingrained in the culture at Lincoln
Electric, yet historically the company from James Lincoln to William
Irrgang was operated in an autocratic manner *except at the production
level.* That changed with Willis, Hastings, and Massaro. Nucor and
Worthington, on the other hand have historically practiced decentralization, radical in the case of Nucor. Decentralization creates the need
for people to stretch and grow, and continuous learning provides the
engine for growth.

Innovation

Lincoln Electric pioneered the development of arc welding early in its
history. Most of all, James Lincoln was a major innovator in the design of management systems to achieve extraordinary competitiveness.
Innovation is essential to survival and to sustained competitiveness in
a global economy.

Notice the way that Lincoln has exemplified one particular insight
of Drucker on innovation: "The business enterprise, its structure and
organization, the way in which it integrates knowledge into work and
work into performance are also major areas of innovation."[19]

Ken Iverson at Nucor introduced the steel minimill on a large
scale. The company has also innovated in many other areas (such as
thin-slab production). Without a doubt, Nucor continues to be one of
the most productive and innovative companies in the world.

The Economic Nature of Business Organizations

Drucker believes that the purpose and mission of a business enterprise
is "economic performance."[20]

It is very interesting to observe how each of the three companies
rank their stakeholders in terms of priority. They are all different in
the first rankings—Lincoln ranks its customers first, Nucor its people,
and Worthington its stockholders. Yet as we have seen, each company
has enjoyed above average economic performance over a long period
of time. In fact, Nucor's long-term profitability has been nothing short

of spectacular. Each of the three companies is a high-wage, low-cost producer. The issue is not the ultimate need to achieve economic performance that is mandatory: The issue is the attitude each company has toward its customers and employees. And on this issue, Lincoln, Nucor, and Worthington appear to be remarkably consistent with each other and with good managerial practice.

CONCLUSION

I have reviewed eight basic tenets of management as articulated by one of the most significant thinkers of the twentieth century on the subject management. I have described how Lincoln, Nucor, and Worthington have performed on these tenets. As you can see, they have done pretty well.

Lincoln Electric has been the primary subject of this book. James Lincoln did not have a book like Drucker's to guide his design of the management systems and processes at Lincoln Electric. He simply had the Golden Rule. And the result has been a century of performance and lasting value. A company worth emulating!

NOTES

1. Frederick Winslow Taylor, *Shop Management,* one of three volumes reprinted in *Scientific Management* (New York and London: Harper & Brothers, 1911).

2. Ibid., pp. 21–22.

3. Peter F. Drucker, *Management: Tasks, Responsibilities, Practices* (New York: Harper and Row, 1973), 271.

4. Ibid., p. 338.

5. The excerpts from *Management: Tasks, Responsibilities, Practices* by Peter F. Drucker, copyright ©, 1973, 1974 by Peter F. Drucker, are reprinted in this chapter by permission of HarperCollins Publishers, Inc.

6. Drucker, *Management,* p. 455.

7. Ibid., p. 456.

8. Ibid.

9. Douglas McGregor, *The Human Side of Enterprise* (New York: Mc-Graw-Hill, 1960).

10. Drucker, *Management,* p. 234.

11. Ibid., pp. 238, 244.

12. Ibid., pp. 251, 252.

13. Ibid., p. 41.

14. Ibid., p. 254.

15. Ibid., p. 285.

16. Ibid., p. 774.

17. "Steel Industry in Need of Engineers, Better Recruiting Tactics," Bloomberg News, Bloomberg, L.P., Chicago, pp. 1–3, July 15, 1999.

18. Ibid., p. 775.

19. Ibid., p. 285.

20. Ibid., p. 40.

Index